Always Remember to Kiss Me Goodnight

A Story of Love, Loss and Healing

LOUISE CRIST

Always Remember to Kiss Me Goodnight
Copyright © 2019 by Louise Crist

All rights reserved. No part of this book may be reproduced or transmitted in any form or by any means, electronic or mechanical, including photocopying, recording, or by any information storage or retrieval system without prior written permission from the author or their representatives.

This book is to be regarded as a reference source and is not intended to replace professional medical advice or prescribe the use of any technique as a form of treatment for physical, emotional, or medical problems without the advice of your physician. The author and the publisher disclaim any liability arising directly or indirectly from the use of this book.

JillyBean Publishing
Coldwater, MI 49036

Cover Art: Jillian Crist
Cover Design: Mitch Chandler, Push Creative
Interior Print Design: Dayna Linton, Day Agency
eBook Design: Dayna Linton, Day Agency
Editing: Jami Lynn Sands
Author Photo Credit: Expressions Design
Photo Editing: Laury DeRosa

ISBN: 978-1-7336514-9-3 (Paperback)
ISBN: 978-1-7336514-0-0 (eBook)

First Edition: 2019

10 9 8 7 6 5 4 3 2 1

Printed in the USA

TABLE OF CONTENTS

Prologue 1

The Sound of Silence 3
Always Kiss Me Goodnight 13
The Aftermath of Devastation 27
Jilly, Phone Home Please 43
40 Weeks 63
Taking Jilly Home 73
Wanderlust and Gratitude 89
Daddy's Hug 101
The Summer of 2013 115
Sign, Sign, Everywhere a Sign 127
Our Family Tent 133
Meet Me Halfway 143
Judge Me, Judge Me Not 167
Out on a Limb 179
No One is Immune 197
At 1900 Days 211
Six Years Later 223
What Not to Say 251
In Memoriam 277

Marriage After Loss of a Child 307
News Flash 335
Out of the Darkness and into the Light 347
Epilogue/The End 377

Acknowledgments 389
About Author 393
Bibliography 395

Always Remember to Kiss Me Goodnight

FOREWORD

It was my privilege to meet the author, Louise Crist, at a retreat given by author, Neale Donald Walsch in Southern Oregon in the fall of 2016. Ironically, the topic of the retreat was based on Neale's book, *Home with God, in a Life that Never Ends*.

I was so touched by Jillian's story and the love and grace with which her family dealt with it, that I knew the world needed to hear it because of the amount of comfort it would bring grieving parents. Consequently, I am proud to call Louise my friend.

True story: Very early in the process of sorting Louise's notes before an edit could begin, I was putting together an email to her. It was broad daylight that morning and the sun was streaming in when suddenly, a lamp across the room turned itself on.

That particular lamp was seldom used. I got up to check to see if the switch was faulty; nope—it had never done it before and has never done it since. I was in awe. There was an aha moment.

It was obvious to me that Jillian had visited, giving her approval to the project. It was clear that not only did she approve, she was instrumental in bringing us together and would inspire and support the both of us as the project progressed. When I told Louise what had occurred, she was not at all surprised because Jillian always has a way of getting her message across.

The goal of this book is not only to bring comfort but to help the reader raise their own vibration so that they too, can be open to communicating with their child or perhaps another loved one in spirit, no matter their age at passing.

May God bless you on your journey,
Jami Lynn Sands

In Celebration of the life of Jillian Alexis Crist
February 18, 1992—November 19, 2011

PROLOGUE

Sharing my journey is for the express purpose of letting parents who have experienced loss, know that they are not alone. Although sometimes the pain seems unbearable, there is help and support available.

Most who have lost a child will be able to relate, even if they weren't able to put it into words themselves. The reader will understand the depth of sorrow and grief a parent feels whether they have experienced it themselves or know someone who has. They will understand why there are some things they ought not say to the bereaved and some of the things they will be responsible for doing when losing a loved one—all through the most trying and traumatic time of their life.

A large part of the message is that there is proof available (if we pay attention) that life not only goes on but does so for eternity. Signs from your loved ones are always there, most of us just don't notice. As you will see, they are profiled throughout and in ways I could never have imagined.

We have a choice; we can let grief destroy the rest of our earthly lives, or we can transcend it and create something positive in honor of our loved one; ideas for doing so are included. It helps us to not only to feel their presence, but to be of assistance to humanity so that it is a win-win for all.

Blessings,

Louise

1

THE SOUND OF SILENCE

There were no warning bells, fire alarms or sirens telling me that in that particular moment, my world as I knew it was changing and shifting on its axis. I awoke from a deep sleep and rolled over to look at the clock. It flashed 06:00 in the darkness of opening weekend of deer hunting firearms season. My husband wasn't in bed, so I assumed he was already on his way to his beloved tree stand in search of the elusive "monster buck" in the woods.

I was not able to figure out what woke me up so suddenly, so I turned back over and dozed until the silence of my deep slumber was pierced by an annoying chime coming from my cell phone at 7:25 A.M. It was an incoming call, not a wake-up alarm.

It was the Saturday before Thanksgiving and I was expecting plenty of company later in the week. I was hoping to get some deep cleaning done that weekend, even though I was on call for surgical cases at the hospital. "Noooo!" I whined. It was way too early to start the day, and my body begged for a few more hours of sleep.

Groggy, I tried to focus on the number on my caller ID. It took me a minute to figure out that although it was not the familiar number of the hospital calling me in for a case, I should answer it anyway. I finally recognized it as belonging to the parent of my daughter Jillian's friend that we affectionately nicknamed "Twinaroo," because she and Jillian look so much alike. I fumbled with the keys until I was finally able to hit the talk button, and in that moment, my world began to slowly shift.

The caller, Twinaroo's mom, anxiously wondered where her daughter and Jillian were. They had both stayed with some friends the night before and were due back in town so that Twinaroo could get to the full-time job she had just started six weeks earlier. This was her first real job as an adult, with full benefits like health insurance and paid vacation, so a lot was at stake if she didn't show up soon. Her mom was afraid that she would be fired. Both girls were chronically tardy to everything it seemed, but Twinaroo and Jilly were overdue by over an hour this morning. I had agreed to allow the girls to stay overnight instead of driving back home late at night. The thought of frightened deer darting across the highway put me into protective mother mode. The girls may have been 19 years old, but the mom part of me did not want to let go of the old habit of worrying about them.

I tried my best to reassure Twinaroo's mom and find out why the girls had not kept their promise to be home by 6:15 A.M. I dialed both girls' cell phones, but it went straight to voice mail. We had discovered that cell phone reception was terrible the night before, because I had demanded that the girls check in with me upon arriving at their destination. They were out in a rural area with limited service. I remembered that texting had worked a few hours earlier, so I tried that instead. No response came from either of them. The axis of my world shifted a tiny bit more.

Assuming they had overslept (or buried the phones under the pillows where they couldn't hear the alarm go off) I hesitantly called the only number I had to the house where they were staying. Getting these girls out of bed in the morning was comparable to moving slugs out of quicksand. One ring. Two rings. Three rings. Just as I was about to hang up, a groggy young voice belonging to one of the twin brothers who lived there answered.

"Oh, hi," I said. "Sorry to wake you up, but did the girls oversleep this morning? They aren't home yet."

A slight pause filled the air before he processed my question and could come up with a coherent answer; after all, I had just awakened him from a sound sleep.

"Hmmm...no, the girls left about 05:50. What time is it now?"

"It's 7:30," I answered.

More awake now, he replied, "They should have long been home by now. (It was only 26 miles from their door to ours.) That's weird. I'm a little concerned. We will get dressed and go look for them. Maybe they hit a deer or something."

"Yeah," I agreed, "I will get dressed and start looking from my end too. Call me if you see them, okay?"

Throwing my robe on over my nightgown, I headed for the door and then thought better of it. If I had to change a flat tire or call a tow truck, I couldn't very well be seen on the side of a highway in my jammies and robe, now could I?

I quickly slid on a pair of jeans and grabbed a lightweight jacket to cover my nightgown instead, snatching up my cell phone, purse and keys as I headed out the door, unaware that when I came back through it again a couple hours later, my identity would be forever changed. My husband Mark was in a deer blind, my youngest daughter Sierra was sleeping upstairs with a friend who had spent the night. It never occurred to me to stop and leave a note.

As I drove in silence, I concentrated on scanning both sides of the road and oncoming traffic for Jilly's car while waiting for my cell phone to ring with any news from the boys.

After searching for about five miles or so without any luck, the twins finally called me back. They asked me an odd question (or at least I thought so at the time). They asked what the color and model of Jillian's car was. They are both severely colorblind and it was already dark when they arrived the night before. I told them that the girls were in a 2004 purple Dodge Stratus.

"Oh God!" one of the twins whispered in a panic. "We found the car! There's been an accident, but we don't see the girls anywhere and the police are giving us the run around. They won't tell us anything. We will call you back as soon as we know something!"

I hung up. My world had not only started to shift, it was beginning to wobble precariously on an unknown precipice.

My car rides are usually spent in silence since I rarely listen to the radio. I know that in that moment, I could hear my heart pounding loudly in my ears. I remember praying these words: "Heavenly Father, please be with the girls. Please, I beg you, *please* let them be okay. And Father... If they aren't okay... and you took them... (No parent even wants to have that thought.) Please have taken them instantly. If you didn't take them and they are badly hurt, please let them heal completely. Whatever the outcome, please give me the strength to handle it. Thy will be done."

Deep down in my heart, I think I already knew what the answer to my plea would be. I traveled a few more miles down the two-lane highway with a magnificent sunrise just beginning to reflect off my driver's side mirror. The ringing of the phone once again pierced the sound of silence. It was the same number as the first call that morning; the mom of Twinaroo. As soon as I clicked on the talk button, my ears were immediately assaulted by the sound of a man loudly wailing like a wounded animal.

It's a sound I have heard many times in my career as a nurse. It's a unique, almost animal sound that people make when their loved one's life is in grave danger... or when they have been told that their child is dead.

Holding my breath, I listened as the mother explained that they had been notified by the police about the car accident. Twinaroo had been airlifted by helicopter from the scene. Not from the hospital five miles up the road, but the *scene* of the accident. My nurse mode kicked in as I rationally thought, "*Well, that can't be good!*" Twinaroo had a brain bleed, a broken collarbone and some facial injuries. She was incoherent, but she was alive... for now. Her parents were on their way to the trauma center 60 minutes away and were not given any reassurance that their daughter would still be alive when they got there. They were not given any information on Jilly, but promised to call me back if they heard anything and hung up.

Once again, I was plunged into silence. The only thing I could hear was the creaking and groaning of my world shifting more ominously toward a razor's edge.

"Oh God, oh God, oh God..." I kept repeating out loud, as I rocked back and forth while driving. These words became my prayer. Over and over again, I repeated them, trying to calm myself as I drove closer and closer to a destination I couldn't get to fast enough, but at the same time dreaded arriving at.

As the phone rang a few minutes later, I became aware that my heart was now skipping in palpitations. Lub-dub, lub-dub... pause... dub, dub, dub... dub-dub, it beat. It was as if my world was suddenly in slow motion. Although the caller ID was now a familiar one, I knew before I picked it up that the answer that I was about to receive would change all our lives one way or the other.

The female voice on the other end was soft spoken and yet a true professional. She verified my name and introduced herself as Amanda, the police sergeant on duty. I think it was around that time, on that crisp November morning, that I felt my heart drop into my stomach and curl up in a fetal position.

"There has been an accident," she confirmed. "We have flown the driver out by helicopter." Even though it was Jilly's car, I knew that Twinaroo had been driving that morning.

"Is it bad?" I croaked. "It was bad, wasn't it?"

Silence. As a nurse, I knew very well what that pregnant silence meant.

"Oh God... My Jilly is dead, isn't she?" I whispered painfully.

The silence was screaming in my ears. It couldn't have been longer than two or three seconds, but it felt like eternity before this trained policewoman, freshly back from maternity leave herself (and working on her birthday, no less) tried to compose the words in a way that she hoped would somehow soften the devastating blow she was about to give. They are words that no one ever wants to say and words that are every parent's worst nightmare come true.

"Yes... I'm so sorry, your daughter didn't make it."

Amanda's voice cracked with the pain that only another parent would understand.

Those nine words registered in my brain first, then slid down to my heart before ricocheting into every other cell of my body and finally coming to rest in my belly, where I had carried this child for forty weeks before birthing her into this world. I suddenly felt empty... and so cold that it was as if I had been viciously plunged into ice water. In those nine words, my former world broke apart and tumbled like an avalanche roaring down a mountain, not stopping until the axis shift of my world was complete and I sat in silence once more, now trembling violently.

They say that cars do not have autopilots, or at least they didn't back in 2011. It surely would have been a nice feature at that time, because I have no idea how I continued to drive a busy two-lane highway while talking to this policewoman, absorbing those unbelievably horrible words: *I'm so sorry; your daughter didn't make it.*

Later, she would explain what had happened. The girls' car had run a stop sign, sailed across a two-lane highway, struck a gas main barrier across the road at 83 mph, then slammed into a small tree about 10 yards away at 72 mph. The car hugged the tree tightly on Jilly's side, depositing bark in her lap as the wood was peeled from its trunk on its rapid, spinning ascent and descent from the higher branches back to the ground. It finally came to rest partially in the roadway. Only three or four seconds had elapsed from the time the car cruised through the stop sign and left the road, marking her last breath in this life.

Jilly's passenger door and the place she sat took the crushing blow. She had died instantly, more than likely on the first impact; her neck breaking as quickly as the time it takes for you to snap your thumb and finger together. Just like that, my beautiful brown-eyed, funny, precious nineteen-year-old daughter was gone. It was quite possible that they had fallen asleep because there were no brake marks to indicate that they had tried to stop.

God must have been my pilot. I don't know how many yards or miles I traveled after that, passing oncoming cars and drifting past intersections where thankfully, I had the right of way.

I remember telling Sergeant Amanda that I would be there shortly, giving her the color, make and model of the car that I was driving. I confessed that I was alone, and currently about five miles from the scene. She discouraged me from coming of course, but I quite firmly informed her that I *would* be there; so, where would she like me to park when I arrived? I somehow managed to listen to the directions she gave me before I hung up. That deafening silence was back.

My nurse brain kicked in again and my 25 years of training snapped to the forefront of my consciousness. I pulled off to the side of the road and put on my flashers. I remember seeing a barren field and a line of trees in the distance to my right, but I was otherwise disoriented as to where I was and how I had gotten there. To this day, the only way I know that I am close to that area is the hollow feeling I get in the pit of my stomach when I travel that section of the road.

I needed help. I prayed. I called my husband repeatedly but got no answer. He was in a deer blind and had left the phone in his truck.

It suddenly dawned on me that I was on call for the weekend, which meant that I had 45 minutes to badge in if the hospital suddenly needed me for a surgical case. That sure wasn't going to happen! I called Jeanette, the nursing administrative supervisor on duty at the hospital where I worked, and told her that I wouldn't be able to take call for the rest of the weekend, so could she please find someone else? Working in a small hospital with extremely limited staff on a weekend, there obviously needed to be a good reason for my request, as it was very out of character for me to ask this of her. I recall calmly telling her that I was on my way to the scene of an accident.

Naturally, she had to know why.

For the very first time, I was suddenly forced to verbalize the words that I already hated, knowing all too well that as soon as I uttered them, they would redefine the path of my earthly life.

"My daughter is dead."

2

ALWAYS KISS ME GOODNIGHT

*I*N 2011, LIFE AS I knew it changed in a way I couldn't have imagined even in my wildest dreams. Earlier that year, in the quiet time of my early morning prayers, I dreamed of talking to Jesus. I told him that I felt ready for the spiritual growth that I had recently had a premonition about. I sensed that something big was soon going to be asked of me.

He answered quietly, *"Yes, you are ready, but the lesson that is coming will be very difficult. To whom much is given, much is asked. Are you sure about this?"*

I hesitated for a bit and finally answered, *"Yes, I think so, but please hold my hand and never let go."*

He assured me that he would not only hold my hand, but also give me constant guidance. I believed His promise and waited nervously for the assignment that would follow. It was indeed the most challenging, difficult, painful lesson I have ever experienced in my life.

Like every other parent that I have met on the tortuous path of grief, our number one question was, "Why? Why her, when there are so many old, frail, sick, lonely ones who have lived long lives and actually *want* to go back Home? Why not a murderer or rapist? She was such a good child, God. Why her? Why us? Haven't we lived our lives in kindness, loving and believing in you and following you the best way that we know how? Why do bad things happen to good people? What possible good can come out of you taking her Home so early? You could have saved her, God. Why didn't you?"

Occasionally, I am lucky enough to "see" Jilly in my dreams. This is the true story of a dream that answered so many of my questions—the greatest of them, "Why?"

As soon as I awoke, I quickly wrote down as much as I could remember, but it was so real to me that I needn't have bothered. I will never forget the details of this dream. This is what I recall:

I was standing in a beautiful grove of trees in a wooded area, reminding me of the Sequoias or Redwood Forest. The air was just right, with a balmy warm breeze caressing my skin and keeping me the perfect temperature. I couldn't help but inhale the clean scent of the velvety moss that covered the huge trunks of those majestic giant trees. Their branches made a lace canopy of shade above me, filtering the sunlight perfectly. Walking down a winding path, I felt the pine needles and cones softly crunching under my feet. I looked up ahead and noticed a warm golden ray of light piercing the shadows of the forest from up above the tops of the trees; it easily illuminated a small, grassy clearing just ahead. It was so beautiful that it took my breath away!

As my gaze followed the shaft of light to the spot where it spilled softly on the ground, I saw a wondrous sight. Jesus was sitting there in a large, comfortable rocking chair with a little girl cozily nestled in His lap who looked very familiar. As I got closer, I realized it was my daughter, Jilly! Oh, my gosh! I wanted to run to her, scoop her up in my arms and claim her again as my own, but it was as if I was glued to the spot where I was standing. Unable to move, I was only allowed to observe from a distance, but I could hear every word of the conversation the two of them were having. It went like this:

Jesus, in a calm soothing voice said, *"I have received your request Jillian, to try life on Earth. You've been talking to the Ancient Ones again, haven't you? They told you that if you want to learn about the things that you can only experience as a human, you must have a physical body, didn't they?*

"Now, I want you to understand that your new body will feel very heavy compared to the one made of Light that you wear now. It will take a while to master how your new body works and sometimes, it will be challenging just to keep it going. It is very fragile

and each one is unique, so you must take very good care of this gift that I will lend you."

Jilly, gazing up at Jesus, with love in her eyes replied, "I understand, but I still want to go. You know me, I just love new and exciting adventures! I want to try some of the things that we can't even practice here, like forgiveness... or faith, for example. We don't get to learn about those things in heaven, because there is nothing here to forgive and all we need to do is want something and *BAM*, there it is! Faith is just as natural as breathing to us here.

"I love being in heaven, I mean it's a perfect place and I am happy here. I love my work, but I am getting restless for a new job. I want to try to really make a difference to someone for just a little while if that's okay with you. No worries though, Jesus. I will make sure to come back here every night to sit in your lap and get my hugs and give you a kiss!"

Jesus chuckled, "*Well, Jillian, that may very well happen, but it will be in a different way than you are accustomed to. I will always be in your heart; sometimes you might feel my arms around you. Perhaps, you may even get little tiny glimpses of me. But you won't be able to come back here whenever you feel like it, the way you do now.*

"*When you are in human form, you must stay that way until the silver cord connecting your physical body to your spiritual body is completely dissolved. Only then can you come back and crawl in my lap for as long as you like.*"

Astonished, Jilly exclaimed, "What? No way! Why can't I visit here whenever I want?"

Jesus patiently sighed and answered, *"Because, if you did, my sweet child, you would be so homesick for heaven that you wouldn't be able to complete the assignment that I am helping you to learn by sending you to the physical realm. I will have to erase your memories of being here or else you wouldn't be able to bear it.*

"I will always be with you though, closer than you can even imagine, but you won't be able to see me with your human eyes. That would be way too intense! You will have to slowly remember all about how much I love you in your own way and in your own time. It may take years... or you may not remember at all."

Jilly kissed him on the cheek and cried, "Nah, there's no way I will forget you! You are my best friend ever! How will I ever find someone there that I love as much as I love you?" She gave Him another hug, "Will you miss me being here with you, giving you hugs every night?"

Jesus, getting a little emotional, whispered, *"Oh, my Jilly girl... you are such a delight to my heart. Your antics continually amuse me and make me smile. Of course, I will miss you, and even though I know in advance how it will all turn out at the end of your journey, I am still willing to lend you to a human family for a while.*

"You see, I am answering a special prayer for them by doing so. I will give you sisters to love and learn from, fight with and protect. They will be your first and favorite best friends; then you will make even more best friends as you get older.

"Each person that comes into your life will bring you a special gift and lesson that only they can offer your soul and you in turn, will give them something that is uniquely yours to offer.

"I will give you parents that I picked especially for you, but please don't expect them to be perfect. They will totally screw up sometimes and make some big mistakes. However, they will love you with everything that they are capable of. Be gentle with them, for they are learning too. They are doing the best that they can with the limited experience they have.

"My dear Jillian, you will have some hard challenges in your life as a human. That is what Earth is all about, you see: learning and growing from your experiences. Don't worry, your parents will always love you no matter what, even when you mess up! I will always love you too ... and I surely will miss having you here in heaven with me.

"Sometimes I wonder how I will bear it, even though I know we will be together again someday. I will let you do this though, because you have asked. You always have liked to stir things up, you little rascal!"

Jilly questioned Jesus, "How will I know exactly what my special assignment is on Earth or when I should come back Home? Will you send me a sign like making the streetlights come on, or will you just appear before me when it's time?"

Jesus answered, *"Well, that's the beauty of it, my sweet girl ... you won't know these things. That is where the faith and patience that you wanted to learn about comes in. I will infuse your soul with a little bit of heaven that you get to take with you* on this journey. You will know you are on the right path when you feel a special kind of love, a warmth down deep in your heart. That is me, hugging your soul."

He continued, "*Now Jillian, you must listen very carefully to what I am going to tell you, because when you get to where you are going, you may not remember this. Sometimes, the lessons that you are going to learn will be just for your own growth.*

"*Other times, you will be part of something bigger that will help others with the lessons they have to learn. Some of it will be absolutely wonderful, and some of it will appear to be outrageously unfair. You won't understand why it IS the way it is.*

"*You will experience joy and sorrow, love and anger, success and what feels like failure, frustration and struggles. You will learn to ask for forgiveness ... and you will be given many opportunities to forgive others. I will tell you a secret though ... every time you learn about faith, love, forgiveness and patience, you are also helping someone else learn about those things too.*

"*You are all My children and are connected to each other in more ways than you will ever be able to imagine. It may look like a jumbled mess sometimes, but trust Me, I know what I am doing. My master plan is much bigger than one human lifetime, it spans eternity. It will be too much for your tiny little shoulders to carry.*

"*I will give you the perfect situations and people in your life that you need to accomplish your goals, and then it is up to you to learn what you need to do to reach them. I will give you a loving family and friends. I will send you multiple teachers in many forms. I will also give you the greatest gifts of all. Choices. Free will. Second chances. And last, but not least, I will give you a great big sense of humor; the ability to laugh at yourself. You will surely need that on this journey!*

"*You will be finished in the blink of an eye, even though at times, it will seem like forever, especially when you go through the rough spots in your life. I know all your days there before you have lived even one of them, but you will not remember the appointed day of your homecoming while you are in your human form. While you will not know your exact last day; you may start to feel homesick for heaven just before it happens. You might begin to catch tiny glimpses of me or even other loved ones who are waiting to welcome you back Home.*

"*No matter how you end up leaving your human body, even that experience will also be part of a bigger lesson that you will help others to learn. You will not mind though, because when the last moment of your human existence arrives, you will hear my voice and leap from your human body right into My arms. You will not feel any pain when you separate from your human body, no matter how it appears on that side.*"

"*It's like an actor exiting a stage after playing out a scene; some exits are more dramatic than others. Any doubts that you may have had about why things happened the way they did will then make perfect sense, and I will explain everything. That is how human life works, you see.*"

They got up from the rocking chair and, still holding hands, walked over to a nearby magnificent prism of light that had suddenly appeared out of nowhere. It was made of colors that aren't even describable in our language. The endless number of sparkly colors merged together to form a twisty tunnel slide, starting at the floor of this glorious forest and descending through a thick bank of misty clouds. I couldn't see where the bottom ended. Jesus placed Jilly at the top of the slide and sat down behind her, lovingly cradling her in His arms once more.

Jesus explained, "*This is a very special kind of tunnel slide that will take you to meet your earthly parents and a big sister who is anxiously awaiting your arrival. In time, I will send you another sister, but she isn't quite ready to join you yet. Are you ready to go?*" Jilly answered, "I guess I am as ready as I will ever be ... but are you sure that you don't want to come with me?"

"*I will be there with you, my precious child, in every sunrise and sunset. I will be there in the smiles of your family, the laughter of your friends and the unconditional love of your favorite pets. I will be there in the warm breezes of summer and the big fluffy snowflakes of winter. I know you will miss me, but I will never leave you, although you may occasionally walk away from me. You can find me in many places ... you will just have to gaze into the eyes of those that you love to see Me.*

"*I can hardly wait for the day that I will hold you in my arms again. When it is time for you to come back Home, I will be waiting right here, ready to get a great big hug from you. Now go and have a wonderful journey and learn lots of new things! I will see you in a little while. I love you, my sweet, funny Jillian.*"

"I love you too! And Jesus ...? I know it must hurt to let me go, because it hurts me to leave you ... so thank you for letting me do this. I will always remember to send you a kiss goodnight."

He embraced her one last time and then softly kissed the top of her head. He gave her a gentle push. She started to accelerate down the slide, quickly picking up speed. He watched her go with a lump in His throat as she grinned from ear to ear at the excitement of this thrilling new experience.

She gazed back up at Jesus one last time as she descended into the brilliant white fog, until at last, He was completely out of her sight. When she got to the bottom of the tunnel slide made of Light, she opened her eyes on Earth for the first time. Her new parents smiled with indescribable joy as she was delivered into their arms. She took her first breath in human form and let out a lusty wail.

He watched them embrace His child.

And Jesus wept.

Hold everything in your hands lightly, otherwise it hurts when God pries your fingers open. — Corrie ten Boom

Why?

OF ALL THE QUESTIONS bereaved families have about the deaths of their loved ones, the number one unanswered question is almost always *why?*

I am taking a writing class and my assignment last night was dialoguing between two or three people. I had exactly 15 minutes to write as fast as I could. I pondered this for a minute and then this question for God suddenly came to my mind. Here is a snippet of that "conversation with God."

Me: God, I just don't understand.

God: *What don't you get?*

Me: Why? I just don't understand why.

God: *Why what? Why when? Why how? What is it you want to understand?*

Me: All of it. Why did you only lend Jilly to me for only 19 years and 280 days?

Why not 60 years? Why not 100 years?

God: *She had done what her soul was sent to do. When you have completed that job, you will get to come Home too.*

Me: What was her purpose? Didn't she have more to accomplish? Couldn't she have done *more* if she had stayed?

God: *There's always more. Sometimes the best way to accomplish it is to start something on your side and let it finish unfolding on this side. That is Jilly's purpose. Just because she no longer carries around an earthly body doesn't mean her job is totally finished. I still have plenty of work for her to do. It's just that she can now do it better from here, with different abilities that she now understands on this side.*

Me: And what is your purpose for me, God? What could you possibly hope to accomplish in my life by letting my child die at such a young age; in the prime of her beauty and only the spring of her youth? How does *that* help the world?

God: *It is a small part of your life's greater plan too. You are helping others survive this journey by sharing your walk on it so* openly. And when you do that, you are doing your best to honor all that I AM. Love. Empathy. Compassion.

Remember, my dear child…Jilly is safe with Me. You are safe with me. I know earth is hard. Being separated from Me is hard. But it's what your soul needs in order to grow to its highest and fullest potential. It was hard when you had to leave your parents to go to school, wasn't it?

Your parents didn't send you to school so that you could stay in first grade forever, now did they? Of course not. They wanted you to grow, to learn and to become the greatest version of yourself that you can be. That is what most parents wish for their children. I am no different. You had to accept challenges in order to have a greater understanding of the tasks I have set before you. And there will be tests! You will get the answer key when you come Home!

The timer went off. I had to put down my pen and contemplate what I had just written. After having this little conversation with God, I feel hopeful that there is some bigger plan; one so vast, so powerful, so beautiful that I can't even comprehend it.

I know my daughter is safe; I know in my heart that I am safe, even if I must remind myself of that several times a day. Maybe, instead of asking *why* I should consider asking *how*? How can I grow and learn from this? How can I make this experience part of the greatest good? Help me, God!

3

THE AFTERMATH OF DEVASTATION

Faith sees the invisible, believes the unbelievable, and receives the impossible. ~ Corrie Ten Boom

IT IS TRUE THAT it is impossible to truly understand the enormity of losing a child until you go through it. The effects on those left behind is something that you never "get over." We may resign ourselves to getting used to living with the loss. We might even begin to understand its purpose; and even come to realize that all really was "perfect" in Gods timing in the grander scheme of things. Since this is a true story, I now want to share with you some of the amazing, incredible things that happened in the week after Jilly parted with her Earthly body.

However, there are some important points I wish to make first:

- I have shared some of these experiences with both clergy and therapists and none of them have described me as out of touch with reality. They couldn't necessarily explain it but said that many people have similar experiences.
- None of this is made up! There have been many witnesses to the "winks" we have received.
- Although it is not necessarily common place, what happened to us is also not that unusual. There are many people with stories like mine that have validated what we have experienced.
- For some of you, this content may be a little too far outside of the box for you to accept as true. No problem. Everyone is entitled to their own belief system. My goal is to help those who may have also had these kinds of experiences to realize they are not alone and that this is a soul's way of giving us peace of heart and mind. I suspect that this happens to many more people than we know. Many are just not consciously aware of the signs or if they do notice, are afraid to talk about it.

For those who feel the need to worry about my salvation, please don't. I assure you that I am committed to the God of my understanding. I gave my life to Jesus when I was 17, and He has held me in his embrace ever since. I wouldn't still be here if it weren't for my faith. Although I don't shout about my relationship with God from the rooftops in an evangelical way, I hope that my life and my actions speak for themselves. It is the best witnessing I know how to do. He is my best friend and I know I will be with Him, Jilly and the rest of my family for eternity.

You may also question my use of the word "angelversary" when referring to the date that Jilly died. I call it this because I believe that the angels swooped down from Heaven and took her Home that day. Is Jilly truly an angel now? Technically . . . no, probably not. I doubt that angels have ever had lifetimes in human bodies, although I do believe they can appear to us as humans when it is necessary for us to have a visual presence. But what else do you call your deceased child that doesn't make you want to break down in tears just saying it? In this sense, angel works for me or simply, "my daughter's spirit."

God gives everyone certain talents or gifts. Some people understand complex mathematics, for instance, but I sure don't! Others can paint, draw or play music well. Some serve others with a joyful heart and others are good planners; some are quite intuitive. My gift has always been that the veil separating this life from the next is quite thin . . . so thin that occasionally, I can catch glimpses of what is on the other side of it.

I have been aware that death is not the end for us since I was a little girl, when my Great Grandpa, whom I adored, died.

At nearly five years old, I didn't understand that death was "permanent" because he came to "visit" afterward and let me know he was okay. I assumed that was a "normal" thing and that others could see him too.

When I lost a friend in high school, the same thing happened. Deeply missing her one night, I was telling God that I wished I could see her one more time, so that I could tell her how much she meant to me. She appeared as a hazy vision at the foot of my bed and asked, "Louise, why are you looking for the living among the dead? I am more alive than you are!" It scared the daylights out of me, even though I did find some comfort in her words.

I have come to realize that thinking of someone who has passed *actually brings them to your side*. By the end of high school, it became clear that not everyone had these kinds of experiences.

With one of the first deaths I witnessed at the hospital where I work, I was stunned to see what looked like the vapors that rise off a hot road or gas grill, coming from the chest of the man we had just pronounced dead. Perhaps this is the reason many of us "old school nurses" feel compelled to open a window when a death has occurred; there are others who have witnessed similar phenomena. For millennia, some cultures have believed that it helps the soul to find its bearings to the next phase of its life.

After witnessing a few more deaths, I realized that what I was watching was the spirit separate from the earthly body. I could see some of them in the corner of the room or above their body. It doesn't always happen, but it has happened to me enough that I believe what I am seeing. Obviously, the end is not "The End."

Jilly was raised to believe the same, that the end "here" is a new beginning "there." She also had the ability from a very young age, to get glimpses through that veil. She had no fear of it. When her grandpa was diagnosed with terminal cancer just a few months before Jilly died herself, I asked her to write him a letter and give it to him to read while he was still alive. I wanted her to say now what she might regret not having the chance to say later, like her favorite memories of him, her love for him, etc. He did treasure it, by the way. The letter said:

> *I don't ever want you to leave me but when it's time, there are some things you have to do. Join my "wolf pack" of guardian angels, that consists of Great Grandma (your mommy), my Grandpa Jim, my old counselor/Godfather Dr. Spink, and my two young friends that died this year, Shawn and Aaron. Every night when I pray to God, I talk to my wolf pack (I have no idea why she called them that, except that she was a huge* Twilight *fan) and thank them for keeping me safe and out of trouble. Once you are a strong enough angel, you should send me signals that you can hear me when I pray at night. That would be cool. I want you to know that when you are gone, we will take care of*

Grandma, but while you are here, make sure you tell her you love her as much as you can and live every day like it's your last. That's what I do! Nothing will be the same without you, but I know you will always be there watching. I love you with all my heart, never forget that!

Love always,
Jilly

She drew a picture of them holding hands and him flexing his muscles. I have included her drawing in this post because it will be important for future reference. Grandpa (she called him Papa) died 67 days before Jilly did. He had a prominent nose. Supposedly, it was what attracted Grandma to him in the first place back in college, besides the fact that he was playing on a collegiate basketball team that made it to the NCAA Sweet 16!

Dear Papa, I never thought I'd be writing this letter. I always imagined you would be around for my wedding, and when I graduate nursing school, and when I have babies. But everything happens for a reason and I think you accomplished a lot in your life for starters you kinda made all of us girls since you made my dad. ☺ I know you guys have had a big impact on all of us girls' lifes. It was because of you $ that I started getting good grades; yeah the money might have got me motivated but after I got all A's it was like I couldn't settle for less, so thank you for that. I have so many great memories with you guys that I will never forget, like always trying to climb the tree in your yard, and when you would take us to the park by your house, or when it was your birthday and all of us girls had a red shirt that said "it's Papas birthday" and you had the hat that said "Papa" 😊 Of all of the vacations we've gone on, my favorites were: The South Dakota trip, Sea World, Florida, and North Carolina. You guys have always been so supportive of everything we've done, especially our sports. It was always good to look up in the stands and see your faces. I dont ever want you to leave me but when its time there are some things you have to do. 1) Join my wolf pack of guardian angels; the pack consists of great grandma (your mommy), my grandpa Jim, my old consilior/god father, and my two young friends that past away this year shawn, and aaron. Every night when I pray

to god and say my prayers
I talk to my wolf pack and
thank them for keeping me
safe and out of trouble.
Once your a strong enough
angel you should send me
signals that you can hear
me when I pray at night,
that would be cool. I want
you to know that when your
gone we will take care of
grandma but while your here
make sure you tell her you
love her as much as you can
and live every day like its
your last. Thats what I do ☺
Nothing will be the same
without you but I know
you will always be there
watching. I love you with
all my heart, never forget
that!

                Love always,
                    Jilly ♥

♥ ♥ ♥

Fast forward to the day after Jilly's accident. As you can imagine, it was a horrible time. We were so numb and so raw that we couldn't even think straight. We weren't sleeping much, so when unusual things started happening, we just took it with a grain of salt... that is, until a couple of days after her passing. I had posted very little on social media since I didn't yet know all the details of the accident myself. In fact, we had to temporarily take down her personal Facebook page because people were posting things on it, like "R.I.P. Jilly" before we had finished notifying everyone in the family. Unfortunately, that was how one of her closest cousins found out about her death. Some of the details we learned by reading the paper!

Public service announcement here: Wait for the *family* to notify the world first via social media about a death. They will decide which details need to be shared! If you want to express condolences before the death is made public, please do so in a private message or an email to the bereaved. There are no brownie points for being the first to post all the details about a death before the family has had a chance to even begin to process their grief. Chances are good that you don't have all the information correct anyway!

When I finally checked my Facebook posts on Monday, two days after the accident, it was flooded with messages. Scrolling through them, I noticed the memorable date and like every other year since reconnecting with him, I wished an old high school friend of mine named Al a Happy Birthday. Al was involved in a serious car accident on his 17th birthday, so that date was of significance to me. Thankfully he survived, but it taught me to never pass up a chance to let someone know how much they mean to me. This was doubly true now that Jilly had been so suddenly taken from this life.

My friend Al told me that his cousin had asked to be put in contact with me. He gave me her private number and strongly encouraged me to call her. *Now,* not later. I was hesitant, as the hour was late, and I was exhausted. He assured me that it would be okay, just do it. Taking a minute to muster up my courage, I dialed this total stranger's number. The phone rang about three times and just as I was about to lose my nerve and hang up, a woman answered.

"I had my phone turned off and it rang anyway! How odd! Who is this?" she said.

I told her my name and the next words out of her mouth nearly made me drop the phone.

"Oh, thank God you called!" she exclaimed with excitement. "Your daughter has been here since 3 A.M. Saturday driving me nuts!" I was speechless . . . I just said, "Huh?"

She repeated those exact words and it sent my mind racing.

"Which daughter?" I asked suspiciously.

She described Jillian, right down to the way she would

"flip" her hair when she met someone new. Hmmm, she must be wrong though. Jilly was still alive at 3 A.M. Saturday. She died at 6 A.M. "Umm, where do you live?" I asked.

"In California." she replied.

On *her* time, 3 A.M. Saturday, would have been 6 A.M. *my* time; the exact time that the police surmised that the accident occurred, since it was not witnessed. (It was also the time I suddenly woke up and looked at the clock, not able to figure out what had awakened me from a sound sleep that morning.) I was in shock. Thankfully, my sister Nicki was recording everything! The woman on the phone told me that Jilly had appeared to her in the middle of a good sleep, jumping up and down on her bed, saying, "You *have* to talk to my mom, she is expecting to hear from me! Please, please find a way to talk to her! I have so much to tell her!"

She compared it to the movie *Ghost* where Patrick Swayze keeps tormenting Whoopi Goldberg by singing the song, "I'm Henry the Eighth, I Am" over and over because he wants her to deliver a message, but she puts a pillow over her head, trying to ignore him. She finally has enough and says "Stop singing already! I'll do it!" I could picture Jilly doing this. She was, after all, very persistent!

This wonderful messenger went on to tell me that Jilly had been welcomed to heaven by an athletic man with a very large nose who had been "waiting for her" to arrive. They were having a grand old time, meeting and greeting loved ones on the other side. She also told me things about the accident that I didn't even know yet and that there was certainly no way she could have known. For instance, another 19-year-old girl was also killed on the same road a year before Jilly's accident. We did some searching and found out that was true. Some of the things she told me were things I didn't find out until three to six months later. For example, she said that if Twinaroo had been able to jerk the wheel a little bit to the left, they might have been able to avoid the gas main. (That was impossible, of course; no one can control a car that is airborne, and they were probably asleep when it left the roadway.) When the police recreated the accident for me several weeks later, the first thing the officer said was, "You know, if they had just been able to jerk the wheel a little to the left..."

She also told me the *exact* words that I swore I had heard Jilly say to me while I was driving to the scene, after the police confirmed that she was gone.

It's okay mom, I jumped out of my body before impact and it didn't hurt a bit!

She knew things that only I would know that happened while I was alone in the car that day. Jilly also relayed specific wishes about things that she wanted handled in a specific way, particularly when it came to dealing with Twinaroo, who was still in the hospital at that point.

We didn't argue with Jilly; we just honored her wishes! It was an incredible phone call and it completely changed the way we looked at her funeral. She preferred that we celebrate her *LIFE*, because she was surely doing that very thing on the other side.

Obviously, this woman was an authentic messenger. She was and is, very well respected in her community and her profession. She is a deeply connected, kind spiritual woman who also happens to have the ability to occasionally see and hear through the thin veil that separates us.

Jilly came to at least two other people from various parts of the country with similar abilities over the next year. They all had the same very specific messages for us. Now that's enough to send your head spinning, isn't it? It certainly was mine. But no, Jilly wasn't done yet. She now knew that we were listening and that we had received her message; she probably wanted to also prove to us that it really was *her*, so she pulled another cool trick or two out of thin air.

Jilly's little sister, Sierra, had gone up to her room and picked out her burial outfit within an hour of me giving her the devastating news. She carefully chose exactly what she thought Jilly would want to wear, right down to the accessories. She decided that Jilly should wear a necklace that had been one of her favorites, since Jilly was seldom without a necklace; she had worn the same plastic stretchy one for nearly two years before it broke. The necklace Sierra picked for her had a cross, the word "Faith" on a silver charm and an old ring that Jilly had been given by her ex-boyfriend (Randolph's) grandma, who had Alzheimer's. She couldn't remember many things, but Grandma always remembered who Jilly was. She had given her this ring on one of their visits. She loved Jilly very much and sadly, Grandma died 25 days before Jilly did. We laid the clothes out on the bed in Jilly's room and placed the necklace on the shirt that we picked out. The family was all in agreement that this was the outfit and jewelry she would wear. On Tuesday morning, the day after the phone call from California, we went into Jilly's room to gather the things on our checklist to take to the funeral director:

- Slippers (pink camouflage)
- Matching socks (I insisted)
- Decent underwear and a nice cozy bra
- Her very favorite gray and pink Victoria's Secret comfortable shirt
- A pink camouflage Columbia jacket and nice jeans
- Make up, perfume, brushes and a curling iron for her hair
- Jewelry for the viewing: her promise ring from Randolph and the necklace with the charm and his grandma's ring on it.

The necklace, the cross and the charm were there but Grandma's ring was missing from the chain! Who in the heck would take a piece of costume jewelry out of her bedroom? It wasn't valuable, and that would be about the lowest thing someone could do to a grief-stricken family. Very few people had been in there since the accident, and we kept the door to her room shut as we couldn't even bear to look in there. We shook out the clothes, shook the bedspread, looked around the room and even suspiciously eyed the cat. That ring was *nowhere* to be found!

We decided it simply wasn't meant to be, placed all the items in a tote bag and set off for the funeral home. Upon arriving, Kathy (who is Jilly's godmother and the director of the funeral home that received her body) exclaimed, "You are absolutely *glowing*! What happened?" Admitting that I was excited, I proceeded to tell her about the phone call from California. Jilly's dad, Mark, hadn't yet heard the recording of the conversation that had taken place the night before. His head was spinning hard enough without entertaining the possibility that our daughter had sent us a message via a total stranger from across the country!

While the funeral director, Jilly's sisters and I were all talking, Mark sat down at a nearby table and started staring off into space, trying to keep from breaking down...again. He was looking down at his feet under the table, when something caught his eye—something *shiny*.

He reached down and picked it up. *It was Grandma's ring!* Right there under the table at the funeral home! It got there before we did...how was that even possible? I could almost hear Jilly giggling...but she wasn't done yet! Not by a long shot!

4

JILLY, PHONE HOME PLEASE

The Quarter Stories

*T*HE FIRST ONE APPEARED two days after Jilly died. Our youngest daughter, Sierra woke up from a short, broken sleep and felt something odd on her chest. She reached up, and there on her chest near her heart was a quarter; a plain old every day quarter, worth 25 cents. She didn't think much about it. Next, she stretched and started to get out of bed. She put her feet down on the floor and stepped on...yes, another quarter! Still not "getting it" she walked over to the mirror where she and Jilly always did their make up together. There was a third quarter by her makeup bag. This was starting to get a little weird.

She told her dad and me about it, but we kind of blew it off. We were so numb and spacey at this point that if you had told us that Martians had just landed in Chicago, we wouldn't have thought it strange. We simply couldn't think straight at that point in time. We had to go out to the wreckage of the car and retrieve some of her belongings. On the floorboard (in the spot where Jilly's foot would have been) was a quarter and another quarter sat on the driver's seat, discolored by bodily fluids.

At her visitation/wake a few days later, people started finding quarters near where Mark and I were standing. They kept handing them to us, asking if we dropped them. I was wearing slacks without pockets. My husband didn't have a hole in his pocket. We didn't know where they were coming from or what else to do with them, so Jilly ended up with a stash of quarters in the casket with her. When she was a little girl and payphones were commonplace, I had told her that she should always have a quarter in her pocket in case she needed to call home. In the dense fog of our grief, it had finally clicked. She had found another creative way to "reach" out to us!

Jilly was calling home!

Quarters have been found in many places since Jilly died that are too strange to be a coincidence: In the fly of a pair of boy's underwear wrapped around a drain under a sink, on the bottom of a riverbed during a brief stop while kayaking, next to the rim of a fire pit while camping, in socks, shoes, boots and mittens that hadn't been used in months, and on carpets that had just been vacuumed and weren't there a minute ago, just to name a few. We have dozens of stories, but here are a few more of the most memorable quarter stories.

To deal with his grief, Jilly's daddy found comfort in the soil. He loves gardening, and since we had a large bare spot in the yard, he designated that area as *Jilly's Garden*, a place of reflection and beauty. We bought this house and yard from my parents in 2000; they had lived here since 1986. During all those years, the area he picked for Jilly's Garden had always been a flat grassy area. It wasn't used for gardening, flowers or even a pet burial spot.

Day in and day out, Mark poured his sweat and tears into creating that beautiful space for her. He designed a raised, round flower bed, surrounded by a mosaic stone path with a granite bench and waterfall in the corner. All the flowers would be purple blooms and a life-sized angel statue with long flowing hair and a beautiful face stands guard in the center of the garden. Solar lights illuminate the angel at night, casting shadows of colorful shapes among the flowers. It blooms from early spring with daffodils and hyacinth, to tulips, irises, peonies, lilacs and lilies. It took him months to plan. The design called for Mark to dig a circular 15-foot wide and 12 to 18-inch deep hole, exchanging it for richer soil. He dutifully picked out rocks and weeded for weeks. It was a labor of love for him and gave him something constructive to do with his grief.

As he got close to the end of his project, he ran into a large tree root about a foot under the topsoil. It was a monster root, approximately five inches in diameter. He dug and pulled, dug and pulled even harder. He finally had to use a power saw to cut through it. He managed to get the root split and pulled with all his might to get it out of the ground. As he checked underneath the root for any stray rocks, his fingers found a small, flat, round object. At first, he thought it was some sort of button, but it was so filthy it was hard to tell. He brought it in the house and cleaned it up. Imagine his surprise when, as the water slowly washed away the dirt, a quarter was revealed in his hand!

He got excited; I mean, what are the odds of finding a quarter, Jilly's sign for us, under a tree root that far down? It got even more bizarre. When the coin was cleaned up, he discovered it was not only a quarter, but a 2009 Virgin Island quarter. It had a seagull (or "Freebird") watching over a tropical beach. Jilly's favorite shirts were Hollister shirts whose symbol is a seagull. "Freebird," by Lynyrd Skynyrd, was also the song we played at her funeral. Her favorite thing to do as soon as the temperature got above 50 degrees was to go lay out on the roof and tan. She loved the beach and all things associated with it.

There it was, a 2009 quarter under a tree root, under twelve inches of soil in an area that had never been broken since at least 1986. Explain that one, because I certainly can't.

In another instance, Sierra was at the crash site (which I refer to as Jillian's Passage) and was about 7 feet away from the tree the car had hit. She found another small piece of the car, even though we have cleaned up the area numerous times. She picked it up and underneath it was a quarter.

At a family gathering later that year, we were all missing our girl, thinking about how much she would have enjoyed spoiling the babies there. Mark sat down on the concrete step and put his hand down to balance himself right on top of...yes, you guessed it...a quarter. A four-year old at the same party walked up and handed me a quarter. I said "Honey, what's this?" She said, "I just thought you would like it." We have a box full of quarters that she has left us here and there. We would not have put quarters and Jilly together before her accident, because they just weren't meaningful to us. Now we can't look at a quarter and *not* think of her. Her friends are the same way. She has made believers out of total skeptics.

She lets us know under no uncertain terms that she is close...so very close. If we could just reach out beyond the cement-like density of our material world and put our hand through the veil that separates us, we would be able to touch her. She is closer to us on any given day than she is when we visit her grave and stand five feet above her body. Does that sound strange? Way too out there? Heretical? It isn't.

Jesus said, "I will be with you, even until the end of time."

I believe Jilly is with God, because in her very own words, written 24 days before she died, she wrote, "I am not scared because I know that God is with me, keeping me safe and strong." Wouldn't Jilly also be with us unto the end of time?

Yet another random Jilly quarter story happened during the winter and there were many witnesses to this one.

In early December, I spent the day with a very special group of people in my life. Each year, several families get together to make grave blankets for our children who have gone Home too soon. In the past, we have shared the signs (or winks, as some call them) we get from our children with each other. By the way, I am not the only one who gets signs.

One year, I was one of the last to finish my grave blanket, because I am a slowpoke and I was the lone person in my family able to work on it that day. Mark was in another state and my daughters weren't available. Sierra had to work, and Erica had gone back home, hundreds of miles away. This is usually a family event, so they were missed very much.

Amid shoving sharp tree branches into a piece of uncooperative Styrofoam (while covered in pine sap), Erica called to tell me that she and her rescue dog, Lucy, had just passed the test to become a certified dog therapy team. They had been working on this for months and Lucy was one of the rare dogs who passed the test the first time. Naturally, I was thrilled for them, but I couldn't talk because my hands were all sticky. I told her I would call her later.

As I was decorating the grave blanket, I was having a mental conversation with Jilly about what she would think of the "bling" on this year's blanket. (It does resemble the skirt of a prom dress.) I also talked to her about her sister's accomplishments: Sierra finishing her first semester in nursing school and

Erica's successful dog training. I know she would be proud of them. I wished she could be here to cheer them on.

I was putting on the finishing touches when one of the dads came around with his push broom, cleaning up the large deposits of pine needles, branches, etc. The floor was nice and tidy as I packed my stuff up to head home. Another mom offered to help me finish up and we moved the grave blanket over to a new spot for easier handling. She looked down on what was a clean floor a few minutes ago and spotted a beautiful shiny quarter... in the same area that had just been swept clean. We called over the sweeper to see if he had dropped it. "Nope," he said, "that was *not* there a few minutes ago!" I had been sitting in that area as he swept; I knew that no one else had been in the area either. I picked it up. It was a Connecticut quarter.

Erica had just moved to Connecticut. The symbol for that state is a tree. What was I working on? A grave blanket... made from tree branches. And here's a little tidbit about nursing in Connecticut. A famous Civil War nurse, Georgy Woolsey, helped to establish the Connecticut Training School for Nurses in New Haven. Sierra was in nurse's training and Erica was currently staying in New Haven! Apparently, Jilly wants us to know that she isn't missing a thing that is going on in our lives. It's so good to know that!

LOUISE CRIST

♥ ♥ ♥

This is one of the most Jilly-like quarter stories ever, which was pretty darn funny. (Warning: it may also be slightly offensive to some, sorry in advance!) To give you a little background on this silly Jilly daughter of mine:

1. She had, and still *has* a wicked sense of humor.
2. She watches over and seems to be with her sisters a lot.
3. She loves, loves, loves babies and older people. She always said she thought they were so cute! She threatened to "steal" several grandparents and take them home.
4. I know this will be gross to most of you not in the health care field, but she also was completely comfortable discussing poop. Many people do, so it's not really that weird ... listen to a group of 90-year-olds sometime and

a conversation about constipation will eventually come up. Listen to a group of nurses over lunch and I guarantee it will come up at some point! She had written a very colorful journey through the digestive system about how our marvelous bodies change nourishing food to waste when we are done using it. Jilly thought nothing of announcing to a total stranger that she "had to go". (I think she did it just to get them all flustered—for the shock value of it.) You have read about the odd places Jilly leaves quarters to let us know she is with us and still very much a part of our lives. Even though we can't see her, we have learned to trust that she watches over us and is near us as much as she can be in her new reality.

This week was the Jillian Crist Memorial Scholarship Mud Volleyball tournament. We raise money for scholarships for future health care professionals, such as doctors, nurses or certified nursing assistants (C.N.A.'s).

Jilly's younger sister was, at the time, a C.N.A. at a nursing home and rehab facility. Part of her job is feeding, dressing and bathing patients with all kinds of mobility issues. Several of them are confined to beds or wheelchairs. They require a special type of device that helps to lift the patient to a standing or sitting position.

Sierra, I should mention, is accustomed to dealing with all kinds of body fluids in her job. It's a nurse thing... changing a diaper doesn't really gross us out, any more than changing a diaper on a baby would gross most parents out. (Although I have changed some pretty awful baby diapers that even make *my* eyes water!) Adult briefs are an awesome modern convenience for people who no longer have bowel or bladder control.

With that being said . . . Sierra was at work one day when she walked into a patient's room; seeing that the patient needed to have her brief changed, she got the necessary mechanical device that helps her stand a patient up from a sitting position. She pulled down the patients brief to change it . . . and a quarter rolled out!

Sierra broke out in a chuckle. The patient asked what was so funny.

"A quarter just rolled out of your butt," Sierra responded.

The client retorted, "I was saving that for later."

Jilly would be rolling on the ground laughing . . . this is her exact sense of twisted humor! It is one of the top five places she has left a quarter. I can still hear her giggling. Only Jilly would pull a quarter out of her butt . . . or someone else's!

Jilly wasn't even close to being done letting us know she was not only okay . . . she was and is *awesomely okay* in her new Home. Isn't that what every parent hopes for; that when their kids leave the nest, they are happy, well-adjusted and content in their new surroundings? This is the entry I made in my journal.

"It's been 78 days and counting since Jilly went home. Most

days it still doesn't feel real. It feels like she is on an extended vacation in Australia and isn't near a cell phone tower so she can't call home."

I don't know why I picked Australia, other than it is probably the farthest spot away from where I live that I can imagine... and they have kangaroos, which Jilly loved. I don't know anyone there, have never been there and pretty much know nothing else about it, except that it has some very remote areas where I am sure cell phone coverage is spotty at best. It was (and sometimes still is) my way of coping. I pretend that she is on a great adventure for a college credit doing international studies and can't call me by phone. Many bereaved parents cope this way for a bit.

About three months later... in May, you can imagine my surprise when I received a private message from, of all places, a woman in Australia! Here is part of the message:

> *Dear Louise,*
>
> *I have been debating whether I should contact you. I have spoken to a couple of my closest friends who have encouraged me to at least let you know about an interesting thing that happened to me, in case it holds any relevance to you. I live in Cardiff, Newcastle in Australia. The other morning, I woke abruptly at 4:45 A.M. and was unable to get back to sleep. My young son and husband were in the bed with me and as the weather here is quite cold,*

I decided to stay in bed but use my phone to go on Facebook.

I was looking at a photo of my niece (who has recently undergone ovarian cancer treatment) and reading all the lovely messages friends and family had put under her photo. When I shifted in bed, my finger must have accidentally touched something on the phone, when the Facebook page dedicated to Jillian popped up. What a beautiful young lady.

Since I didn't know Jillian, I tried to exit out and back onto my own Facebook page ... I couldn't do it. My phone wouldn't go back, wouldn't manually switch off or respond to anything. I thought it quite odd that my phone seemed to be frozen in place. So, I began reading through the beautiful messages that everyone had left for Jillian. I sat in the dark, crying over a girl that I didn't know, who lost her life and was undoubtedly loved by many. I got up and went to the computer to look up more about Jillian (having a daughter of my own compelled me to find out more.)

A newspaper article about Jillian's accident caught my eye and as I read it, I saw that the date of the accident was Saturday, the 19th. I looked down into the corner of my computer. Saturday the 19th.

> The article said the accident occurred about 6 A.M. As I read, the time on my computer clicked over to 6 A.M. I thought it just a coincidence, but I couldn't get it out of my head. The continuous signs that Jillian sends to her loved ones can't be ignored and I have been wondering whether this is a sign for you, or is someone trying to tell me something? I have noticed that every time I go on Facebook on my phone, the message symbol keeps popping up—when I don't have any unread messages. I didn't want you to think I was some weirdo from the other side of the world which is why I didn't write to you sooner, but I cannot get it out of my head and I would like to think it was more than just a coincidence and it may hold some relevance for you. I apologize if this means nothing to you, and I wish you all the best in such tragic circumstances.

And she signed her name, (which contains Jilly's initials) I would say that Jilly found her cell phone tower. In Australia... it was through this dear woman, a total stranger half way around the world!

January 19, 2012
Top Ten Favorite Things About Heaven

*I*T HAS BEEN TWO months since our beautiful Jilly Bean went HOME. It seems like just a second ago and yet a lifetime ago. She has come to people in dreams, in signs, in quarters, in blown light bulbs and even in visions. Today I was thinking about what she would want to share about the ten best things in heaven. Here is what she would say:

- It's always sunny.
- I can travel at the speed of thought.
- I can see *everyone* all the time and hear their thoughts. (No secrets!)
- The love is unimaginable by humans.
- I am more alive here than I ever thought possible when I was there.
- Tomato soup and grilled cheese sandwiches really do have pictures of Jesus on them.
- Doing a standing back tuck, aerial cartwheel and full twist is now a piece of cake. (This was part of her gymnastic routine that she struggled with for years.)
- The music is ... well ... you just can't even imagine.
- Now I can know anything I want to know, because I can just ask God!
- Did I mention the *love*? It envelopes every single molecule of my being. It is the ultimate tummy hug!

Always Remember to Kiss Me Goodnight

Kisses from Heaven,
Love,
Jilly

February 18, 2012
First Birthday in Heaven

*L*ooking back on it, I can't tell you how we celebrated Jilly's last birthday on earth... her 19th. I am sure it was with her friends. We probably took her out for dinner, and she got to invite someone. I wish I had pictures of that day, but if I do, I can't find them. That makes me sad.

I clearly remember her first birthday in heaven though... what would have been her 20th here on earth. We decorated her resting place with lots of bling-bling. We invited friends and had cookies and hot chocolate at her grave. We set off twenty sky lanterns at the cemetery, which was breathtakingly beautiful. The crowd that had gathered spontaneously sang the "Happy Birthday" song. I don't think I had a meltdown that day, but nothing I did eased the deep ache in my heart. I was so lost in my deep grief with no map to guide me. It was all so new and raw.

Only three short months had passed since her death. I am sorry to say that I don't remember a lot of that year, including her sisters' 23rd and 17th birthdays, my husband's 51st or even my own birthday in 2012. I was wandering through life in a dense fog. Some days that fog still returns and with it, the sadness of missing her comes back.

There will always be a place in my heart that is the exact shape of Jilly and no one else can ever fill that particular hole.

Time doesn't heal all wounds, but I have found that they have become different somehow. Not as raw as those first two months, softer perhaps on most days as an emotional scab begins to form over that area in my soul ... but bumping against a strong memory or important date can make it bleed all over again.

♥ ♥ ♥

If God sends us on stony paths, He provides strong shoes.
~ Corrie Ten Boom

March 4th or MARCH "FORTH!" (not Fourth)

Some people have New Year's resolutions. I have always had "time dyslexia" (as in procrastination or a poor concept of time.) I don't make my resolutions on New Year's; instead, I make them on March 4th.

Why? Because to me, March 4th literally means "Begin anew! March Forth into the future, strong and steady!" That means I have had over two months to think about my goals for the year.

My first goal is to finish my children's book and have both it and this book published. This will allow me to get them into the right hands at hospices, children's hospitals, etc. and help fund Jillian's Memorial Scholarship.

My second goal this year is to move forward with Jilly. Notice I didn't say leave her behind. Her body is part of my past. Her memories are in my present...we share a future together somewhere, at some time that only God knows.

I remember the first time I really laughed after she died. I quickly clapped my hand over my mouth and thought in horror, "Oh my gosh, I just laughed! I can't do that! My child is dead! What kind of mother would I be if I laughed when my child hasn't been gone from my presence for very long?"

I have come to realize that I would be exactly the kind of mother that Jilly loves and wants me to be. Her whole life was about shenanigans, making goofy faces, random totally crazy moments and making her friends laugh until their sides hurt.

Why should that change? Because she isn't "here" to instigate the fun and pranks? Someone has to carry it on.

She is here, all around us in essence; we just can't see her as well as we used to... but trust me, she *is* still close by in many ways! What would happen if I decided to be happy? If I decided that it is okay to smile, to laugh until my sides hurt or I had to gasp for breath?

Does it mean I am "over" her death? Absolutely not. You don't get "over" burying your child any more than you get over giving birth to them. Part of me died with her that day... but part of me still lives. It is high time I started to live the way she would want me to. Each person who is going through grief will find the time that feels right to do this; and some people are ready sooner than others.

I will go on, trying harder each day to find something Jilly would have smiled or laughed about, and I will appreciate it. I will marvel at the beautiful colors of a sunset or sunrise. I will make goofy faces at babies to see them smile, without a second thought.

I will honor Jilly in this way... and I will do it because my love for her is greater than my grief. I trust that she is with God, safe and sound, still laughing and pulling shenanigans in Heaven. I will not leave her behind in my past; rather I will carry her with me as we go forward together. We will *March Forth*...

5

FORTY WEEKS

August 25, 2012

It has been forty weeks since you went Home, my Jillian. This is the exact same amount of time I carried you in my womb. It took forty weeks for you to develop from two random cells joined together by an act of love into an embryo, and then a fetus. At the end of those forty weeks, I had to let you leave my body. You were ready and there was no keeping you safe inside me anymore, where I could always keep you warm and protected.

I loved being pregnant with you. I carried you under my heart, next to my soul for 40 weeks and helped you come into this world. I nursed you in the middle of many nights, watched you grow from the shy baby to be the cool individual you turned out to be and then... when God called you Home, reluctantly gave you back to Him for safekeeping. Someday, He will let us hug you again. I am sure of that!

The labor of it was challenging, exhilarating and exhausting. One minute you were a fetus, the next you were an infant. You were my easiest and shortest delivery, and despite being a whopping nine pounds, it only took ten hours for you to arrive. I remember telling your Daddy in the delivery room that I would be ready for another child soon. Part of me was saddened that you had left my body, but at the same time, I was happy that you were outside of it, where I could see you and hold you in my arms.

We could communicate either way. From the time you were conceived, we had always had that "mind-meld" thing going on. I did with all my daughters, but it was most apparent with you, my "Jilly-Bean." You came out studying the world so seriously. The night you were born, as I kissed your beautiful face and each of your fingers and toes, you gave me the first of many looks that spoke volumes. It was a look even back then that said, "This is my temporary home." You were a wise old soul in a petite little body. I had taken care of many babies at that point in my nursing career, but you were just different somehow. I asked for His blessing on your life and offered my thanks to God that first night, a few hours after your birth; I wondered how long He would lend you to me. Somehow, I always knew deep down that you weren't meant to stay. For us, 19 years and 280 days was *much too short!*

I wondered if the difference I saw in you was because you were such a sponge, soaking up the emotions I was going through as I carried you. My own Daddy died when I was 30 weeks pregnant with you. I sobbed, and you kicked. I cried all the way to Virginia, where we laid him to rest. You got very quiet, as if letting me grieve and just being quietly present, holding space with me in the darkest hours I had ever known up until that point.

I rubbed my tummy a lot, trying to stroke and comfort you. Instead, you comforted me. Those forty weeks I carried you were so precious. I loved you with all my heart before you were ever placed in my arms. Now, my sweet girl, we have given you back to God, and he carries you in His arms. He has held you, loved you and cherished you even more than we can ever imagine. You are safe with Him; I never need to worry about any harm coming to you now or ever again. It is no wonder that you heard Him calling your name and leaped into His arms. We can't begin to fathom the intensity of that love while we are in human form. But you can, because you experience it always.

Forty weeks seems like so long ago. An eternity for us ... and yet, it's just a fraction of a second for you. Your room still has your scent. I have given away a few things and loaned out a couple others to bring friends comfort, but it is largely unchanged. We are just not ready to have your room be anything else yet.

Just two days before you died, you hid notes of love and

gratitude on Daddy's and my dresser. The day before you left, we spent the day together. You laughed at me as you cranked up the radio and taught me the words to "Red Solo Cup." We shared lunch at the mall. You ran errands with me that evening and belted out the song, "Bohemian Rhapsody" in the parking lot. Then you hugged and kissed me goodnight, told us you loved us and walked out the door.

Was it only 280 days ago that I looked upon your very beautiful, but oh too still, body lying on that gurney behind the fire truck and officially identified you for the police? One minute you had a body, the next minute your soul was flying. Even without closing my eyes, I can still see the red and gold leaves in your hair and the little smirk on your lips. Did you leave at the beginning of a smile as you saw the angels coming? Was it because you knew all along that your work here needed to be done quickly and that your stay would be short? Perhaps, it was because you heard your Heavenly Father's voice, calling you to come Home now and were delighted by the sound of it.

Has it only been forty weeks since our world shifted on its axis? I can't even remember who I was before that time! My life is defined by "before and after *that* day." Our world still turns, but differently. We have all changed. You changed us, both with your life, and with your passing. We love each other more deeply and appreciate the trivial things much more intensely. We make more of an effort to communicate with others who may also still be hurting.

Some days, there are even tiny amounts of joy and laughter. We have learned to keep going somehow, to keep putting one foot in front of the other, as we look ahead to the date that we will all be reunited in our eternal Home. This journey is every bit as difficult as childbirth was, even more so. In the end, I know it will be worth it, just as you and your sisters were worth every single labor pain I felt.

I miss you, sweet girl. I miss your big brown eyes and your wonderful sense of humor. I miss your mischievous grin and the way you would hug people tummy to tummy. You really didn't get away with half the things you thought you did, but your antics still make me smile just thinking of them! Thank you for the constant reminders that you are still close by and safe, still loving us and doing your very best to bring us comfort during our "labor."

Perhaps, you have become the nurse that you always wanted to be after all!

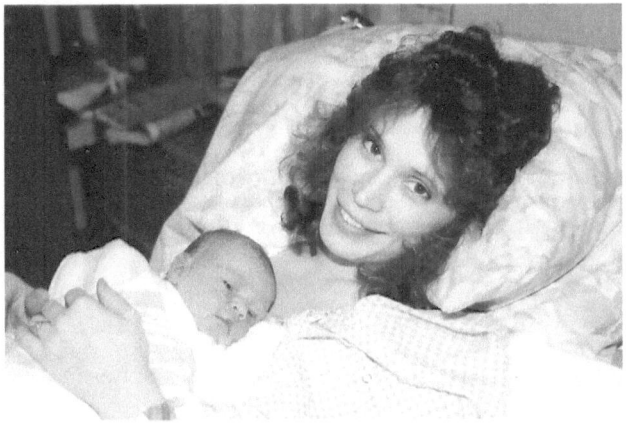

LOUISE CRIST

♥ ♥ ♥

No Such Thing as Time

I HAD BEEN PONDERING A conversation I had last week with a very wise, dear friend. We were discussing time. We don't really have a concept of "forever" here on Earth. Food takes "forever" to prepare. Red lights take "forever" to change. It takes "forever" for our computer to boot up. Our vacation destinations take "forever" to get to. (*Are we there yet?*)

Oddly enough, it seems like it only takes a minute for our kids to grow up. It was just a "minute" ago that I was in college and became a nurse. Ask a 90-year old when they watched TV for the first time in their life. They would likely say, "it seems like just a minute ago, but it was years; forever ago."

When our kids fall down, or get a shot at the doctors, or get stung by a bee, we hold them close, let them cry and try to soothe them by saying, "Shh, it will be okay. It will only hurt for a minute, and then you will be fine." Of course, to them it feels like much longer than one minute.

I believe that God is holding us close in our time of hurt and pain. He is also trying to soothe us; saying, "It will only hurt for a minute, and then you will be fine." It really *does* feel like the pain will last forever. In the grand scheme of eternity though, our lifetimes *are* only "just a minute." Although we on earth are bound by bodies, space and time, Jilly is not. Where she is in eternity, we are already together again. There, we are flying at the speed of thought, exploring all that there is to explore and happily doing whatever work God would have us do. Can you imagine? How weird it must be to not actually have such a thing as the constraints of time! We have "all the time we need" there.

Many of us will hurt "forever" because of a loved one's physical death. We want so badly to see them again for "just another minute," although that would never be enough. The scars we bear from the pain are those created by loved ones coming into our lives, dancing all over our hearts and then leaving us to explore parts unknown. I will bear my scar with pride. I would rather have had my girl for those too short, 19 years (which seemed like a minute) than to never have had the joy, love and heartache of not knowing her at all. She is not gone, she is simply not here for now. Like beloved family waiting for us at the end of a long journey, she is at the other end of our destination. I just don't know how many more "miles" it will be before I get there. She has been gone "just a minute" and "forever" all at the same time. I will be with her again for eternity someday. I will try very hard not to keep asking God, "Are we there yet? Are we there yet?" as I come closer and closer, day by day to our final destination. I will be there when I get there. In the meantime, I will try very hard (and fail on many days) to enjoy the scenery and my companions along the way. I would be honored if you would join me.

♥ ♥ ♥

Jilly's Day in Heaven

Since time does not exist in Heaven as it does here on Earth, you will have to use your imagination just as I do.

Jilly's starts her day by rising and singing God's praises with the angels. Their voices all blend to make the most beautiful tribute to our Creator. To be in the midst of this song gives every being in Heaven new energy and fills their souls with an all-encompassing love. Afterwards they go to "work." For some, this is creating new things... music, art, dance, knowledge. For Jillian, I think this encompasses two areas of work. First, would be the infant area of Heaven, where she would go from baby to baby, picking them up, cuddling them, kissing them and saying things like "Ohhh, you are going to be just right for my friend _____. (Fill in the name of her many friends yet to have babies.) But in the meantime, I am going to keep you and give you lots of tummy hugs!"

Then she would move on to the doggy section of Heaven, loving all the other animals along the way. She would find the ones she knew here on Earth who have gone before her and the ones who have since heard the Master's voice and obeyed the command to come Home. She would toss balls endlessly and give the best tummy rubs. From there, she might peek in on our lives down here, seeing how we are getting along and what we are doing with the points of light she left us with. Have any of us carried on the light she started here? Have we learned anything from her passing? Are we better people because she was a part of our lives? What impact did she make? How do we show it? Do we smile at strangers?

She might guide a butterfly to land on us, or perhaps drop a quarter here or there. She might even decide that the light bulbs in your house need to go out... several at once and smile as you catch on that she is close by. Maybe she will pop in on a dream to let someone know she loves them or give someone else an irresistible urge to pick up the phone and wish someone else a happy day.

She would do her best to let us know that, "Sad means you think I'm not here! I'm here, I'm *here*! Right inside your heart!" She might take a little break, work on her eternal tan, eat some pizza, ramen noodles, bean burritos or grilled cheese sandwiches. Or she might make the best chicken noodle soup to share with the angels and pour ketchup all over it! I doubt they eat in Heaven, but who knows? I personally hope there is chocolate in Heaven.

She might meet up with her "wolf pack" of angels that she talked to while she was here on Earth. Maybe do some fishing with her grandpas. (Catch and release, of course.) I bet she has made all kinds of new friends there too... other kids who have come Home before their families were ready for them to leave.

Maybe she is showing them how to let us know that they too, are safe, close by and we can only "see them on special occasions" like the above-mentioned butterflies, quarters, dreams, etc.

Whatever she chooses to fill her time with while waiting for us to join her, I know in my heart she is incredibly happy. She is with God, in the greatest most wonderful loving light that exists. She is Home. And someday, when it is my turn to go Home, I will see her again and get the longest tummy hug ever from the "angel" with the longest hair in Heaven. Knowing that makes it almost bearable to wait here.

6

TAKING JILLY HOME

November 28, 2012
Speed of Light

It has been just over a year since we laid our daughter's beautiful body to rest. Most days, it still doesn't feel real...I wonder if it ever will? There are certainly days when the enormity of the accident comes and smacks me upside the head, sending me reeling into a meltdown, but those days, thankfully, do not come as often as they used to. They say that grief doesn't ever go away, but it does evolve into something different. That one day, instead of thinking of her and crying, I can think of her and smile, or even laugh. Sometimes those two things happen in the same day, or even the same minute. Grief is so indescribable sometimes!

Most of the time, it still feels like she is off on vacation or away at college. In some ways, she is! She has graduated to the greatest "Universe-city" or University ever! Her teacher is the greatest Being in existence! She only must ask what she desires to know, and it is shown to her.

One of her favorite phrases was, "everything happens for a reason." Now she knows what all those reasons are; everything makes perfect sense as God shows her who, how and why things were in her life here. She is being shown how everything and everyone is interconnected. Just like a pebble in a pond sends out ripples, her actions and reactions here on Earth also sent out ripples. From where she sits, she can see the ripples she made while she was here impacting other lives.

She is "Home" in the light. We all know how fast light travels, right? 186,000 miles per second. A traveler, moving at the speed of light, would circumnavigate the equator approximately 7.5 times in one second; that is physical light. How much faster does divine light travel? Think about it...can you imagine wanting to be in Paris and BAM, you are there. Or wanting to be with 10 of your friends all at the same time and whoosh, it happens?

I believe that when loved ones "go to the light," part of their job might be to shine a little spark of that light back at us...in many forms. It could be a gentle breeze, a sunny day, a rainbow, a butterfly, or "pennies" from heaven (or in Jilly's case, quarters), etc.

I know with every fiber of my being that she is safe, loved and treasured where she is. I do not have to worry for one second that she is feeling pain, heartache or loneliness. She will never have her heart broken again; never have to learn something the hard way. That brings me peace and comfort beyond measure.

I didn't "lose" her, because I know exactly where she is. What I lost was a part of myself... a part of my heart and soul. I will find it again when we all meet again on the other side. She will take my hand and lead me to those I love who are also celebrating the joy of being with the Creator. God will knit my soul back together and I too, will see the reason for everything.

December 29, 2012
56 weeks after "That Day"

A DAY OR TWO AFTER Jilly went Home last year, I called up Kim, a dear close friend of mine who has lost not one, but three children. I have always looked up to her, as she has a wisdom that continually amazes me. She had recently carried a baby nearly to term when it was discovered that this sweet child had deformities that would be fatal. She was told that the baby she had looked forward to meeting for months, and had already named Catherine Faith, would die either during birth or very shortly afterwards. My friend was bedridden for several weeks while waiting for the baby to be born, separated from her other six healthy children who waited for their mom, their rock in the storms of life, to return to them.

She handled the whole situation lovingly, gracefully and with such an intense faith in God that I was simply in awe. Baby Catherine lived for two weeks at the hospital, was sent home on Hospice and died that night in the arms of her parents, surrounded by angels and blanketed in lots of love from her siblings. She joined her brother Johnathon in Heaven who had been there for several years. Yet another brother, Noah, would follow Catherine back to God with the same lethal deformity. In all, my friend would eventually be left with eight living healthy, happy children to bring her comfort.

I begged this wise woman to tell me how to walk this path. How could I go on for days at a time and continue to live, when I couldn't even get through a single minute without my heart breaking repeatedly?

She gave me a strange answer... or so I thought at the time. She gently and lovingly gave me this piece of advice.

"On the day that you can get down on your knees and thank God for taking your sweet Jilly Home," she said, "you will have a peace that transcends your own understanding."

I shuddered as I thought, "*You want me to do what???*" Perhaps I didn't hear you correctly! God could have made things turn out differently. If He had been there, maybe Jilly wouldn't have died!"

She answered softly, but it took my breath away, "Don't you understand? He *was* there! God and his angels were with both girls in the car that morning as it soared through the air. He was with the driver, helping her soul to understand that because she still had things to accomplish on Earth, so she had to stay. He promised her that he would always be with her.

He was with Jillian the entire time too. When the accident happened, and her death was inevitable, He took her hand just before impact as she leapt from her body into His warm, loving embrace. He sent His angels to stand on either side of her and watch the scene play out from above, allowing her to observe without having to feel the physical pain of being in her body. He let her see why things happened the way they did. Her work here on Earth was done and He helped her understand that although her physical life had come to an end, her eternal life was just beginning. God showed her how her journey here had affected (and will continue to affect) others for a very long time, in ways she couldn't begin to imagine while she was in human form. He took her Home as instantly, painlessly and lovingly as possible."

I knew my sweet girl didn't suffer... this was evident when I looked at the total peace on my daughter's beautiful face at the accident scene; the faint little smirk she wore on her lips. She was just beginning to smile at something... perhaps she had a glimpse of Heaven.

This wise mom continued by asking if I had ever lost Jilly in a store? Kids can hide in clothing racks or behind displays when they are bored with shopping, finding ways to amuse themselves. Like many children, Jilly had done this to me once when she was about 4-years-old. Even though she was born a wise old woman in a little girl's body, I still freaked out. Panic set in ... where was she? Where was my baby girl?

I am sure many parents have had this experience. I was nearly at my wits end, when some kind stranger found her, took her to the nearest intercom and announced that little Jillian was lost. Would her mom please come and get her by the dressing room? This caring adult entertained her until I got there; by the time I arrived a few seconds later, Jilly was totally engaged in telling this person all about her life.

Jilly wasn't worried in the slightest. She *knew* I would eventually come for her. She wasn't particularly missing me right then, because at that moment, Jillian was completely enthralled and amused by a very interesting grown up who was giving her their undivided attention. She was loving every minute of it.

This wise friend of mine who had endured more grief than I can ever imagine, then asked me, "What did you say to that wonderful angel in disguise who kept your daughter safe until you reached her?"

"Well, I said thank you very much, of course! I was relieved and grateful that she was not forever lost, only out of my sight temporarily!"

"Exactly!" she whispered.

That was her point. God is keeping Jilly safe and "entertained" (or perhaps she is keeping *Him* entertained with her antics and unique sense of humor) until we get there. No harm will ever come to her with Him at her side. She could not possibly be in better hands or loved more deeply than she is at this moment as she snuggles in the lap of God.

The next day, as I stood in the shower with a river of tears running down my face, I did the very thing my wise friend suggested. I fell to my knees sobbing and thanked my Heavenly Father for taking my girl Home ... for keeping her safe and sound, happy and loved, until the day that I will get to see her again.

My friend was right. The peace and understanding which came over me was indescribable. It still is, many months later. Don't get me wrong; I still miss Jillian, and yes, I still have meltdowns and grief quakes whenever I try to wrap my heart around the magnitude of our loss. After all, I am still a human mom.

However, since that conversation with my friend, I have taught myself to try to start each morning with a prayer of gratitude that goes something like this:

> *"Thank you, Heavenly Father, for my family and for the people you lend to me each day, however long they may be here, that I might grow in love and faith and joy. Thank you for loving and comforting my family while we learn to bear this incredible human pain with some semblance of grace. Thank you for sending us other parents whose children also live with You, so that we can hold hands on this journey together, and take comfort knowing that we are not alone in our grief.*

Thank you for taking our precious Jilly Home to your awesome Kingdom.

Please give her lots of hugs and kisses from us from now until the moment we are reunited, and she is once again able to go from your loving arms back into ours for a wonderful, eternal hug. Please keep her so excited and occupied with the babies she adores up there, that by the time she turns around to make sure we are standing right behind her... we will be.

May the blessings be abundant.

Amen."

♥ ♥ ♥

♥ ♥ ♥

January 19, 2013
Grief is Like a Leaky Tire

While driving today, I noticed that if I let go of the wheel for just a few seconds, my car wanted to veer off to the left. I must have a slow leak again in my front tire. If you stop and think about it, grief is kind of like a leaky tire.

Let's pretend that the tire is a part of my soul, or "vehicle." In the first minutes, hours, days and weeks after losing Jilly, the magnitude of the grief was so overwhelming that I had to "pull off to the side of the road" in my life to be able to even focus three feet in front of me. My tires were all completely flat. Much of that time was a blur as I watched others in their "vehicles of life" whizzing by, their tires (souls) largely intact. Some wonderful people in the community, friends, family and most importantly God, stopped to re-inflate my "tires" with kindness, love, hugs and lending a listening ear. I could get back on the highway of life, although I was certainly not up to speed. I felt vulnerable in my "vehicle." My tire had a patch on it, which might hold up for a little while. That first season of grief felt like driving on a bumpy gravel road filled with ruts, just waiting for another blowout to occur. Thankfully, God had my back.

The next season of our grief was that of steady leaks, but not blowouts. We would go along day to day trying to have some normalcy, only to notice that we were frequently veering off to one side or another along the journey, grief again pulling us to the side of the road. Sometimes when we least expected it, we would have another blowout, wondering what caused it and how it could have happened; it just made no sense. It might have been a song on the radio, Jilly's favorite food at the grocery store, or seeing some quote on the internet that set us off. We cried a lot, the numbness of the initial weeks slowly beginning to melt, like an icicle in the direct sunshine on a cold winter's day. Our tears helped to fill the slow leak and re-inflate our "tires." Tears can be a wonderful thing, releasing stress and soothing the ache in our hearts like a warm bath on a wintry night. Again, we managed to get back on the road.

Now we are in yet another season of grief...we know we have a slow leak and occasionally, we feel brave enough to let go of the steering wheel (our control in this life) to see if our vehicles will steer straight. Nope. While they can go longer distances in time without veering off to the side of the road, our tires with the patches on them will never be as smooth as the original ones. We will always feel the bumps more acutely. We can never trade them in for new tires; we are stuck with them the rest of our lives.

We have become more observant of others traveling this "road" who also have patches on their souls. We have seen families broken down on the side of the road and pull over to help them as best as we can, giving them hugs and re-inflating their tires, like so many have done for us. We have learned to "let go and let God" when it comes to trying to map our journey. We don't have half the control we thought we did over life before our blowout with loss taught us otherwise.

God re-inflates my tires frequently. I only need to ask Him, as he is now a permanent fixture in my "vehicle." I am working on giving him the job of driving it full time...He would do a much better job than me. I am 14 months closer to my final rest stop, where Jilly awaits us with hugs and kisses. I will do my best to enjoy the scenery until I get there, even with the "pit-stop" delays; I know they are a part of my life now. Those rest stops are a time of healing and rejuvenation and they will continue to be for the rest of my life. It is amazing to see the strangers that those unplanned breakdowns bring us: they become friends. Sooner or later, they too, will have patches on their tires and we will stop to help them when we can. It is like belonging to a spiritual AAA or ambulance club! Their motto might be: "You fall, you call, we will haul!" They do not need the specifics on what caused the "vehicle" to lose its power; they just know that they are there to help fix it.

We are all simply holding hands and driving each other Home.

Winter Weather

> "When someone you love dies, and you're not expecting it, you don't lose her all at once; you lose her in pieces over a long time—the way the mail stops coming, and her scent fades from the pillows and even from the clothes in her closet and drawers. Gradually, you accumulate the parts of her that are gone. Just when the day comes—when there's a particular missing part that overwhelms you with the feeling that she's gone, forever—there comes another day, and another specifically missing part."
>
> —John Irving, *A Prayer for Owen Meany*

As I watched the snow fall yesterday, it occurred to me how much winter weather can be like grief. Sometimes grief comes in like the snow—gentle, slow steady large flakes, coating our world with just a light dusting. It brings tears to my eyes at the beauty of it and brings back memories of first snowfalls in years past. It makes my heart ache to do all the activities we did together... building snowmen, our skiing adventures and making snow angels. The tears are sweet and tender with remembrance... and then it is over, and I go on.

Sometimes, the grief is more like a white-out. One minute I can see clearly and the next, I am blindsided by a memory that leaves me unsure of how I will go one more step without falling. It is then that I have to trust it will pass... and it usually does, sometimes as quickly as it came.

At other times, grief is like a blizzard with unrelenting snow covering my life, and negative wind chills that make it feel as though I will never feel warm again. I have to deal with frozen, then thawed, broken "water pipes" in the form of tears. There is nothing to compare it to. It feels as though the hope of spring and the bright sunshine of summer will never happen again. It saps my energy, and there are days that are only good for staying in my pajamas and sitting near whatever heat source I can find for comfort. It's difficult to see beyond the endless storm of memories.

I must try to remember everything I can, every detail and nuance, because I am so afraid of forgetting. Forgetting would be like she didn't exist. That is my worst fear. The question is this: Which parts of her existence do I need to relive over and over again in order to find peace in this storm? (Most of them, probably.)

The parts I focus on, so that I can keep going:

- My joy of becoming pregnant with her and feeling her grow under my heart, complete with the gymnastics she performed even as a fetus.
- My awe as she would act like a 90-year-old when she was two, reading people so well it was uncanny.
- Her intense tenaciousness (immovable stubbornness) as I homeschooled her. She would get up early, hide pillows and blankets in the bathtub, then deliberately

bait me until I put her in "time out" in the bathroom. Odd that I never caught on to how happy she was to be sent there until I found her sleeping in the bathtub one day, cozy as a bug in a rug! Of all my daughters, she was the one I had to stay on my toes with the most. It didn't help that she was so good at reading body language that I swore she could read my mind.

- Her transformation into a social butterfly in 8th grade. She could look straight into my eyes and tell gigantic fibs and I would fall for it. (I was not alone; she had this ability with many people!) One of her famous pranks that came back to "bite her in the butt" was telling all her classmates that we were moving to Florida during Christmas vacation. She was so convincing that the other kids actually started buying going away presents for her! They were tearful and sad as they would tell her how much they would miss her! Watching her get herself out of that pickles still makes me smile. When she finally confessed, no one would talk to her for about a week! She wrote endless notes of apology for that one.
- Her ability to befriend someone so quickly by the time she was done talking to them, they felt as though they had a new best friend. She would greet them from then on with a smile and often a hug. It didn't matter if they were her age, or toddlers, or senior citizens. She made a difference in many lives, getting other people to believe

in themselves, or offering them encouragement. She had friends from ALL walks of life. She gave people second chances...and 3rd and 4th ones, too.

- Her love of animals and babies...and baby animals. "Mom, can we go buy another squirrel at the store?" after we nursed a baby squirrel back to health that had been pushed out of its nest by a sibling. "No, Jillian. Squirrels don't just fall out of trees, you know." To which she responded: "That one did!" We had pets of all shapes and sizes, from squirrels, to iguanas, to rabbits, turtles and briefly, even a baby raccoon.
- She loved, loved, loved those "real" baby dolls that schools pass out in parenting classes. Even as an older teen she loved them. When Sierra had one for a babysitting class, she snuck in her room and clipped the bracelet key off Sierra and her friend. Then she stole the babies and kept them in her room. Apparently, the babies continuous screaming in the middle of the night eventually got to her because she got up, buried the doll under a large pile of clothes in her closet and went back to sleep!

Her life here was such a unique combination of laughter and love, depression and sadness, empathy and compassion, outgoingness and shyness. She was flawed and yet so perfectly Jillian. She always said she had to learn things the hard way...and in the end, she did. It was the hardest lesson she ever had to go through and the hardest one for those of us left behind.

During the times that I can only see her last day, not her life as a whole, I have to remind myself that what I focus on makes the difference between existing and living. Sometimes, my greatest wish is to live somewhere that only has blizzards of the happy memories. I will be there someday. We all will—thank God for that. Until then, I can only do what Jilly would do when faced with the "snow" in her life—gather some friends and go make some memories.

♥ ♥ ♥

7

WANDERLUST AND GRATITUDE

February 18, 2013

*J*ILLY'S 21ST BIRTHDAY IS upon us... the age of being "legal." The restrictions placed on underage young adults would have been removed, allowing her to make adult decisions and choices—and experience adult consequences. I would imagine that like many college kids, her buddies would have taken her to a bar, or six, and before too long, the memory of her 21st birthday would have been a blur, if she remembered it at all.

Why does society place such a big emphasis on drinking when you turn 21? We have become close with several exchange students over the years. They can drink much earlier but can't drive until age 18 or 21. They first experiment with alcohol and have the chance to see how it affects their body before they are given the responsibility of driving a vehicle. Public transport is a given. Those who do drink young know to get on a bus, subway or train to get home. They work hard to get their drivers licenses... and the penalty for drinking and driving is so severe most of them would not even consider doing it. They lose their license the *first* time they get caught. (That's a good thing, as their speed limits are much higher as well... can you imagine driving 100 mph on the Autobahn while you are drunk?) Besides, drinking no longer holds the appeal it did in those first weeks or years.

Maybe, we have it backwards here in the U.S. as far as that is concerned. We trust our 14, 15 and 16-year-olds to control 2000 pounds of steel on an icy road before we trust them to drink a glass of wine. Go figure.

March 2013

I BELIEVE GOD PLANNED FOR me to learn about and experience gratitude when He sent me to this life, because that seems to sum up my journey so far.

My father had a chronic case of wanderlust. He loved to travel the country, visit new areas and take in the local natural beauty of an environment. In his Army years, he had served in the China-Burma-India Theatre. He lived in Alaska after the 2nd World War, and Hawaii was his last vacation destination. Before he drew his last breath on Earth, he had been to every state in the country. He even managed to move after he died! In the 20 years that he was married to mom, they racked up 28 moves with five children in tow. Our parents had us convinced that we were luckier than most children because we got to see various parts of the country and go to many different schools. Some children had never even left the state they were born in! I have memories of sleeping on the floorboard of a Rambler station wagon as our family took in the breathtakingly tall buildings of New York City (the World Trade Center was being built the first time), the sights of Philadelphia and Washington DC. Every summer we would travel from wherever we lived at the time to Nebraska, a diverse place of cities and long lonely stretches of highway where the only thing to see are cows and corn. We wandered from the sunny white sandy beaches of the Bahamas (and the hurricanes that go with island living) to the deep snowdrifts and blizzards along the shores of Lake Michigan. I am grateful for the many miles I have traveled in my life.

My mother Vera, having grown up during the Depression, was able to hold our home together move after move by counting pennies and making do with what we had. We didn't starve, but there wasn't anything wasted either. Blissfully ignorant, we assumed all children lived that way. A couple years after my parent's marriage dissolved (partially due to all the moving), God put another parent in my life, a 29-year-old man named Dean. He was younger than mom by twelve years and had no children yet. I think we raised him as much as he raised us. (For the record, he also loved to travel, and although mom swore that she would never move again, he talked her into another eight moves.) He gave mom fresh ideas on child rearing and provided us with a stable home, taking care not to uproot me until after graduation. He was there, proud as a peacock, to walk me down the aisle when an airline strike prevented my biological father from making it to my wedding. In future years, he was present for the births of my children. When I married Mark, I inherited two more parents, Donna and Larry, my in-laws, making a total of five parents. Each of them taught me about the values of hard work, persistence, being financially responsible, morally accountable and how to love, even during challenging times. I am so grateful to each of them for those lessons.

God brought my husband to me when I was a shy, sensitive, 19-year old, totally lacking in confidence. I had a strong faith going for me though. He helped me to grow by encouraging me to try new things. Sometimes I failed, sometimes I succeeded...but I always learned. I am still learning 35+ years later and am no longer shy. My confidence has grown. I am still sensitive, but now use that as a tool to help others. I am grateful for my husband's patience and love.

God then blessed us with three beautiful daughters, each bringing us their own special talents and gifts. Our eldest, Erica, brought an imagination that has given us joy beyond measure. Our youngest, Sierra, has the compassion and gentleness of her ancestors. Our middle daughter, Jillian brought us the gifts of humor and faith, both in God's promises and a faith in our fellow man. I am blessed beyond my wildest dreams to still have two daughters to walk the Earth with and one who waits in Heaven to teach me how to fly.

My career (I can't call it a job because I have never thought of it as work) has helped define me as a person. I am in the healing profession on many levels and I feel that is what I do best. Healing does not come "from" me, but rather, "through" me, from my Heavenly Father as I touch those that I am lucky enough to encounter each day. The joys and sorrows, the trials and triumphs of the human spirit, I witness these each day and having experienced them myself, am able to understand and feel them in others. We are all deeply connected to each other. I see the fragility of our human existence in everyone, from newborns to those getting ready to make their trip back Home. Each person's life matters and they are the entire world to someone. They matter to me, too. The friends I have made on this part of the journey, both in co-workers and patients is indeed priceless.

It is these experiences that have helped to make me who I AM, for which I am grateful. Looking back at my life, God has not made a single mistake. He has a plan for each event that has happened in my life. He allowed nothing to happen to me that was not first screened by His protective love. I am His child, and he loves me more than I can fathom. I am eternally grateful to be able to serve Him; I look forward to the day He lets me come Home too. I will have a joyous reunion with so many on that side who I love and who have gone ahead of me and will be waiting for me at the gates of Heaven. I continue to have joyous reunions each day that I stay here with those that I love. I am grateful beyond measure.

♥ ♥ ♥

Ever had a song stuck in your head? It isn't playing on the radio anymore, but it comes unbidden when you are trying to concentrate on something else? Try as you might, it just keeps coming back to the front of your mind repeatedly.

Grief is kind of like that. Instead of being the song we hear out loud, it is the background music of our lives. It is always there no matter what we do, where we go or who we are with. In this case, I can't run from it, can't play something else louder to drown out the song and I can't change the station. It just IS. We learn ways to incorporate it into our lives. We eventually learn how to hum along with the memories.

The ache of missing Jillian comes without warning so often that I have begun to think of it as "normal." I guess this is a good thing; I drive down the road, see a sign for pizza and remember her fondness for food. I see babies in shopping carts, I think of her love for them and how she would find any excuse to get near one so she could ask a mom if she could hold it. Many moms did give their consent. I hear songs on the radio and think of her breaking into an impromptu dance wherever she happened to be. I go past the school and think of her years there and the wonderful friends she made and brought home for us to love.

When Sierra turned 18, I thought of how Jilly wanted to take her to get her 2nd set of ear piercings for her birthday. When Erica turned 24, I thought of how Jilly would have wanted to go celebrate with her now that she herself would have been 21 and "legal." Those days were bittersweet for us. I am so grateful for Erica and Sierra. They are terrific young women and I love them with all my heart; yet we all acutely feel that empty spot at family celebrations. I have a feeling we always will.

When I see pit bulls, I remember how Jilly would pick up Emma (her own puppy) like a baby and try to burp her or dress her in baby outfits. She is everywhere ... and yet she's not ... and yet she IS. Does that make sense? She is the "background music" of my life now ... the song stuck in my head most of my days. She is the first thing I think of in the morning, the last thing I think of at night, and about every other thought all day long. I have friends who are 20 or 30+ years further along in their grief journey and they tell me that even after all that time, it is the same with them. They think of their angels every single day. It's not an obsession, more like they just can't turn off the "background music" of their loved ones any more than I can. It never ever goes away; it becomes the new "normal."

I almost find that comforting ... because it means I won't forget ... which is something that I fear. I am afraid of not being able to remember her smile, her scent, the way it felt when she gave me a tummy to tummy hug or how it sounded when she gave me a squeaky kiss on the cheek; her mischievous grin when she was about to do a "sneak attack" and run up to someone and jump on their back or into their arms. I fear not being able to remember what she sounded like when she would say, "*Mother!* You *are* my mother! I *do* love you, my mother!" in her weird nasal voice... I don't want to forget the way people would stare and then smile when she would belt out a song, slightly off key (but so enthusiastically, you would have thought she was trying out for a talent show) in the middle of a store. I miss seeing her pour ketchup on just about everything... finishing a meal and standing up and asking, "Does my butt look any bigger now? I am trying to grow a bigger butt!" I miss watching her wrap a lock of hair around her finger and caressing her eye or cheek with it. She would then turn to whoever was sitting next to her and rub their face with her hair too, as if it were as comforting to them as it was to her. I love remembering her claim to have the "longest hair in school." (You did *not* want to be the person sitting in front of her in class if your hair was longer than hers!)

If I can remember something about her every day for the rest of my life, that is background music that I will enjoy having stuck in my head. I don't think I want to turn the station. I will go forward with my life, tucking these memories in my mind. It's like being able to carry a little piece of her wherever I go, right next to my heart. The memories make me smile on most days. I think that makes Jilly smile too, from wherever she is watching and singing along with my background music... slightly off key, with gusto, in her new angelic voice.

♥ ♥ ♥

December 14, 2013

As I drove through the newly fallen snow, making new tracks in the cemetery where there weren't any previously, I thought about how that reflects the direction my life is taking. I am doing things in my life I never imagined; going down roads I never thought I would be traveling.

The snow was dangerous, but beautiful, glistening like tiny diamonds as twilight fell. The solar lights around your place of rest flicker on and off, using what little energy they had gathered on this cloudy day. They were only good for a few minutes before they fell back to sleep, awaiting a day with more sunshine. They just didn't seem to have the energy to keep going. Some days that is exactly how I feel.

The area I visit frequently was pristine today. Snow hides all the mud, tracks, imperfections and new graves that dot the section you are in, my Jilly. The grave blanket stands guard; a testament of love made by the family you spent your short 19 years with. The evergreen branches are a stark contrast to the sea of white snow. The purple and green ornaments are perfect and festive; they seem to mock the solitude of this place. The soft, snowy blanket of fluffy white crystals covers the area where your body now rests, safe inside your beautiful ivory casket with roses, tucked gently into your light purple vault. The cold and snow can't reach your body there. I wish I had remembered to bring a blanket to cover you with before we closed the lid to your casket.

I think about those things a lot. I visit your grave often, something I never dreamt 25 months ago that I would be doing. It brings me comfort to be five feet from your earthy remains, although it feels like a million miles. I know you aren't really there, but your body is... and I miss it terribly. I miss the feel of your silky long hair, the sound of your voice and your smell, a cross between Hollister perfume, Olay body wash and a slightly soft, spicy kind of smell that was uniquely yours. I miss your laughter, your way of telling stories about the most mundane things that would have everyone cracking up. I miss your sneak attacks when you wanted someone to "hold you like an infant." You always got your way with that!

One night before going to bed this week, I got out the lock of your hair that we saved before we put your body to rest. I twirled it, just as you would have, found the "good part" and rubbed my eyelid with it. I am so glad we have that little part of you to cherish. We have given away almost all your shoes and bras (you must have had 40 of each!) We have found homes for your tiny little size 0-2 jeans. Your shirts still hang in the closet the way you left them. Your pajamas are in the drawer. I can't seem to make myself part with those yet. It is so incredibly hard, even after two years, to wrap my head around the thought of you no longer needing them. My mind just can't go there! I start to panic when I think of it. I keep the outfit that you had on when you died in my closet, occasionally taking out your bright pink sweatshirt and hugging it, the way I wish I could hug you instead. I study the hole in the arm and am so thankful you didn't feel your body breaking; I believe with all my heart that you were gone before that happened.

I know you are spending Christmas with Jesus this year. I envy you on one level. You got to go Home. Some days, I can hardly wait to get there myself! The lights down here can't compare with what you are seeing every minute. You are with so many people that I love. They are helping you watch over us and none of you are missing anything that goes on in our lives each day. What a glorious reunion you must have had! I wish I could have seen it when your grandpas welcomed you to Heaven with big hugs.

The only way I can survive your physical death is to keep telling myself that it is just a matter of time before I can see you, hold you and hear you say, "I love you mama," as we cry tears of joy when we embrace. Will you still look like you did when I last saw you, or will you just be a being of light? Will you be 19 or will you age? Will you still smell like you? What will you be wearing? How soon will we see you again? Will it be days, weeks, months or years? None of us know. One minute we are alive here on this plane and in an instant, we are Home.

These are some of the things I think about as I drive through the newly fallen snow at the cemetery. What used to terrify me no longer does. I never imagined the need to drive out there in the dark to see how pretty it looks when all the solar lights come on. I could pitch a tent and sleep on your grave and it wouldn't phase me in the slightest. Death no longer frightens me, your dad or your sisters. We know it is just the turning of a page and that you are waiting at the beginning of the next chapter. We will stay here until we have completed whatever assignment God gives us and we will gladly do whatever that assignment might be.

All too soon, it will be our turn to come Home...to God...to all our loved ones, and to you, our precious Jillybean, forever and ever. Until then, my darling girl, I will visit often, whisper how much I love you and draw hearts in the snow. I will always remember to kiss you goodnight.

8

DADDY'S HUG

*I*NTENSE GRIEF CAN CAUSE a delay in seeing signs that our loved ones send, because we can't see them through our tears. It's like covering up with a thick canvas and expecting to see the sunshine. Let's go back a bit.

April 29, 2013

*M*Y HUSBAND MARK AND I stopped to see an old friend the other day. She is a widow who lost her husband the same week Jilly died. We talked about the intensity of the feelings of grief; how it *still* doesn't feel real. It makes you have the most peculiar thoughts... things you would never in your wildest dreams imagine yourself thinking about.

Even in the same family, we grieve and mourn differently. When I walked through my kitchen a couple weeks ago and saw one of Jilly's friends who looks uncannily like her from the back, I almost ran up to her and yelled, "You are home!" I still expect her to walk through the door, even after 17 months. I know she can't, but it's hard to explain, so allow me to tell you a true story. I have shared with many of you my grief stories, so I will now share with you my husband's story.

As we shared a cup of tea, Mark told our widowed friend that he forced himself to go the cemetery *every single day* when he got off work for almost four months after we buried Jilly's body. He hated going there, but he also could not stay away from there either. It was the only way he knew how to face the grief, since it does not come with an instruction booklet. Even though you fantasize that you *might* have some idea, you really do not have a clue how you will handle it until you do not have any other choice. Some days, Mark sat in his truck staring mindlessly at her grave. There were days he laid on the ground and made snow angels next to her. Other days he cried until no more tears would come. At times, it was all he could do to keep from clawing at her grave with his bare hands, wanting to dig her up and bring his little girl back home, because that is *not* where she belonged! She isn't supposed to be in the cold hard ground before we are! That is not the natural order of things!

(The thought of digging up your child probably sounds totally bizarre, but most parents who have buried a child completely understand this. Many of us have had it cross our minds at one time or another.)

My husband understands the accident...and it *was* an accident. "It" could have happened to anyone. He needed to channel all his anger toward something or someone. In the first insane moments of grief, he was angry with Jillian, but felt guilty about being mad at his dead child. ("She should have stayed home last night! This would not have happened if she had not gone out!) Then he blamed himself for not being able to stop the accident from happening, even though he was out deer hunting that morning. Eventually, the driver in the accident (one of Jillian's best friends) was unfortunate enough to become the face of "it" and most of his anger got directed toward her. I had to give the driver, Jilly's "Twinaroo," time alone with Jillian's body at the funeral home after Mark had left. She found sanctuary in the balcony of the church during the funeral so that he could not see her. He is usually a rational guy, but he did not trust himself not to verbally and emotionally cut her to shreds if she was in his sight.

Mark still occasionally struggles with the senselessness of his beautiful daughter's death. Why Jillian? Why didn't God choose some crazed murderer or rapist at the prison he worked for instead? Or, why not him? Why had he survived cancer two years earlier only to lose his daughter now? He would have traded his life for hers in a heartbeat. Why, why, why? It is the number one question every bereaved parent asks. There are no good answers, but we are slowly figuring out some semi-plausible explanations as life unfolds before us.

Mark just wanted *one* more hug from Jillian, which of course, would never be enough. Could you live with only *one* more hug from your loved one? He yearned for it so badly that it was constantly in his thoughts, day in and day out. He could not come to terms with being unable to hold her, embrace her, feel her warm breath on his cheek when she hugged him, hear her laugh, call him Daddy, or see her brown eyes widen just the tiniest little bit when she wasn't telling the truth. Even though she hugged us both before she walked out the door the night before she died, my husband wanted that final hug he didn't get to give her, before sending her off to the greatest "Universe-city" of all... the final "college" where all knowledge is—Heaven.

After reading many grief books, he followed one of the suggestions for mourning, which was practicing controlled breathing to help him relax. He tried to wipe his mind completely clean of everything, which in the initial stages of grief, is much harder than it sounds. He begged God to please, *please* send him some sign that Jilly was okay; that even though the physical body we knew as Jillian was in the frozen ground, her gloriously free soul was working on an eternal tan in Heaven.

My husband has always been a very concrete thinker. He is Mr. Skeptical. He must feel it with his own hands and see it with his own eyes to believe it. Mark has always been leery of my ability to "think outside the box." He sometimes wondered if I wasn't just "a little bit nuts" for my beliefs about life continuing on the Other Side. Good thing I am reasonably comfortable in my own skin.

I did not know that he had started practicing relaxation exercises every morning and would have been shocked if I *had* known! People who live in the same house can grieve differently and quite frankly, at that time, I was doing well to find matching socks and remember to put on underwear in the morning before I left the house for work, much less help him grieve. Looking back, I was on autopilot maneuvering through a dense fog and some days, I still am. Grief is not unlike a traumatic brain injury. It permanently changes your brain, both physically and mentally.

Alas, on this one particular day, he decided that he probably would not get his hug, dream about, or feel Jilly very well, if he did not release his anger and work on forgiveness. He felt . . . no, he *knew* deep down that the anger was blocking something in his heart and his mind. He felt he needed to forgive himself, forgive the driver, forgive God for taking Jilly, forgive Jilly for dying with so much "unfinished business," forgive the "if onlys" and the "what ifs," etc. that had rolled around in his mind for months.

That very same night (in what was truly an amazing turn of perfect events) he decided to forgive the driver. In the middle of a crowded high school gymnasium, he embraced her and told her that Jilly loved her and so did he. It was incredible, breaking down his barriers. He cried so hard on his way to work that night that he had to pull over because he couldn't see through his tears. He continued to cry most of the night. I had been with my husband for over 25 years before I ever saw him cry the first time, so that tells you he is not an openly emotional kind of guy.

The next morning, feeling relieved, exhausted and lighter, he climbed into bed and practiced clearing his mind. We were alone in the house. I was lying next to him and at that very moment, was having one of my very first dreams about Jilly since her death.

In my dream, she had come up behind me, tapped me on the shoulder and before I could get more than a quick look at her, did one of her famous, "I am up to something *really good*" mischievous laughs and then quickly disappeared through a gymnasium door. Still asleep, I was not aware that Mark was also having one of the first of many experiences that would change the way he grieves forever.

As he lay there, picturing a blank slate in his mind... he felt someone come in and sit down on the bed. When you are lying a foot or so from the edge of a bed and someone sits on it, it is unmistakable. He *actually felt* the mattress indent. His eyes flew open and he commanded, "NO! Close them! Go back to where you just were in your mind!" He did and then he felt the most incredible thing. The whole side of his body closest to where the bed was being indented started feeling tingly from his knees to his shoulder, followed by a slight warming temperature change that he only felt on that half of his body. He was finally getting his Jilly hug! After a few minutes, the warmth he was feeling slowly dissipated, but the feeling of incredible love stayed with him.

I want you to know that he made me recreate this experience a few minutes later, just to prove to himself how it would feel if someone came and sat in that exact spot. It felt the same, except I weigh more than Jilly did. He could feel the difference. He knew then that his own anger was so dense that it had been blocking Jilly's ability to reach him, to touch him, to comfort him. Forgiveness wasn't just for the driver... it was also for him.

Now, some of you whose loved ones have also gone Home might think, "I've never had anything, heard anything, felt or seen anything that would give me that kind of comfort that my loved one was still around." I guess I would have to first ask you if you believe it is possible. If you don't believe it, our loved ones on the other side will have to work that much harder to convince you.

The friend we were visiting was an experienced educator. She had taught school for many years and had a scientific mindset. She really wanted to explain away certain odd things that had happened since her husband died. One day, however, her husband literally dropped something (a coin with an angel on it) in her lap out of thin air. There was nowhere in her office that it could have come from. He had to show her signs a few more times before she was finally able to go from "suspecting" that her beloved was still with her, to "knowing" he was there when she needed him most. She feels his presence and is so peaceful about it. Heaven isn't some far-off place...it's all around us. She is so comforted with the knowledge that he is waiting just beyond the veil for her, and that veil is closer than she ever imagined. Sometimes it is thin and sometimes, when we are experiencing deep and intense emotions, it is like a thick piece of canvas that we can't feel anything through, no matter how hard they try to comfort us from that side. If these two skeptics can get signs, believe me, so can anyone! It may take a while, but it *will* happen if we are open to noticing. Be patient. When you believe it, you may very well see it. Remember that our loved ones are in a place where the communication reception is always good but trying to get the signal to us in the perfect moment can be a little sketchy.

If your loved one goes to all that trouble to send you a bird, or a coin, or a song on the radio, or a particular car, or light bulb that blows when you walk under it, or some other sign repeatedly and no one notices, I would imagine that those on the other side would find that frustrating. (But who knows, they may not get frustrated there.) Sometimes those of us on this side simply dismiss it as just a chance occurrence. However, in our family we have learned to say, "Thank you, God," when we get a sign from Jilly. And the more we thank God for them, the more we seem to notice.

After all, Jesus promised—"Blessed are those who mourn, for they shall be comforted."

And we are. We truly are.

An hour after finding out that Jilly had died, Mark was on his way to break the awful news to his mom in person, when he pulled over to the side of the road to write the first poem down.

WHEN THE WIND BLOWS

I hear her name.
When the sun shines brightly,
I see her smile.
When the clouds move through the sky,
I think of Jilly flowing through our lives.

I also found this piece that Mark wrote two days after she died.

> "My Beloved JillyBean,
> I'm so afraid. Afraid that as years go by, your memory will somehow be diminished. It will not be the fierce love and pain I am experiencing today. Other significant events will somehow, piece by piece, slowly push you to the background. This cannot be.

I'm so afraid that I won't be able to look at a photograph of you or reflect deeply on what you meant to me without falling down and rolling around in clenched pain. I want to be able to sing your name, not scream it. I want to be able to say that my beloved Jillian went to the place of warmth and wisdom that we who are left are denied; went to heaven, without sounding like a crying, blubbering mess. I pray that I will find that strength and confidence someday.

Jilly, as a child, you measured new situations so carefully. You were the one standing back, watching other children interact, trying to figure out what people were up to. More importantly, why people did the things that they did and trying to solve the unknown equation of how you fit in. One day in Junior High, it just happened for you. Once you deemed it safe, slowly becoming involved on your own terms, you became the teenager who wanted to give to all. You were at home with any group or clique. You openly gave your love and friendship freely to anyone, knowing perfectly well that all the other cliques were judging you. You found the beauty in each person. I think that is why you were so drawn to babies. They have unconditional love and can't hide what they are feeling. I believe it was their pure genuineness that drew you to them.

You became my "spider monkey warrior" as you found new strengths and challenges, singing, laughing, smiling and bringing joy to all who entered your world. You had to learn to ward off the ugly face of anxiety and energy draining depression. You took advice and eagerly accepted counseling, turning even those relationships into deep friendships. It was during your struggles that you had to sort out coping mechanisms and "crutches." Sometimes drugs, sometimes alcohol, but finally through the love of God, family and friends, our old Jilly was back. Back as the one who leaped at the world in Junior High, back as the one who had to hug and kiss you in greeting, back as the one who made my heart sing for joy. Just as my eyes were reopened to the limitless change of our little chameleon, to the surging love and joy of our baby girl, Heaven called out to you. I sit here in pain, unable to sleep, looking at the joy and hope she gave back to me. How can I see her face and not hear her voice or get that hug as we lay you to rest? I want my Jilly back. I'm so afraid.

LOUISE CRIST

Mark's Love Notes (2/12/14)

*Slowly, slowly
Minute by day,
Life has got me
Spinning away.*

*Drifting down
The spiral I go
Hoping someone
Will rescue, sorrow.*

*Faith, hope
A hand reaches down
Tears from my heart
Still drip to the ground.*

*Move, run . . .
Dodge the torment.
Feet are stuck
As if in cement.*

*I trust that time
Will do its work
Fearful that it's truly
The end's last look.
Love, Daddy*

Song Mark wrote to Jilly (3/30/2014)

I'M CRYING OUT YOUR NAME

Lying here in solitude,
Living life destitute,
Something needs to go,
And come my way.

My heart lies trampled underneath
The growing burden of this grief
Where's the sunshine
To brighten my day?

I'm crying out your name...
I'm crying out your name.

Being tortured by the thought
Of living life where you are not...
Still hearing the words, you used to say.

Give me just one more chance,
I'll even take a single glance
Don't let the memories fade away!

I'm crying out your name...
I'm crying out your name.

You are gone and I must stay,
Living life in a whole new way

LOUISE CRIST

Never realizing if it's night or day.
It's time to start and build anew
Not quite sure what I'm going to do
I only know I wish you'd stayed
Because I'm still crying out your name.

♥ ♥ ♥

9

THE SUMMER OF 2013

July 4th Fireworks

As I sat watching the fireworks last night from our local outdoor community pool (a tradition with our kids for the last 10 years), I had a mixture of feelings. It will be the last time we do that, because after this year, the pool will cease to exist. It will be filled in and transformed into a fountain. We will never be able to watch the fireworks exploding over our heads again, as we sit on a lounge chair in the water or poolside with other lifeguards and their families... at least not in that exact spot. All we will have when we go to that location will be the sweet memories of Independence Days gone by. Ironically, the timing coincided with my last child leaving home.

I couldn't help but be awed by the beauty of the displays of light. Fireworks are made of volatile substances mixed with some color, the bang being the "firecracker." They are sealed in neat little packages. Their true colors don't show until a catalyst, such as a flame, is added. Only then do they become a spectacular light for all to see. It struck me then, isn't that kind of like our lives?

We happily anticipate the holiday, perhaps planning family get-togethers, enjoying a day off work. We go to a special place for the best view, pull up a chair or blanket and wait, and wait and wait... for darkness, because only in the darkness can you really appreciate these beautiful lights. It is one of the rare days each year that we want the daylight to end.

We watch a plume of light go into the sky, then a quick silence, followed by a *BOOM* and a spectacular spray of light illuminates the darkness. We ooh and aah over the patterns made. Along comes another and when it too shatters the darkness, we can see the smoky shadows still left by the previous one. It always seems to be over too soon. We pack up and head home, the lights having brought us joy.

It occurred to me how life is very much like those fireworks.

When our children are born, it is the same cycle. We anticipate the day of birth. Family gathers around. We go to a special place and wait. However, in order to see the beautiful "light" that is now exploding from its cocoon, we must endure a time of darkness and pain. Only then, can this beautiful child come forth and light the world with its presence. We *ooh* and *aah* at the pattern this child has made; when other children follow, we go through the same process and the light brought forth by that child illuminates the life of someone before it. (Why, she looks just like her sister, mom, her aunt or grandma!)

The child grows up, meandering through other people's lives, touching them all with his or her own special unique spark of light. Sometimes this leaves a long trail of light...a long life...and sometimes it is a shorter burst of light. When they leave this earth to go back Home, there is a sudden burst of color, a *boom*, as our hearts are exploding with the loss and it leaves sparks on anyone within viewing distance.

Sometimes those burning embers are enormous; sometimes smaller, but they all make an impact. They all show how that person's life illuminated others. Each of those sparks are the things that person did that touched another life. Sometimes, only in the darkness of death do you truly appreciate how wide reaching those fiery sparks were. Occasionally, a stray spark will land on someone or something and a new spark is born, again lighting the area around it with the memory of the original firework.

It would appear to us that after the explosion of loss, our world goes dark. I personally believe that those who have gone Home are in the presence of eternal glorious Light. There is no darkness after that burst of color. They will always be radiant and in full bloom where they are. Only on this side do we experience the darkness after the boom. Those in Heaven only know the Light. They are full of joy and wonder. It would be like having the happiest, most content moment of your life magnified a thousand times for eternity.

When I look out at my garden each night, lit by solar lights, it reminds me of my loved ones who have gone Home before me. The solar lights (representing my loved ones) that I see in my yard (representing the landscape of my life), can bring some comfort, some joy and even a few *oohs* and *aahs*. Each one throws a unique pattern of light to the area around it, continuing to light the darkness with the love they brought to my life. That light can never be extinguished. I carry it with me in my soul. It is eternal.

Perhaps from Heaven, our lives here look like those solar lights, blinking in this shadowy world. The love we give to others illuminates the darkness in the lives we lead; each random act of kindness joins with other lights to create a bigger one. Our loved one's lives absorb the light from God while they are here, during the daylight of their lives and when they go Home, those who are left behind are plunged into the darkness of our "nightfall." It's easy to lose our way. We stumble and sometimes fall hard in our grief. It takes time to open our eyes and see the light left behind.

When I examine my life, I feel blessed to have three beautiful daughters who light the world with their love and kindness.

Jilly was a pretty light... not just physically, but also in the way she loved others and was loved by so many in return. I believe each of our lights will make a difference in the life of another when it is our turn to go Home.

Maybe she is watching and singing that sweet little song she learned in Vacation Bible School so many years ago: *"This little light of mine, I'm going to let it shine. Let it shine, let it shine, let it shine..."* You shine on, my Jilly Bean. You shine on!

♥ ♥ ♥

The 5K Marathon Man

As a nurse for almost 27 years, I truly *love* my job. Some days, I love it more than others, but becoming a nurse was the best idea God ever put into my head. Usually, I say a prayer on the quick drive to work, as I never know whose path will cross mine. I ask my Heavenly Father to lead me to those whom I need, and those who need me and to let something I do that day have some lasting significance.

God heard me recently and here are just a couple examples of the way He answered that prayer. Let me share a sample day at work with you.

I started the day in outpatient surgery. My job there is to prepare people for various surgical procedures. My first patient that day was well known to me, our lives having crossed repeatedly while our children were on a high school sports team together. He was nervous about his surgery, very nervous. (By the way, your mouth can say that you aren't afraid, but your vital signs will never lie.)

He and his wife had sat through multiple surgeries on their daughter, who is a lovely, compassionate brave young woman, but when dad was the patient, it was a different story. I think he was afraid of losing his independence, even if it was only for a few hours while he was under the effects of anesthesia. His family and I said a prayer and asked God to watch over him and guide the surgical team. I did my best to help keep him calm and gave him the same care I would give to any of my own loved ones. His surgery went well, and he did great! I got a hug when he left, which really made my day. I was feeling happy as I moved on to the next patient, an older man who also came in with a nervous smile.

This gentleman, although we had never met, somehow already felt like an old friend. A few days earlier, I had done his pre-anesthesia assessment on the phone (which seems like a million questions on your health history), so I had the advantage of knowing a whole lot more about him than he knew about me! He had never, in all his almost 70 years, had a surgery because he kept himself in great shape, often running 5K races and usually winning his age group.

He struggled to put on a brave face. He was a delightful fellow and made my job a pleasure. His sister sat by his bed, offering support. His procedure went well; afterwards, we chatted while I took out his IV. He asked me about the "Always Remember" bracelet that never comes off my right wrist. I explained that my daughter had gone Home 19 months ago, and he began to cry. He shared that he had lost his wife just 15 short months ago. I sat down across from him, put my hand on his knee and offered my sympathy. The tears flowed as he told me of her illness and eventual death from cancer. We bonded deeply in that moment, both of us having been stung unmercifully by the beast we know as Death.

He then asked me how I did it, how did I manage to smile, to keep going on each day after such an enormous loss? He told me that when he closed his eyes and thought of his beloved wife, all he could see was her lying in bed, taking her last breath and closing her eyes forever as death finally claimed her. He could not get that picture out of his mind, no matter how much he wanted to. (This is a classic "Post Traumatic Stress Disorder" (PTSD) symptom.)

I could relate to that. I struggle each and every day with the mental image of walking around the side of the fire truck and seeing Jillian's body in that gray bag on the gurney. It was zipped up to her neck, hiding most of her injuries and allowing me to see only her beautiful face. I have witnessed many heartbreaking things in my job, but no amount of experience in my nursing career ever prepared me for the moment I identified my child's body. It took every ounce of strength I had to remain upright and hold onto my brother and sister-in-love's arms. My legs were shaking violently beneath me. I wanted to fall down and die right in that very spot. I remember silently pleading with God to bring her back and take me instead. I don't even have to close my eyes anymore to see that image... it's just there.

But, as bad as it was, that horrible snapshot in time was *not* what my daughter's life was about. That moment in time was just the end of her chapter, not the end of her book. Her book will never be over, because her energy will never cease to exist. She has simply turned the page while I am stuck on the previous chapter! She is now just a different *form* of energy. Although it is still traumatic for me, how she got that way no longer matters to her, because she is in a perfect body now.

I asked him this question: "Why are you defining the 60+ years that your wonderful wife lived on this Earth and all the love and memories you shared, by the very last moment of her life? Is that all she was? Her last day, her last few seconds? Is that what her entire life was about?" I asked him to picture in his mind for just a minute, the time when his wife was the most beautiful to him, the happiest and the most loved. Magnify it by a million. That is who she IS now... forever. She will never know another second of sorrow, pain, grief or unhappiness. We can't even begin to fathom that joy. We can't comprehend being the recipient of the magnitude of love that can only come by literally being the presence of God. If we truly understood this, we would be crying when babies were born into this world and throwing Celebrations of Life, instead of funerals when people leave it. It is said that to be absent from the body is to be present with the Lord.

I shared with him the phrase that has become my mantra on the many days when I still get stuck in that last moment of Jilly's life, instead of celebrating all the other days and years she was here.

The phrase goes like this: "I'll be your legacy; I'll be your voice. You live on inside me, so I've made a choice. I'll honor your life by living again. I love you. I miss you. I'll see you again."

That little verse brings me so much comfort. I *will* see her again.

I asked this kind sensitive man what his wife's passions were. He did not skip a beat before answering that she liked to read, she liked flowers, she liked to watch ball games; they had season tickets. I suggested honoring her life by sharing the things she loved to do. Donate some books to the library in her name. Plant some flowers in a garden for others to see and enjoy. Take someone to the game that has never had the chance to go; watch the joy on their faces. "That is a way to remember someone's life, by bringing them along in your journey as you make new memories that honor them," I explained to him. What if he did one random act of kindness each day as a way of saying, "I love you," to his wife? Would it make a difference? I honestly believe that it would.

Now, don't get me wrong. It doesn't magically make the pain disappear. I still cry...a lot! Tears are allowed! We cry as often as we need to, as tears are one of the signs that we loved deeply. Grief is the price we pay for love.

By the way, tears of joy are allowed too. I had some good tears of joy this week! Whatever you feed often will multiply and grow, so what would happen if you fed the good memories each day after feeding the moments of missing our loved ones deeply? It may not work for everyone, because each person grieves differently, but that is what works for me right now.

Through the tears that were now falling softly down his cheeks, he looked at me and said, "Well, I never really thought of it that way!" He pondered it for a minute. Then he smiled, we both thanked God for letting our paths cross and he and his sister hugged me on the way out the door. I smiled and shed some tears at the same time. Just for an instant, I felt my Jilly very close by. God led me that day not only to those who needed me, but to those whom I needed. God answered my prayer.

I will remember this man every day for as long as I live. He came into my life exactly when I needed him and trusted me, someone he had never met before, enough to share the most tender part of his heart; his obvious love for his wife. Death can do many things, but it cannot steal that love. That kind of love never dies. I only took care of him for a few hours that day, but I feel so incredibly blessed to have met him and look forward to the day I get to meet the lovely woman named Fronie that he so clearly adores in Heaven. (She and Jilly probably orchestrated the whole "random" meeting!) We have become good friends since that day.

Witnessing that kind of love is so powerful. Having a job that I still get excited about doing after all these years? Absolutely priceless. It just doesn't get any better than that... until the day when we all get to go Home.

10

"SIGN, SIGN, EVERYWHERE A SIGN"

To offer some clarity and make it less confusing: I refer to my biological father (Jim) as Daddy, my stepdad is Dean or "Bumpa Dean" to my kids. Mark's dad is Larry, or "Papa" to his grandchildren.

August 13, 2013

I think that nearly everyone who has lost a loved one wishes and hopes for a sign from them. The problem is, we wait for a sign *we* think they should send, instead of one that *they* want to (or are able to) send, so we don't always recognize it as a sign.

When I was pregnant with Jillian, I lost my biological daddy (Jim) to lung cancer. He was buried a few days before my 30th birthday. I was his baby girl. After he died, I asked him to send me an "Eeyore" sign so that I would know he was still with me, still close by. As a little girl, the last present I received from both my parents before they divorced was a little stuffed Eeyore from the Winnie the Pooh family. It became my most treasured possession, a link to the time before we were a "broken" family, and I was the only kid in my class with divorced parents. One year, Daddy took me on vacation, and I accidently left Eeyore in the hotel room. We were hours down the road when I realized he was not in my suitcase; I was one heartbroken teenager. I had slept with this stuffed animal every night since he was given to me. My dad called the hotel and had Eeyore shipped across the country so that he was waiting for me when I arrived home. I cuddled with him until after I had my own children; long after his eyes fell out, his tail got lost and his fur got rubbed off by my endless hugs, tears and kisses. He now sits in my china cabinet, barely recognizable as the fine gray stuffed donkey that he once was—but to me he is still beautiful.

I looked and looked all over for an Eeyore sign from daddy for over 10 years. I had some close calls. I saw John Edward (the medium on the Crossing Over TV show) three separate times as part of a large audience. He came out once saying,

"Christopher Robin? Tigger?" and then proceeded to read the woman in front of me, the man behind me and finally the woman sitting next to me, whose life and circumstances were very similar to mine. We didn't know each other at all, but most of the things he said to her were also very specific and unique to my situation as well.

I sometimes felt Daddy around, especially while walking along a beach. The only big sign I ever got was a dream I once had where Daddy and I were sharing our thoughts over coffee. It was three or four years after he died. It was so real that I got up the next morning and looked for the empty coffee cups. I ached to hug him again, to feel his gentle arms around me and have him comfort me the way he had done when I was a little girl. If only I would see or hear about a random Eeyore, I would know that Daddy was still watching over me. But no Eeyore signs ever came.

Ten years after he died, I attended a 4-day class on energy balancing. We had to use the techniques we learned on each other. When it was my turn, I climbed up on the massage table and closed my eyes. Within a minute, I went in to a very relaxed, almost dream-like state. I saw myself walking into a church and there, standing near the altar, about 10 feet away, was Daddy! Oh my gosh! I was so excited to see him!

I told him that I really wanted to hug him, but I was afraid he would be cold and stiff. (I can't touch dead bodies without nearly fainting... Don't laugh, I know that is an odd confession from a nurse!)

Daddy said, "I promise, I am not cold or stiff; I am nice and warm, just like you remember. Come here and give me a hug." I did. It felt every bit as real as when I hug someone here! I was *so* happy! Then I asked him where in the heck he had been, because for 10 long years I had been looking for an Eeyore sign from him! He laughed and said, "You have been so busy looking for the sign you *think* I should have sent, that you missed all the signs that I *did* send! I have been right here, very close to you the whole time! I haven't missed a single moment of your life." It felt so wonderful to be hugged by him again! I stayed with him for what felt like hours. However, when I finished the session on the massage table, a mere five minutes had passed.

My youngest daughter, Sierra, was missing her sister fiercely one morning this summer. As she sat there stirring her bowl of Lucky Charms, thinking about Jillian, wishing she could "hear" from her, she looked down and noticed that Jillian had sent a sign to let her know she wasn't too far away. The marshmallows randomly all stuck together and made the letters "JC" in her cereal bowl. Explain that one!

I guess what I am getting at is this. If you have lost a loved one, don't put limitations on the signs they can send you. If they were a quiet shy person here, you might have to look a little harder. Jilly was loud and visible wherever she went while she lived here, and she continues to be quite boisterous on the other side. I have talked to people who find random coins, feathers, hearts and stones. They see their loved one's cars, orbs, red tail hawks, eagles and other birds, butterflies, dragonflies and lady bugs. They hear songs, catch a whiff of certain familiar fragrances and yes, even actually swear they caught a glimpse of their loved ones. Dropping their vibrations down to our physical level so that they can send a sign is a bit like holding your breath underwater. It can only be done in very short spurts. If your loved one can't find a way to reach you through your grief, they may use someone else to send the message. It isn't because that person is more important to them, they just find the most open channel. Please don't take it personally that someone else has dreamed of them before you have. They are trying to tell you of their love in whatever way they can.

Sometimes, like Jilly's initials in the cereal, they make it more obvious and fun. We have learned to just say *thank you* and smile when we "get" the sign they are trying to send to comfort us. If you haven't gotten one from your loved one, it doesn't mean they aren't sending them; it is often just too hard to see the signs when we are under the heavy blanket of grief. We can hardly see anything under there; it is so dark and heavy! We wouldn't recognize those signs if they hit us on the head. When we start to peek out from under that heavy canvas of grief and shock and see life going on around us again, we will often be able to see a sign that our loved ones are okay.

Quarters never meant a thing to us before Jillian died. After the accident, there were quarters everywhere we looked. I can't look at a quarter now and *not* think of her. She has sent us so many of them and when she does, it is always extraordinary. Perhaps it is her way of "paying us back" for all the trouble she used to get in to. I don't know how, but I do know she sends them to us, her friends and often to people that she wants us to have in our lives. I have no doubt that one of these days when you find an odd single quarter in a place that it shouldn't normally be, or that you could swear wasn't there a minute before, you will wonder if it isn't our Jilly telling you that she is glad you are in our lives, sharing our journey. She is doing her best to show us that her life didn't end on November 19, 2011. She is letting us know that it really had only just begun!

11

OUR FAMILY TENT

February 18, 2014
Third Birthday in Heaven

For those of you who think I am so strong and wonder how I keep going...I am *not* strong, just stubborn and there are days I just want to throw in the towel on this whole "grief thing." I had one of those days this week.

I have not had a meltdown in almost six months. I knew one was lurking dangerously close. I was having a very bad day the day before Jilly's 22nd birthday. Usually, I think of her birthday and I feel joy. It's a happy but bittersweet day for me. It's the day she came into the world and changed us all by being a part of it. It is filled with wonderful happy memories of Jilly and the past celebrations with her countless, precious friends that she brought into our home and our hearts.

In one way, I dread it and yet on another level, look forward to celebrating one of the three happiest days of my life; the days that I gave birth to my daughters. A good friend, who has also lost a child, recently had an epiphany that we should treat our children in heaven's birthday, with the same joy that we have when we celebrate our children on earth's birthdays.

The day they came into this world changed everything about our lives... even our identities. I became the mother of two daughters (instead of one) the day Jillian was born. No longer did I only have one child, I had children; Erica became a big sister. Our family unit changed completely. As my belly swelled with her pregnancy, I wondered how on earth I would ever have enough love for two children... and I couldn't fathom loving anyone more than I did my firstborn. Jillian taught me that love doesn't have a limit that must be divided among a certain number of people. Instead, love knows no end. When more children come along, the love you have somehow multiplies so that there is plenty for everyone. When Sierra was born into the family, I learned that my cup of love simply gets bigger and deeper with each addition.

But that day, I was blindsided repeatedly by "grief quakes." Talking about her, thinking about her, seeing her birthday looming on the calendar all brought tears to my eyes the entire day. (Not a good thing when you are at work!) I just couldn't get a grip on the sorrow. I tried hard but couldn't seem to stop the tears from rolling down my cheeks throughout the day.

My last phone call at work was to a mom I later learned had lost her son as well. I barely made it through the phone call without blubbering. I crawled into bed after crying in the shower and snuffled myself to sleep that night. I asked Jillian to help me and asked God to bring me comfort. I was at the point where I just didn't think I could stand *one more* minute of life without being able to hold her and hug her again.

When I awoke the next morning after a restless night, on what would have been her 22nd birthday, I noticed that the street was unusually quiet. It is usually filled with the sounds of little kids on their way to school. The weather the night before had been terrible, but it was sunny when I opened my eyes. School had been cancelled. The kids all got the day off. Hmmm.

Jilly's idea of a totally awesome birthday would have been to skip a few hours of school and go tanning. The day turned out to be the sunniest, warmest day we have had in weeks. For those of you who knew Jillian well, she would have been in her bikini on the enclosed sun porch trying to get a tan, as she had done in years past even when it got to be freezing. (Only in Michigan do we do that!)

I thought to myself that it could possibly be a Jilly sign, humorous but slight. It did make me smile though. Next, I got my morning cup of tea and logged on to the computer. I belong to a local online group where people sell things they no longer want.

There was a car for sale, but not just *any* car. It was a purple Dodge Stratus. That is very significant for two reasons; the first being that is the *exact* car she took her last breath in and the second is that it is her "just for you, Mama," special sign for me. It always gets my attention when I see one, as they aren't that common. Try to remember the last time you saw a purple car? I always thank her for putting one in my path at the perfect moment, so I know she is with me. This person did not know anything about Jilly or me. It was just "random" that he chose that day to list the car.

Okay, Jilly girl, that sign was definitely stronger! I smiled a little more. A few minutes later, I received a private message from one of the former coaches Jilly had when she was little. This is a mom of two boys with health issues and it had been an exhaustingly hard week for her. Her husband told her to go take a nap and she willingly did so. She dreamed her boys were in danger, but Jillian showed up and helped her fix everything. She and Jillian sat and talked for a while. She asked how Jillian was "really" doing and Jilly smiled and said:

"I am doing *great!* Can you please tell my mom I said Hi and that I love her?"

This person did not even know it was Jillian's birthday until after she sent the message. Wow! No mistaking this sign. It was loud and clear. Smiles and now tears of happiness and gratitude started leaking from my happy eyes.

Jillian had *always* believed that it was possible for our loved ones to let us know they were okay from the other side. She asked her grandpa as he was dying, to "send her signs when he got to Heaven and got to be a strong enough angel." She didn't ever doubt that it would happen. She *expected* it to happen, just as I do. And it does. I am so grateful to God for allowing me to see these "Jilly winks." They usually are not huge "right in your face" signs; they are subtle; "having to be at the right place at the right time" signs. I am 100 percent positive that she found a way to comfort me on her birthday. She found messengers to give me the best birthday hug she was capable of without being in a body.

It turned out to be a Happy 22nd Birthday after all.

Camping, anyone?

I ONCE READ THAT A family unit is like a tent. When it is just a husband and wife, your life resembles a pup tent. Big enough for two, but if you take out one of the poles, the tent will collapse. As you add children and other loved ones to your family, your tent gets bigger and more complex, with each person representing one of the poles. They all help to support and hold up the family unit. When one person in the family dies, the tent temporarily collapses, and the family must figure out how to get the tent back up using one less pole. It is a difficult task.

When Jilly lived on earth, she brought many people into our family to act as supports for our tent. Our tent grew to epic size. We had many wonderful memories in it and each one of the people who were important to her, will stay in our hearts (and in our "tent") forever. In some ways, Jilly was our center pole. She was the middle child, the best friend to both siblings, the go between for each one. She physically resembled me but had Mark's sense of adventure and fearlessness.

She didn't look like her sisters and yet in so many ways, she did. When she went Home, our tent collapsed under the weight of grief and tears. Our community, friends and family members rushed to our side and helped us reconstruct our tent, filling it full of love. It isn't the same as it had been and never will be again. One of the poles is missing. In its place, many people brought their own poles and used them to offer support. Our new tent is beautiful, and part of its beauty is the patches and scars both on the outside and inside, along with the way that it was built with such a hodgepodge of many poles of love. Jillian managed to take all our love with her, yet somehow return that love tenfold to those left behind.

As her birthdays come and go, we will always miss her and feel a certain sadness that she is not physically here to blow out the candles. In her place though, she leaves her spirit of laughter and silly pranks, her compassion for others, her tender heart and her precious witty sense of humor.

She no longer fits inside the confines of our tent now because she is *love* and her love is now truly endless. It will never go away and cannot be destroyed.

I want to say thank you to all those that she has brought into our tent. Just by sharing her life, her love and her memories, you help us stay strong enough to keep going each day, to keep celebrating her life and her birthday each year; to have the courage to continue to love, even though we know the tent will go through many reconstructions before we ourselves go Home.

Jilly couldn't ask for a better present. Neither could we.

♥ ♥ ♥

June 01, 2014
"Uncle Carl"

Upon receiving the news that our Uncle Carl was in his final hours on Earth, I felt the urgent need to drive to Dayton, Ohio. Carl is my father-in-law, Larry's brother. He had been fighting metastatic prostate cancer for months when he suddenly took a turn for the worst. He is one of my favorite uncles and we never missed an opportunity in our travels to stop in and see Carl and Aunt Leatha for a quick visit. She called and wanted me to come right away, so I quickly packed a bag and hopped in my car for the four-hour drive.

Just a few years before, Carl and my father-in-law Larry both had open heart bypass surgery a few months apart. They both recovered well enough to take to the dance floor at my oldest daughter's wedding, earning them the nickname of "the Bypass Brothers." Carl was the spunky, silly uncle who would let the five girl cousins do his hair and practice make up on him at Thanksgiving get-togethers. As a truck driver, he shared many of his goofy adventures with us.

I came up one dining room table short during one of our famous, annual Thanksgiving card games of "Spoons." Carl grabbed for a spoon, flying toward the prize at the opposite end of the table, but instead landing squarely in the middle of it. He wasn't a tiny guy and the poor table creaked and groaned and finally gave out. It's one of our family's favorite memories of him.

In 2011, he made several long trips to our state to be with his brother Larry in his final days of battling cancer; he then turned around and came right back for his funeral. Nine weeks later, he came when Jilly died.

Both men loved our girls, but Jilly especially seemed to adore Carl. I have a picture of her sitting on both of their laps at a family reunion the summer before she died, like she just couldn't decide whose lap was softer. After her visitation at the funeral home, I remember missing Larry deeply and putting my head on Carl's shoulder, exhausted, as he put his arm around me, offering me the comfort I wished his brother was still around to give. I finally felt safe enough to relax and doze off. He never moved; he just let me sleep, even though I am sure it was uncomfortable for him.

Throughout the drive to Ohio, I prayed I would make it in time to kiss him goodbye. Sadly, Aunt Leatha called when I was still about 20 miles away to tell me that he had passed before I could get there. As soon as I hung up from that call, I started talking to Jilly, asking her to welcome Carl Home and give him a big hug... and, by the way, if she would please send me a sign that she could hear me, and that Carl was with her—that would be dandy!

I am terrible with directions and have never been anywhere else in that city, except to Carl and Leatha's house. I punched in the name of the hospital on my GPS and took a deep breath as I relied on it to guide me there. I frantically followed the voice prompts telling me to turn here and turn there until it finally said, "You have arrived at your destination." I was turning into the hospital parking lot when I looked up; what I saw brought me to tears and laughter at the same time.

Jilly took her last breath in this life on a street named Big Hill Road... and there, right in front of me, was a street sign in large letters... *Big Hill Road.* But I was in a city four-hours away from where she died. What are the odds?

I had asked for a sign; Jilly, still the prankster she always was, literally sent me a "sign," a street sign! I knew Carl had arrived Home safely and had probably helped her set that "wink" up. It would be just like their personalities.

I got up to Carl's room and said my "goodbye for now" to this wonderful man and offered to go back to my aunt's house.

On the way out of the hospital, I was in line to leave the parking garage behind a small blue car with a decal on the back. When I got close enough, I could see that it said, "Team Edward." Edward is Jilly's teddy bear (she was a huge *Twilight* fan) and the subject of the children's book I wrote on grief. She carried her sense of humor with her to the other side. Love never dies. Life just continues somewhere else when we are done here.

Jilly, Larry and Uncle Carl have simply stepped into the next place.

12

MEET ME HALFWAY

June 6, 2014
The Art Assignment

A COUPLE YEARS AFTER JILLY died, I finally got up the nerve to go into her closet and start sorting stuff to put into totes. Before that time, it had been difficult to even open the door to her room without that familiar sinking feeling hitting me like a sucker punch to the gut.

Heidi, a very dear friend (bless her) was helping me. She sat on the bed just watching as I picked up a treasured item and would bring it close to my face, looking for any lingering scent and shedding a tear or two. She helped me organize and put away the mementos from the last weeks of her life, the last sheets Jilly had slept on, the many pictures, trophies and varsity letters that we had borrowed off her bedroom wall for the visitation before the funeral. We gathered all the sympathy cards and letters together to put in the hand carved hope chest that she had received for graduation the year before. Sadly, she would no longer need it.

My friend was in Jilly's closet, putting something away for me and noticed a paper barely peeking out from behind the dresser. We carefully pulled it out and studied it. I had never seen it before, but she had drawn it in her high school Art class sometime in 2007 or 2008, three or four years before she went Home.

Somehow, amazingly, she had drawn the last day of her life and in uncannily accurate and great detail. The picture setting is at dawn as the sun rises, which is the time Jilly went Home. There are two distinct scenes in the picture.

In the lower half, a car is crashing into a dump area. (The accident happened catty-corner from an old dump.) The closest thing to the car in the picture is a gas can. (They hit a gas pipeline and then a tree, but I am sure she was already gone with the first impact.) She drew an empty lifeguard stand and a school nearby. (She had just finished signing up for winter/spring semester at college and her very last job was life guarding.)

Off to the bottom of the picture are the Twin Towers and an airplane flying into them. That stumped me until it was brought to my attention that not only was it a set of *twins* whose house she stayed at on her last night on earth, but they *also* had a September 11th birthday! Jillian also affectionately called the driver of the car, her "Twin-a-roo!"

A giant pencil seems to be saying, "This history is already written in the book of Life." The words, "Decisions, Stress, Work, Life, War and Troubles," are each scattered in the dump. There is money scattered in the dump. (She leaves us quarters, but is she also trying to tell us that you can't take your "riches" here on earth with you, because the true riches are really in heaven?)

Above that scene of chaos and destruction, there she is, my Jilly girl happily sitting on a cloud, holding the hand of the guy she was no longer dating at the time of her death, but was her first true love. He will always hold a special place in our hearts. At the time of the drawing, he was a very important part of her world. I think a part of him went with Jilly the day she died. Her "fur-baby," Emma Jane the puppy, is also with her because love never dies. She is very serene in her usual Hollister shirt and jeans sitting on her cloud.

Balloons, including purple and green ones, are holding the cloud up. (We sent up green and purple balloons at her funeral.) There are purple and green butterflies, and a rainbow. She looks very content on her cloud. She has a big smile on her face.

When I flipped the drawing over, the title of her drawing said: *"I'm in a box!"* (Okay, I had to sit down for that one;

her body literally is in a "box!") It goes on to answer questions about the sketch...and to say that the box is made of a big cloud; she is happy and has no worries there. She isn't alone, but she can't get out, nor would she want to. No one else can come into her box either. The point she is trying to make with her illustration was, and I quote: "I don't want to grow up and have all those worries."

Wow. Wow. Wow. Jilly, *how* did you know? *How* had you known since you were a small child? Is that why you told your grandma you would never have real babies? Is that why you lived life to the fullest, made friends everywhere you went and ate pizza to your heart's content? Was it because, although it was your greatest ambition, you knew your butt would never get any bigger? Is that why you had such an obsession with how you would look in your casket? Because you just knew?

When I need a big smile, I simply think about you in heaven; I only have to imagine you in big Victoria's Secret fluffy white angel wings, twirling your hair and rubbing other heavenly faces with it and grinning from ear to ear. You are always smiling in my visions. Always! It is a radiant, fun, full of mischief Jilly smile that warms my heart. I imagine that smile will bring lots of comfort to the "newbies" that have recently joined you. Please help make their Homecoming as easy as possible. I can't imagine any reason that God would not put you on the welcoming committee on the other side...you make new friends feel comfortable everywhere you go!

When it's my turn to come Home and you reach out and pull me into your warm loving embrace, you will tell me all the answers to these questions. You always were a wise old soul in a young girl's body! I miss your special "knowingness." We all miss you so much, our Jilly Bean. One of the things that gives us great peace is knowing that without any doubt, we will see you again. Oh yes, we will. I will find your "cloud" and join you there.

By the way, she got an A on the assignment!

Jilly's drawing, "I'm in a Box."

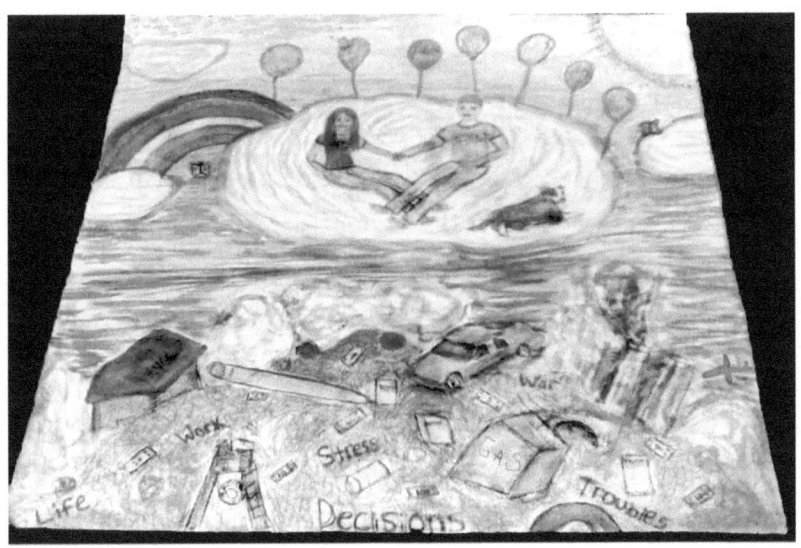

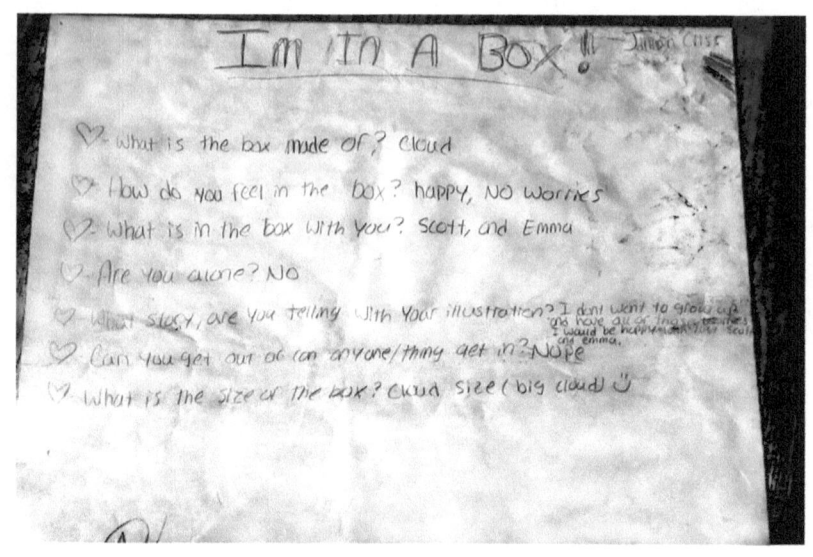

♥ ♥ ♥

October 12, 2014
"Freebird"

*L*AST NIGHT I WENT out with some dear ones in my life to a special event. We saw the "Long Island Medium," Theresa Caputo in person in Kalamazoo. What a hoot she is! The nails are just as long and high heels are just as sparkly as they are on TV.

Now, I would be lying if I said that I didn't wish that Jilly would somehow talk to me through Theresa and her ability to channel spirit, but I wasn't holding out any hope. If that happened, I would gladly settle for a single word from Jilly. I would also be content to just watch this woman talk to others who probably needed her far more than I did. The main reason I went was to watch how comforts and inspires thousands of people; I love to watch inspirational people!

Long before I knew of Theresa, my husband and I met someone who was gifted at peeking through the thin veil separating us from our loved ones. Her name is Lynn.

This was Mark's first experience with any kind of mediumship and he was the world's *biggest* skeptic. Before meeting her, Mark had a little "talk" with Jilly. He told her that he didn't believe much in this "nonsense," but if it was real and it was truly her (Jilly) and she could somehow still communicate with him, he wanted one specific sign: Somehow, he wanted Lynn to say the word, "Freebird." (By the way, this is not conducive to a "good" reading with a medium. It is suggested that you go in with an open mind with no preconceived expectations of who might come through.)

Since "Freebird" was one of Jilly's favorite songs, we played it at her funeral. For us, it symbolizes her new freedom in a spiritual body, having shed her physical one.

Mark walked into the office to meet Lynn. She introduced herself and asked his name. His response was, "I'm not telling! I'm not giving you any information."

She told him to have a seat, then proceeded to tell him there was a beautiful young woman whose name began with a "J" present, calling him Daddy. She said her daddy's name was Mark. They chatted for a few minutes; then Lynn said, "Does

"Freebird" mean anything to you?"

My husband, the world's biggest "former" skeptic, sobbed. What a gift Jilly gave us through Lynn! "Freebird" has always been Jilly's special sign to her daddy, just as the quarters are a special sign for the rest of us.

Anyway, back to last night with Theresa Caputo. She was walking through the audience of about 3000 people, stopping here and there to pass on messages to loved ones. She got within 20 feet of us and I got a little excited! And then she turned around and walked away, almost to the center of the stadium. She started a reading on a lovely couple. It was beautiful and touching.

Suddenly, she stopped, and said. "Wait...rock band!" She looked up and out of nowhere she yelled, *"FREEBIRD!"*

She then went right back to talking to this couple, picking up where she had left off. My loved ones and I squealed with joy. Amazing how one single word can mean so much. Mark wasn't with us last night, but Jilly still managed to tell him, "Hey, I love you Daddy!"

> *"If I leave here tomorrow...*
> *would you still remember me?*
> *I must be traveling on now, 'cause*
> *there's too many places I got to see.*
> *I'm as free as a bird now*
> *and this bird you cannot change..."*
> ~ Lynyrd Skynyrd

Jilly has only changed form. Her personality still shines. Thank you, God, for allowing us to see that wink. Love you, our little free bird!

Another Jilly/God wink to this story: A couple of friends from my area were also at this event, hoping to hear from their children. They knew when they heard Theresa say, "Freebird," that I would be overjoyed. They sat in the front of the audience and when the show was over, they walked up the aisle where Theresa had been during the reading. The janitor had already swept the area. Looking down, there was a quarter on the floor, right where Theresa had stood when she said Freebird! They picked it up and sent it to me.

November 10, 2014
I'll Meet You Halfway

I can remember every detail of this most vivid visit in a dream, even years later. I say visit instead of just a dream, because there is a difference. You might forget a dream. You never ever forget a visit, no matter how many years go by. I have had many dreams of her, but only a few that were of this intensity... so real I know that deep down in my soul, we were somehow together.

I went to sleep last night thinking about what she was doing three years ago at this time and like every other night for past three years, missing her deeply.

Here is what I dreamt:

I was in a gravel parking lot near an old building. There was an old red car with a white top on it. It was the only car in the rather large parking lot; the windows were all fogged up, like they were dirty on the inside. I was alone, but I wasn't afraid. I walked over to the passenger's side and wiped off a small area of dust so that I could see inside.

I was astonished to see Jilly sitting in the driver's seat, hands on the steering wheel, like she was pretending to drive the car. She made direct eye contact with me and in that moment, I knew that we had met "halfway" somehow, somewhere. I don't know how else to explain it.

I am not sure how I got the rules, but I also understood that she could not roll down the window, nor could I attempt to reach into the car in any way. We had to talk through this small clearing in the window and she could only stay a short while.

We gazed deeply into each other's eyes, as if we were somehow able to see each other's *souls*. Now, wouldn't you think that if your deceased child were sitting there right in front of you, and you could have a conversation with them, it would be pretty deep?

Nope. It wasn't anything I had imagined I would be saying to her in this situation.

I said, "Jillian, honey... how *are* you, *really*?"

She flashed the most beautiful ear to ear grin and said,

"Mom, I am fine! Really, I am! See?" as she pointed to her healed body and face.

Then she said, "How are you, *really*, Mom?"

I uttered softly, "Day by day, sweetheart. Day by day."

We still couldn't take our eyes off each other.

I whispered with all the intensity that my heart felt, "I love you so much, Jilly."

She replied, "I know."

She somehow gazed even more deeply into my soul and said, "I love you, Mama."

And I cried, "I know..."

We looked even *more* deeply into each other's eyes, sharing that love for a few more seconds, and then she suddenly exclaimed, "I'll be seeing ya!"

Just then, the alarm clock went off. I woke up sobbing tears of joy. I have been weepy all day remembering it. They are happy tears.

Love is eternal. Love never dies.

LOUISE CRIST

♥ ♥ ♥

November 19, 2014
Hello from Heaven
(The letter Jillian Crist would give me if she could)

Dear Mom,

Hello from heaven! I still love you more than the world, bigger than the sky! I am whole, healthy and happier than you can ever imagine. There is no darkness here, Mom... absolutely none. There is nothing scary here at all... not at all like where you are. It is always light and always warm and cozy.

I know I left in a hurry, I am sorry about that; but I really went in the quickest, most graceful way I could. I know it might have looked bad from your point of view, but I promise you that I didn't feel any pain... just a loud snapping sound for half an instant as my soul separated from my body —and poof! There I was, just chillin' outside of my body, watching everything from above like a bird would.

I watched the crash happen and thought for sure it would hurt, but it didn't! Or if it did, I sure don't remember the pain of it. I watched my friend jump out of her body too, but it wasn't her *time yet. I told her she would have to go back. I hugged her and told her that I love her and will always watch over her until we meet again. She didn't want to stay there, but I convinced her that she had to. She will change lives too. That's the path her soul chose. Somehow, I probably picked my most spiritual friends to spend my last hours with, because I am hoping that they will bring understanding to others. They know the pain of the choices that we made and will help others because of it. It is such a heavy load they carry, and not many people could bear it, so please pray for them often, okay?*

I helped that nice guy Dave (who had planned to go hunting that morning) find the wreckage. I convinced him to stop and help my friend instead. I was with the EMTs, the firemen and the helicopter crew as they came to help too. I was especially with the policewoman Amanda, who woke up that day, hoping her birthday would be a good one, even though she had to work. (It wasn't.) She will remember me on her birthday for the rest of her life.

I watched as she figured out who I was by running the plates of the car and I could see the heaviness come over her heart when she knew she had to make that call to tell you. I was with them all, Mama...and I was also with you, Daddy, Sierra and Erica that morning. (In fact, I was able to be with everyone who was hurting that day!) Everyone was so sad...I tried to explain that I was okay, but I guess no one could see or hear me.

I was with you as you drove your car down the road looking for me. I was sitting right next to you, with my arms wrapped around you when you answered the phone call that changed your world. I held you tight in those moments giving you the biggest hug I could. I know you felt it Mom...and I know you heard me tell you that I jumped out of my body before impact. The angels just swooped down and pulled me out...that's why I didn't feel any pain. It made me sad to watch you get that news and I could see your heart breaking, so I gave it lots of kisses. Our hearts connected then, as they have several times since I came Home...not in a physical way, but in a timeless spiritual eternal way, kind of like they did before I was born.

I was with Daddy in the tree stand at sunrise as he felt that strange comforting warmth come over him, all the way through his clothes. That warmth penetrated his skin and seeped right into his soul. That was me hugging him when he looked at his hands and wondered why they were glowing. That was my love reaching him and preparing him for what you would tell him less than an hour later. God helped me touch his heart. We can do that from this side, you know.

I was with my big sister, Erica, as you called her and told her from across the country, as gently as you could, that I wasn't here anymore; I had gone to be with Papa. I held her as she screamed, and I whispered to her that it would all be okay someday. She didn't believe me, but now she is working on that as best as she knows how. I was with my baby sister, Sierra, as you told her I had gone Home too. She knew that Papa had called to me and I had flown into his arms. (By the way, he is playing basketball and tennis here and loves being a stud muffin again!) I left her the very first quarter the next morning. I am with both of my sisters every day; especially when they drive. (Speaking of driving, some of my friends are keeping me very busy watching over them... you know who you are!)

I helped Sierra pick out my outfit, because quite frankly, Mom, you would not have picked the right one (unless you picked my footie pajamas and robe... those would have been okay, too!) But that princess dress you thought about having me wear? Nuh-uh! I am glad my baby sister picked my camo outfit...and the necklace was perfect. Did it blow your minds when the ring you chose for me to wear on my necklace disappeared from my bedroom and then turned up at the funeral home before you did? Ha-ha! I had to get your attention and let you know I was watching!

I was with all the rest of our family and my friends as they found out, one by one, about the accident. I watched each of their responses, from dropping to their knees in disbelief, to screaming, to thinking it was a really bad joke, like the one I pulled in 8th grade when I told everyone I was moving to Florida over Christmas break and they believed me and started planning a going away party. Remember how embarrassing it was for me to confess that fib? The kids at school wouldn't talk to me for a week!

I watched as their innocent belief that, "things like that don't happen to people like us," shattered. It happens every day, all around the world. It was hard to see and feel their pain. Most of them refused to believe that I was gone...and they are right! I am not really "gone" despite how it looks to you. When you think of me, it is like dialing my "heavenly cellphone" and I come to your side...and sometimes I barge right into your dreams. (Sorry about that, it would seem that there is a time warp between my intention to comfort you and when I get there, because time doesn't really work the same way on this side as it does for you.) I watched as hundreds came to comfort you and our family on visitation night. They each brought back a piece of your broken heart. I helped you guys plan the funeral; I gave you the ideas while you catnapped, walked around like zombies and cried in the shower. (By the way, please tell my godmother, Kathy, thanks for the "eternal tan." I sure do love her! She did such a great job with my body that I looked like a princess!)

While I was on your side, I knew that I had lots of friends, but I had no idea how many people truly loved me and cared about our family. I was so surprised! That kind of love is so incredible, Mom. If I could only explain it... Love lights up heaven with a color that you can't even imagine. The closest thing we have to it is the color of the sky on the most beautiful sunrise or sunset you have ever seen; and even that doesn't come anywhere close. Love on this side is something that you can see, feel, taste and even hear. It tastes like the best food you have ever eaten. It sounds like a million angels singing. It makes my tummy quiver in delight and happiness.

Wait till you get here and see if for yourself!

When you pray for me, Mama, it is like sending love on a credit card... it helps me get stronger so I can send you love right back. I try to send you signs, so you know how close I am. You only get a few of the many that I send every single day. Sometimes, in your grief, you just can't see them or hear them. It takes practice.

I can be in lots of different places at once, because time doesn't exist here. You just think about someone and BAM! It feels like you are right there with them, even if several people think about you all at the same time! (Flying is the closest thing we have on earth to this, except we can do it a million times faster.) It is sooo cool! It is a billion times better than the Ripcord at Michigan Adventure or the coolest ride at Cedar Point!

I thought it was very original to have an all-girl team of pallbearers. Who better than my best friends and my sisters, who I love more than anything, to round out that team? There were so many people that I wish we could have included that day. I hope they know how much I love them too. I felt their love. I still do. Tell them thanks for not dropping the casket; that would have been so embarrassing that they never would have lived it down. *(And if they are ever pallbearers again, note to self, do not wear high heels!)*

I loved having the cheerleaders lead the "cheer Jill into heaven." I was glad the gymnastic team came to lead me out of the church. I loved the funeral, because it really celebrated my life and did not define me by just the last day of it. Pastor Jeff did an amazing job reaching out to everyone. And if you could see how hard my teachers, Kim and Jessica, were shaking reading those poems, you would never believe they stand in front of children all day and talk! LOL. I am glad my baby sister got up and shared the page I had read to her that week out of the Daily Bread booklet too. I hope that my Celebration of Life made people appreciate what they have and love each other a little more. That is what I wanted it to do.

There were so many friends that I know you wanted to be part of that service, but there just wasn't a way to do it, but then a couple of my friends' moms, (Linda and Marcy) came up with the balloon launch. That was totally cool! I got every single message attached to the balloons. They reached me all the way in heaven (the messages, not the balloons...if you had thought a message and sent soap bubbles skyward it would have had the same effect and would have been better for the environment!)

The messages were delivered as instantly as they were written by some kind of telepathy that I can't explain very well. I am glad that my puppy dog got to come and see my body one last time. I visit her a lot and she can see me. There are animals here, just like on your side. Our pets get to come Home too! I listen to every person who talks to me. It's not weird or silly to do that. I really can hear them! They just can't hear me quite as well.

I can see how things are turning out and how my life will impact other lives for many years. We are all connected, you know! I love that you and many others have worked hard so that other children can go into the health care field with my scholarships. Thank you for that! The ripple in the pond from that will surprise you some day when you least expect it!

I see you when you are sad. I laugh when you talk about the crazy things I used to do. I hug you when you cry, and I watch you when you sleep. It's okay, Mama... it will all be okay in the end. You must trust me on this one. We will all be together again, I promise! When you come Home, I will teach you how to "fly" like I do and how to leave signs for those still there on that side. You will be a pro because you already know it's possible to do it; you taught me that before I left! I will show you how to let little children and animals sense when you are near. They pay a lot more attention.

And when your time to come Home happens, Mama... I will reach out for you, give you the greatest tummy hug and take you to meet Jesus. He is my absolute best friend on this side. You will love Him, mom... He is so easy to talk to and He gives the best hugs I have ever had! I can hug Him as many times as I want to. He just smiles and says, "Again, Jillian Alexis? Oh, all right then. One more hug for you!" and then He gives me another one! When I have a question, He always answers me patiently, no matter how random it is. (I even asked Him that question about the hippos that you always wanted the answer to!)

He makes me feel like I have His undivided attention for as long as I need it, although millions of other people are also talking to Him. And he is so funny! You would never guess how much He makes me laugh! He holds me close to Him the way He holds anyone close who wants His hugs; they only have to ask. Sometimes I even sneak attack Him and jump in His arms and ask Him to hold *me like an infant, like I did to you and my friends when I was there! He just shakes His head and laughs at me.*

Occasionally, He lets me hold you, too... like when I sneak right into your dreams and talk to you. It feels real to you, because it is! I am there, giving you a hug the only way I know how!

He holds parents whose children are already here especially close, because they have a hard time walking by themselves for a really long time. He knows that you don't usually understand His big plan, so He sends special angels to help you guys keep going so that you can finish the plans He has for you. (It will all make perfect sense when you get here!) We pray for you. Do you think it is coincidence *that you have met so many other families like ours whose children are already Home? Nope, us children all got together and planned it that way, so that you cross paths and can support each other. We love it when you talk about us to each other, because we are all talking about you guys on this side, too!*

I won't miss a thing in any of your lives, Mama. And I will be here waiting... for you and Dad, Erica and Sierra, for the rest of our family and all my friends. I will be there with you for as long as you need me to be, *so it's okay to* live, not just exist. I'm right there with you! It's okay to be sad some days and it's okay to be happy and to smile and even laugh too! I do that on this side, and I want you to try as often as you can to feel joy again in life there, even if it's only baby steps. I understand that you miss seeing me and I miss being able to really touch you too, but *I truly* am in the best hands in the universe Mom, so don't worry about me, okay? I am so much closer than you can imagine.

I can't get into too much trouble in heaven; at least, I don't think I can. Jesus hasn't put me in "timeout"... Yet!

I love you forever, I love you for always, as long as you're living my mama you'll be. Forever and ever, Amen, okay?

XOXO (x1000), Jilly

December, 2014

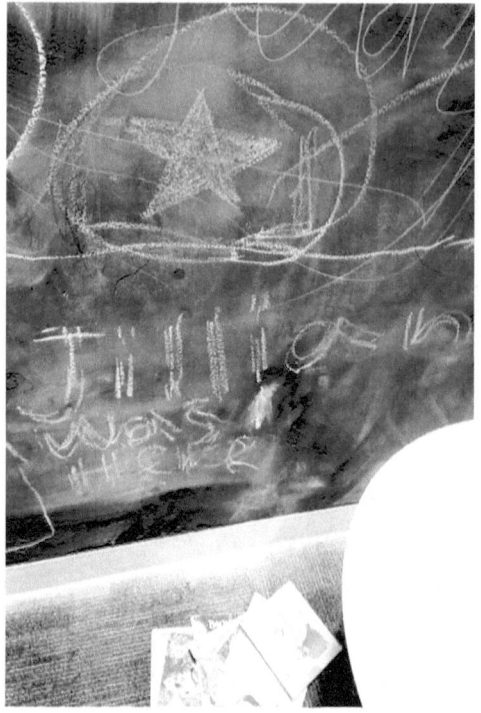

Sierra, Jilly's younger sister, goes to an auto shop to have the oil changed in her car. To pass the time while they were working on it, she walked into the children's playroom waiting area and saw this on the chalkboard. Jilly used to have her oil changed there as well ... and this is definitely her handwriting! Odd that no one would have erased it in three years, don't you think? Thank you, God, for the Jillywinks!

13

JUDGE ME, JUDGE ME NOT

December 27, 2014

Although my Christmas this year was full of family togetherness and wonderful presents (I was thoroughly spoiled and am very grateful), I still struggle hard with the depression that usually hits at this time of year. The "winter blues" have been trying to bring me down again...darn those cloudy weeks with no sun!

This Christmas Eve was especially hard. I was missing Jillian with a deep longing, an ache that sometimes can only be soothed with a good cry...which happens when I least expect it and sometimes at the most inconvenient times! Thankfully, this cleansing cry happened in the safety and privacy of my own shower on Christmas Eve night. I skipped church services because I knew I would be a blubbering mess if I went.

There I was, crying out to my Jilly girl and I asked her to send me a sign.

Just a little, "Hi, Mom!" would do. (I don't ask for much, do I?) I really needed a little something to help me keep going forward without her here this Christmas season. I asked her to send it as soon as she could.

I waited all Christmas Day; nothing... but I believed a Jilly wink would come. The day after Christmas dawned brightly. My oldest daughter, Erica and I went shopping in Kalamazoo, looking for after-Christmas bargains. We went to Joann's Fabrics for some mommy-daughter decorating time.

Kalamazoo is a large college town, with a population of about 75,000, so it's safe to say that several thousand people travel through there on any given day. The parking lot to the fabric store was fairly full, so we parked quite far from the door, with empty spaces all-around us. That way, I didn't have to worry about someone carelessly putting dings on my car doors.

Now, I should tell you that Jilly has special signs for each of us... quarters are her favorite and she likes butterflies, too.

But Jilly's very special, *Just for You, Mama* sign that is significant for *me* is a purple Dodge Stratus. Perhaps it is because that is the car that she went HOME in. Maybe it is because the memory of seeing it terribly mangled at the scene is etched forever in my memory... I don't know. She loved her little purple Stratus, but the day she went home, her close friend was driving it.

This much I can tell you though... seeing an intact purple Stratus both takes my breath away... and makes me smile at the same time. Jilly had so many adventures in that car! The fact that it was shown to me "intact" lets me know she was showing me that without a doubt, she is indeed "intact" and wow, what a ride she had on earth!

Purple cars really aren't that common; she liked that her car was different from most. Purple was also one of her favorite colors.

So, when Erica and I went out to my car after shopping, I was putting the bags in the back seat, when a small sweet little Jilly voice in my head said, "turn around and look!"

So, I did. Right there next to me... a purple Dodge Stratus.

That car wasn't there when we went in. I definitely would have noticed that!

Now, I suppose any one of the thousands of people in Kalamazoo last night could have been in that parking lot... but how many of them drive a purple Dodge stratus and happen to park next to me in a huge lot, two days after I beg my daughter for a special sign?

When I most need it, one will "somehow" be put directly in my path, so that I can't miss it. Just like it was that night.

Thanks Jilly! Love you sweetie!

Was it a wink from her?

I believe it was. I have to believe it! It's how I survive.

♥ ♥ ♥

February 18, 2015

Happy 23rd Birthday, our sweet Jillian! Are you dancing wild and crazy with the angels? Did Jesus throw you a party? Are you eating some heavenly cake? Are you grinning from ear to ear the way you always did here when we sang to you?

It doesn't seem possible that 23 years have gone by since you made your brief appearance in our lives after 10 hours of a fairly easy labor. Some of your best friends had already been born this month, Alanah, 12 days before and Kara yesterday...Hannah would arrive in another nine days. You would grow up celebrating your birthdays with these wonderful girls for many memorable years.

You had an unusual intensity about you...it seemed that you aged backwards. In the beginning, you were so serious, like an old lady afraid to laugh in church...and as time went on, you became more social and so outgoing that many found you irresistible to be around. You were so silly and so much fun! You didn't know many strangers. Whether they were tiny babies or "sweet little old people" or kids your own age, you pulled people from all walks in life into your loving embrace and made them feel special. You would say, "Mom, I just want to steal them and bring them home and love them!"

That is one of the gifts God gave you to use freely while you danced on this earth. Your infectious, loving, random enthusiasm. You got excited about eating—sleeping—ketchup—friends...and of course, baby animals and infants! You left your footprints on so many hearts. You brought so much joy and craziness to our lives; there was rarely a dull moment with you around! Oh, how we miss that!

Even though you didn't take your earth suit with you to Heaven, your personality went with you, so God must be chuckling every day at some of your antics! We are so blessed to have been chosen to be your family, our JillyBean. You made our family what it is and the void of your absence here is felt with each and every heartbeat.

Today though and on each of your birthdays for as long as we walk this earth, we will celebrate the life you had here and offer our thanks and gratitude to God for the best birthday present He ever gave us; the gift of *you!*

Our love always and *all ways.*

♥ ♥ ♥

March 12, 2015

By now you know that I am very open to receiving "signs" from Jillian. Some people might refer to them as synchronicities. Random butterflies, quarters, smiley faces and Dodge Stratus cars get me excited. I will admit that I sometimes get *super* excited, especially when there is simply no other explanation, or the timing is just too ironic for that "coincidence" to happen.

How can I not? It has become increasingly evident that there is no such thing as coincidence. In addition, if I didn't believe that Jilly is somehow putting signs in my path, hoping and waiting for me to find them, checking in on our lives every so often, then I would have to believe the alternative:

- that she is forever gone, unreachable to me.
- that she ceased to exist.
- that I must wait a lifetime to feel her presence again.

I can't even go there... I just can't.

Without faith in a heavenly afterlife with our Creator, I would have no reason to keep going, to put one foot in front of the other on this journey, trying to make some semblance of a "new normal", much less try to make something positive out of the situation.

If this side is *all* there is, and death is the be-all-end-all of life, this suffering would be unbearable. I could not survive it; I wouldn't *want* to survive it. I would have curled up and willed myself to die the day she did when my heart shattered. I don't believe this is what God wants for his creations.

I believe that my loved ones... my daddy, grandparents, aunts, uncles, good friends, clients and co-workers who have left their bodies behind still exist somewhere that is so amazing, so beautiful, so peaceful and full of *love* that we can't even begin to imagine.

It is a fact that Jilly believed that too. She had some experience with grief, having lost several people she loved in her 19 short years. She lost her grandpa nine weeks before she herself went Home.

She would talk to her "pack of angels" each night and whenever else she needed that comfort (which seemed to be a lot of the time.) She swore they sent her signs in return, letting her know that they heard her and were indeed okay. She would get all excited too and share stories of those signs with me.

It's obvious to me that she would try to do the same for us from that side, if she could...and I personally believe that she does. However, even members of the same family sometimes believe different things. That's okay too.

Jilly's daddy had a vivid life changing sign from her a couple of months after the accident (and he still receives little "winks"), but he had to let go of his anger before that started happening. That took a lot of work, time and tears on his part. Her sisters get winks too, each one getting a different "special sign" from her. They just don't get as excited about them as I do. (Or at least they aren't as verbal about it.)

I tend to get *excited*, sometimes even weepy about signs that I believe she sends. I always give thanks for them, no matter how small the sign. I figure if she works that hard to send them, the least I can do is acknowledge the probability that they are from her.

My family, well, they sometimes smirk and roll their eyes at me. "Oh boy, Mom got another "sign." It will be on Facebook or something soon." I don't know what it feels like to be a daddy or sibling of a child lost. We each walk our own path of grieving...and it's all just as intense for one as it is for the other.

I only know what it feels like for me, as her mama... the one who helped her grow from an egg and a seed to a fully formed beautiful human. I was the one who offered her to God on the night of her birth after all the visitors left the two of us alone to bond.

I was the one who thanked Him for lending her to me for 19 years a couple of days after her death (on my knees sobbing in the shower) and reluctantly gave her back to Him. I can only know what my own mourning feels like.

Each of us, her dad, her sisters and myself, all received signs from her (pretty much in the same hour) on the day of her death, despite not being in the same room, or even the same state. Mark was in a deer blind, Sierra and Erica were both sleeping, thousands of miles apart. Yet, we all got signs that we were able to corroborate later.

My first sign from her was probably the most important one she ever sent me. She tried to comfort me as I was driving down the road toward the accident scene. I had just been informed of her death. I pulled over to the side of the road and tried to make phone calls but was unable to reach anyone. I started driving again, in a daze and clearly heard Jilly's voice.

She said, "I'm okay, mom! I jumped out of my body before impact! I'm okay!" And she *is okay*... even if that is not quite the way that we on this side, tend to think of "okay." She still exists, I know she does... just not in physical form. She no longer needs an earthly body to do her work, but she stays mighty busy.

So, now I return to my latest sign story. Jilly's sisters both had birthdays this week; Erica on Monday and Sierra on Wednesday. They are exactly six years and two days apart. It is always a happy occasion. I love watching the beautiful young women they are turning out to be. It's exciting. It's also kind of weird and bittersweet. Sierra is now older than Jilly ever was on this side.

Every family celebration is tinged with the knowledge that we have an empty chair around the table. Individually, we cope with that the best way we know how. I had asked Jilly to stay close to all of us this week, but especially to her sisters. I asked for a sign that she was and is with us during these important milestones, so as not to miss out on any part of our lives.

I waited ... and waited ... and not so patiently waited some more, hoping for a birthday sign. A few days ago, an almost unheard-of cheap airline ticket to Hawaii popped up for Erica. One of her best friends is stationed in the Navy there, but only for a couple more weeks. Erica had wanted to go visit her for almost a year, but had given up on the idea, as ticket prices were way too steep.

BAM! A ridiculously inexpensive flight to Hawaii pops up last minute, right around her birthday! It made a once in a lifetime present when a few of us went together to get it for her. She was so excited! Who wouldn't be?

Erica kept asking, "Which island am I flying into?" She couldn't remember, "Oahu." We teased her about this ... hoping she would get off on the right island. We put her on a plane to Hawaii yesterday morning, on Sierra's birthday. After work, I went through the mail, which I hadn't done in a few days... and there it was, our first "sign," a Bath and Body Works (my favorite store) flyer addressed to Erica. Although she hasn't lived here in five years, it even had my address (not hers) and her married name. Odd. And what does it say? "Let's go to *Hawaii*!" (The words, "Free travel-sized item" also jumped off the page at me.) I opened the flyer and "Oahu" is right there in big letters, of course.

This just had Jilly's sense of humor written all over it. Jilly has her "wings" now, so she certainly can go for 'free' and she would be a 'travel-sized' item! In addition, there is no way that Jilly would not somehow find a way to go with Erica to an exotic location like that. Her favorite vacation destination involved anywhere on a warm beach! That little flyer just 'happened' to arrive smack dab between both of her sisters' birthdays. What are the odds of all that being a weird coincidence?

I am doing a little happy dance over this obvious sign. My family, meanwhile, is rolling their eyes at me again.

"Oh boy, Mom got another sign. It will be on Facebook." It sure will. Judge me... or judge me not... but only after you have walked a mile in my shoes.

14

OUT ON A LIMB

May 2015

On a beautiful late spring day about four years after she died, one of Jilly's best friends took a walk alone in the woods. Kara is a "nature girl" born in the wrong decade. She would have made a great hippie of the 60s, as she is into yoga, meditation, health food, nutrition and exercise. Even as a very young child, she was fascinated with the meaning of life and the possibilities of what we experience after death. In high school, Kara was co-captain of the gymnastics team and a cheerleader with Jilly. Kara is so full of love and light that she couldn't hide it under a bushel basket if her life depended on it... and for that reason, she was Homecoming queen her senior year. Like Jilly, she is a sweet "old soul" in a young body.

Jilly and Kara met in fourth grade in gymnastics. They both had the same watch, and both loved "Tweety Bird." They instantly clicked. They also discovered that they were born less than 24 hours apart. They both loved animals and had over the top creative talents. One of Jilly's favorite places to hang out was Kara's house, because she had zebras, kangaroos, emus and peacocks in her pastures. (Yes, real ones!) They would get the video camera out and make the craziest, funniest home movies together. One winter day when school was called off due to a snowstorm, I came home and found them dressed in pirate and poodle costumes, talking pictures of each other in the woods. The two of them were part of a group of girls that grew up together and stayed friends throughout junior high and high school. Kara and the other girls of the group led a cheer for Jilly at her funeral and were also her pallbearers.

When Kara gets sad or depressed or just needs some time to rejuvenate, she goes for nature walks. On this fine spring day, Kara was helping her mom adjust to a new home. Her mom moved frequently (as she is a free spirit as well). Kara had never lived in that house during Jilly's life, and Jilly had never been to that property. She didn't know anyone who lived on that road. It was a perfect opportunity for Kara to take a break and explore the woods across the street from her mom's house.

As she walked through the woods, inhaling the natural

perfume that the woods give off as it comes to life in late spring, she was making mental notes of the different trees in that grove, probably so she wouldn't get lost and could find her way back. She says she had been thinking of Jilly that day, wondering what one of her days in heaven would be like and if she ever *really* knew how much she was loved on this side.

Within a few minutes, Kara had the unexpected, unexplainable answer. As she walked near one unusual little old tree, Kara noticed that some of the limbs hadn't grown leaves. She wasn't sure if the tree was dying or just a late bloomer, so she stopped for closer inspection. Something about that tree just piqued her curiosity, almost calling out to her. As she studied it, she was intrigued with what looked like *writing* on one of the small limbs; then she noticed writing on another nearby limb. Perhaps it had been two lovers, writing their names to declare their love for eternity on the branches of this tree or graffiti drawn by a budding artist. But the writing looked strangely familiar somehow, even though she had never been there before. It was neither of those things.

As she read the words written on the limbs, Kara gasped and then giggled with delight. She might have even wept with joy as her heart sang. (I know I would have.)

Kara got her answer that day; out on that limb and *no one can explain how it got there.*

♥ ♥ ♥

**June 22, 2015
The Longest Day**

It has been two weeks ago today since my mom last spoke to us (It was garbled, but at least we heard her voice.) Each day since then has been very long. Mom is now resting comfortably at a rehab center since a massive stroke suddenly took her ability to speak, swallow or move one side of her body. Sometimes, if she is having a good day, she can wiggle her eyebrows, do half of a smile at us, or make expressions that look like surprise, love, depression, confusion, fear, pain or frustration. She moved her mouth in an attempt to speak today. Nothing came out, except her tears.

She holds onto a clear, soft plastic squishy ball filled with beads of every color for hours with her left hand, mindlessly rolling it between her thumb and forefinger...but she still doesn't seem to be able to feel or control much of anything on her right side. There are some random movements that stir our hope, but it's as if that side of her body isn't a part of her anymore; it seems it no longer exists. Much of the day, she just stares intently, almost in a trance-like state. It is often at the plain wall near her bed that her gaze is directed, or the upper corner of the room to her left, or the grassy lawn and trees just outside of the window near her bed. She tilts her head to that side and appears to be looking with absolute wonder at something the rest of us can't see. Her eyes rapidly dart back and forth, watching something play out on an unseen stage.

Maybe, just *maybe*...she can see Jilly or other loved ones who watch over her from Heaven? That thought gives me much comfort! I am sure it would give her comfort too. Other times during the day, we can't rouse her at all. Her sleep is too deep, her breath is too shallow. We don't see her chest rise and fall for 1, 2, 3...10...15...or 20 seconds. We hold our breath, wondering if *"This is it,"* as we move closer to check on her; then she takes another deep breath in and exhales...and finally, so do we.

I can't think of anything much more devastating than being trapped in a body that you have little control over. It was mom's worst fear. It is beginning to become mine too, especially with a strong family history of strokes.

The tears come and go for all of us, but especially for her, as we go down this unpredictable path. We don't know how long the journey will be. Are we at the worst part of it, the middle part or is this the best it will get? Will she get any better? What if she doesn't? If she does, then what?

What is she feeling, sensing, thinking or processing as she lies in that bed, with the right half of her body not functioning and robbed by a stroke of the ability to speak, swallow or move at will? Is she aware of all the love that she receives, or does she forget our kisses as soon as they are given? Does she have any concept of time? Is each day the longest day for her? Communication has always been hugely important to her. In the beginning, only one eye watered, now when she cries, the tears roll down both cheeks, making her sadness and frustration more obvious. The mom I know would sooner hold something like a mouse or a snake, rather than cry, I do believe!

The woman in the bed *looks* like my mom. She wears the same clothes, has the same hair and beautiful skin as my mom... but my *real* mom is trapped inside that body! I know she is in there somewhere and sometimes, for very brief periods, I can connect with her. I get her attention, look deeply into her eyes and smile. I say, "There you are! I see you!" and she smiles back at me (with just her eyes) before suddenly slipping through my grasp. In an instant, she has once again gone somewhere that I can't follow. When this happens, I don't know when or if she will come back to us or stay "out there," wherever it is that she goes.

My 29 years of experience as a nurse, everything I was taught in school and all the skills and knowledge that I have learned so far in my healing profession, isn't worth a darn right now. I cannot fix her and that frustrates me to no end!

All we can do is love and encourage her in each moment that we have, however long that may be. I guess this is another test of our faith. I know that many others have taken the same test with their parents and loved ones. I have seen it and grieved with them as well. There are so many things I am grateful for in my life:

- I am so grateful to the love of her life, my wonderful step-dad, for the incredible amounts of love and patience he has for mom. Each time he walks in the room, he cups her face gently in his hands and says something silly to her or kisses her cheek. I am grateful that my daughter, Sierra, works at the place where mom now resides. She can look in on her frequently during her shift and give her kisses and pep talks. I am grateful to my daughter, Erica, for traveling hundreds of miles to be here to help out, while also trying to pack up her own house and move to another state. She took her therapy dog in to visit mom, did her funny "Erica-isms" that make me laugh. Mom smiled a brief crooked smile. My daughters are very compassionate; that is the best gene I have handed down to them.
- I am grateful that my siblings and my uncle, mom's

brother, came from several states last week to encourage her, to sleep near her, to try to strengthen her mind and body and to give her lots of love. It was one of the hardest kisses goodbye that they have ever given. They may or may not see her again on this side.

- I am grateful to friends who check in on me frequently. I know they are there for us, as they have always been, my beacons in the storm. Jilly's friends, who always seemed to be at our house during her life, have also been there, taking turns holding Mom's hand, sending bright colorful flowers for her to look at, whispering stories or watching over her at night as she slumbers. I am grateful to my co-workers for understanding that I am just not myself these days. Part of me, no matter where I am physically, is with mom, holding her hand. They are picking up shifts, taking up the slack and keeping me as sane as possible during this chaotic time. They know... they have either been there themselves or walked families through it before. I will do it for them when their time comes too. I am so blessed.
- Most of all, I am beyond grateful to God for lending Mom to us, just as He lent Jilly to us for a short while. I am glad for the opportunity to give her back some of the love she has shown me in my life. She always believed in me. Now I must believe that whatever difficult choice she makes... whether she decides to stay

here with us and work very hard to regain some of the functions we all take for granted or go on Home, where Jilly awaits with joyful open arms, a squeaky kiss and a tummy hug, there are lessons to be learned from this for all of us. God has a bigger design in this difficult, seemingly endless, longest day than my tiny little human mind can comprehend. He is the Greatest Healer of all. I must give this to Him. One way or the other, He will heal her... in His own time... in His own way.

♥ ♥ ♥

October 2015
Halloween... Hide and Seek Jilly Style

Lord make me a rainbow, I'll shine down on my mother
She'll know I'm safe with you when
She stands under my colours, oh and
Life ain't always what you think it oughta be, no
Ain't even grey, but she buries her baby
The sharp knife of a short life,
Well, I've had just enough time
—If I Die Young by The Band Perry—

(One of Jilly's favorite songs. She even wrote a college paper about the lyrics!)

I AM NOT A SAINT; I'll admit that right now. Jilly's prankster ideas are somewhat genetic, mostly from her dad though! They say confession is good for the soul, so here I go. This story is so wild and crazy that even today, I can't believe I did this! It was a humorous experience about something a bit bizarre. In memory of Jilly's love of silly Halloween stories and pranks, I will share it with you. It's kind of long, so please don't pass judgment until you have read the whole story.

Back at the time that this event took place, it never crossed my mind that it was not a rational thing to do. I suppose that what I will tell you is kind of twisted and morbid to anyone who:

- Is not a forensic science major
- Is not on the cast of CSI or Criminal Minds
- Has not experienced the loss of a child. (For those who have, I know they "get it." At least I hope so, because otherwise maybe I really am crazy!)

First a little background. You may find this hard to believe, but a common thought that many bereaved parents have is wanting to be able to somehow reach out to their child and hold them again. It's hard to explain; it's not that we want to hold their dead bodies; that is way too creepy even for me! We just want to be near our children again, the way we remember them before "that day." There's an enormous difference! If we could just put their caskets in a glass case and be able to look at or touch that box now and then...

In the first few months after Jilly died, when the intensity of my grief would run wild with me, there were times that I would go out to the cemetery, sit on her grave and fight the urge to claw my way through the dirt to find her. I guess I wanted to make sure it really was her. Maybe it was a mistake, and I was just in a horrible nightmare that I couldn't wake up from! (Although I am not one of them, I know of bereaved parents who have thought this same thing and have asked judges for exhumation orders!) I can tell you that after four long years, I still expect her to walk back through the door.

So, keeping all that in mind, here is my confession. A couple of the names have been changed to protect the guilty parties on this escapade... and oh, what an adventure it was.

A couple of years after our sweet Jillian died, we finally picked out the perfect headstone for our family and had it okayed by all the different people who must approve such a thing. (Lots of paperwork!) The order then goes to the cemetery crew, who comes out and prepares to pour the cement foundation for the stone, so that it doesn't sink or shift once it's placed. (I understand the cement must cure for several weeks.) The bigger the headstone, the deeper the foundation and the stone we designed would be for 12 people, so it was rather large.

One evening when I stopped by the cemetery, I noticed that Jilly's flowers and decorations weren't sitting in their usual spot. Instead, there was a green board covering a large hole near the top of her grave. The crew must have been out preparing the area for the headstone foundation earlier that day and they are very diligent about safety. This large hole was completely covered by wooden boards so that no one would accidentally trip. As I stood there, my grief finally got the better of me. I had flashbacks to the last time there was a hole nearby with boards on top of it and a purple vault inside that hole...before we tucked her in for the very last time...and in that moment, all my rationality went right out the window.

Making sure no one else was around; I carefully lifted one of the boards off and looked in the hole. The hole was about four feet deep, five feet long and about 24 inches wide. I knew that Jillian's purple vault (which holds her casket) was in close proximity, just mere inches of dirt now separating her and I. The overwhelming crazy urge to touch that purple vault one more time got the better of me.

It was so close that I had to find it. *I just had to!* The hole would be filled with cement in a few hours. I would never get another chance. So, I picked up a long stick and began poking around where I thought the vault might be located. No luck.

Lying on my belly along the side of it, I got so absorbed in sneakily trying to poke that stick into the side of this big, gaping hole (without making it noticeable) that I failed to hear a car pull up...or see that suddenly, I was no longer alone! I looked over to my right and panicked when I noticed a pair of feet standing right next to me. It turns out that a well-known important person in our small town (I'll call her "Lucy") was out visiting her loved ones grave and leaving flowers for a birthday.

Lucy stood there staring at me. I was still on the ground, trying desperately to hide my little poker stick. I was quite embarrassed and trying to figure out a good explanation for what I was up to.

"*What* are you doing?" she demanded. "You are trying to find her vault, *aren't* you?"

What could I say?

"Um ... well, yes. Yes, I am."

There. I admitted it. I waited for the judgment I was sure was coming next. Instead, Lucy looked at me, broke into a big smile and said, "Hold on, I have a snow-scraper in my car! This has always been on my bucket list!"

She ran over to her car, came back with a snow scraper and jumped in the hole! She whispered, "You just stay there like a grieving mom and keep a look out!" What else *could* I do? I was too stunned to do much else at this point!

Instead of the dainty little pokes I had been making with my stick, Lucy starts digging craters in the side of this big rectangular hole with her snow scraper. It looks like every single woodchuck in the cemetery had been having a party in there! Lucy is happily digging away when suddenly, another car pulls up. (I heard that one!)

"*Hide*!" I tell her. "Duck down so no one can see you; maybe they won't notice!"

She is bent over double in the hole but peeks out ... and it turns out to be her elderly Auntie also coming to visit a loved one's grave!

"Stay down, Lucy! Don't you dare pop up out of there!" I said in a loud whisper. After a few minutes, she whines, "I can't stay bent over like this for much longer!"

Just as her elderly, somewhat frail looking auntie looks over in our direction (probably wondering what I was doing laying down), up pops Lucy from this big hole in the ground like a jack in the box!

Auntie turns white as a sheet. I think she may have started to sway a bit. I am mortified. Lucy crawls out of the hole, dusts off the dirt and nonchalantly goes over to greet her Auntie. She somehow manages to come up with a plausible explanation for what we were doing; like she accidentally dropped her cellphone in the hole and was just retrieving it or something, and Auntie finally drives off. Whew!

Back we go to digging. No time to waste, it's getting darker by the minute! Another car pulls up. It's "Fred", who also has a loved one buried in our section. He walks up and says, "What are you guys doing? Oh! Are you looking for her vault?"

Lucy and I just look at each other and don't say a word, holding our breaths. Fred looks at us blankly for a minute and says, "This has always been on my bucket list! I have a flashlight in the car, I'll go grab it!" (Seriously? Who knew?)

He comes back with a flashlight and a long stick kind of thing that you might use for roasting marshmallows. I get in the hole; Lucy and Fred keep watch. We have very little daylight left and I am getting desperate. I asked Lucy to lay down on the grass where I know Jilly is buried for a reference point. (I think she did, bless her heart!) I start poking with the marshmallow stick. Fred shines his big flashlight.

Wait! Here comes another car! (What? Is this Grand Central Station? The cemetery is *never* this busy!)

It's my oldest daughter, Erica. She drives up, jumps out of the car, sees me standing in this big gaping hole, Lucy with her snow scraper and Fred with his big flashlight, and stares at me in disbelief.

"*MOTHER! Are you digging Jilly up?*" she demands to know.

"*Of course not!*" I reply.

If the tables were turned, however, I just want to say that Jilly would have dug me up long before this, because she watched way too much CSI and had a weird fascination with it. She used to go on archeological expeditions in our backyard trying to find deceased pets. Ask any of her friends; Jilly would have instigated this adventure in a heartbeat if she were here.

"I am just looking for her vault," I said as innocently as I could, as though people do this sort of thing every day.

We go back to digging. Just before it gets completely dark, I finally find it! A little tiny piece of her pretty purple vault! I can see it and can finally touch it! It's the closest I have been to her in years!

I am so excited! Lucy is excited! Fred is excited! Erica is

excited! Erica calls Jilly's phone number (which we hadn't canceled yet) and I put the phone on the vault within inches of where I know Jilly's little head now rests, so that Jilly can "hear" it.

"*We love you!*" we yell.

We snap a picture. We climb out of the hole. It's very dark by now and unfortunately, it no longer resembles the tidy little neatly dug rectangle that it did an hour ago before we started all this craziness. We do our best to minimize the damage. (Epic fail!) The dirt doesn't go back in the craters nearly as easily as it came out of them!

"Wait!" says Erica. "We might as well give the cemetery crew a good chuckle."

We decide to place Jilly's picture in one of the craters that Lucy made near the top of the hole, so that when they pull the boards off the next morning to pour the cement, Jilly is peeking up at them from below.

Erica and I go home absolutely filthy, covered in dirt. My husband says, "Wow! Rough day at work?" We just smile. I'm still wearing my scrubs from the hospital.

My youngest daughter, Sierra, comes home about an hour later and says, "Mom! Did you know there is a giant hole by Jilly's grave? It was covered with a board, but I so wanted to jump in and find Jilly's vault."

Erica and I can't control our giggles now. True story. Would I recommend anyone else do this? Absolutely not. Would I do it again to find one of my children? Hope I never have to!

P.S. My sincere apologies to the cemetery crew! My sincere gratitude to Lucy, Fred and Erica for their support.

15

NO ONE IS IMMUNE

December 2, 2015

It is human nature when a tragedy strikes to silently thank God it isn't us and wonder how we would cope. "Can I talk to you about something? It's personal." Several times in the last few weeks I have had conversations with acquaintances that start like this:

Them: "Can I ask you a question?"

Me: "Sure."

Them: "It's personal; I don't want to upset you."

Me: (Thinking, "personal?" Like the intimate questions about bodily functions I must ask my patients every day? For example,

"Are you passing gas yet, Mrs. Smith?"—kind of personal?)

"Uh, sure, go ahead and ask."

Them: "It's about Jillian."

Me: (hugely relieved): "Oh, gosh *yes*. You can talk to me about Jilly all you want!" I may be a little crazy, but I love to talk about my kids! (And I am aware that I talk about Jilly a lot!) I talk about her sisters a lot too; just not as publicly, to give them some privacy (which wasn't quite so important to Jilly), so why would I not talk about Jilly too? I think it's a mom thing for me; that's what moms do, isn't it?

After all, I had three daughters... I *still* have three daughters. I have been hopelessly in love with all three of them since the day I felt that first flutter of life from them. That part will never change.

One of them is in a different form though and I can't kiss her goodnight quite like I can the other two. I can drive 10 miles and kiss Sierra goodnight... or drive hundreds of miles and kiss Erica.

Jilly is different though... I can't plant a squeaky kiss on that soft cheek the way I used to. The best I can do is drive a mile up the road to the cemetery and blow a kiss to the place her body rests. I know she isn't really *there*. She is in a different form, but I still like to tell her goodnight.

Someday, I will be in that different form too (as will we all.) Why is that so scary? We all know that we aren't given a warranty at birth that guarantees us a lifespan of 100 years... but we take those sunrises each morning for granted and assume that we will see or be able to talk to our loved ones again whenever we want.

For some of us, that time may not be "very soon" as we think of it. Jilly's sisters might be grandparents before I see her again... or I could wake up next to her in Heaven tomorrow. I am good either way, because I am absolutely not afraid of death... but admit that like most people, I am a little nervous as to how it will happen.

Talking about my children makes me happy. I can tell you about the current things Erica and Sierra are doing; how they are doing in school and new developments in their lives. With Jilly, I can't exactly do that. (Although I do like to pass on her latest winks.)

For those of you who have children, can you imagine telling them good night and then *poof* in the blink of an eye, you suddenly are not able to say your child's name without blank stares or uncomfortable glances from loved ones? It's the most natural and comforting thing in the world to talk about your kids!

When our children are conceived, we post pregnancy announcements, maternity pictures and finally, tons of pictures of our beautiful babies when they are born. Total strangers smile at them, give us encouraging nods and ask how old they are. With advances in media trends, you now get to share pictures of their latest smiles and developments on Facebook.

Can you even fathom that after a few months or years,

people would expect you to *get over* giving birth to them and not want you to speak of them again because it makes them uncomfortable, or to only do so on special occasions a few times a year? Try it for 24 hours! Try not to think of your child. Don't say your child's name. Pretend you can't talk about them without "turning people off" or making them want to avoid you. Pretend that you must wait years or decades to kiss them goodnight again. Can't do it, can you?

Why does talking about someone who has gone Home make people so uncomfortable? It's a normal part of life! Just as we are all born, we are all going to pass from this worldly existence someday; every single one of us! Why not talk about that?

Is it weird to talk about a graduation party when our kids are just starting school? Is it strange to talk about what they want to be when they grow up? Have you ever fantasized about their wedding day with them? Why is it so taboo to talk about the day they will go back to God again? Why can't we say, "Hey, when it's my turn, I want … "

I am so thankful that Jilly had many conversations with us about what life might be like for her someday in Heaven. It brings me incredible comfort, peace and gratitude that she prepared me long ago for this time of intense longing on my side. She assured me that if it were possible to do so, she would send me signs to let me know that she is okay and somehow, she has managed to do so. I would lose what's left of my fragile mind if I had to go the rest of my life only saying her name on special occasions. I could not do it. (When it's my turn, I certainly hope that people talk about and share memories of me for a long time. Don't worry, if possible, I will be right there listening to what they have to say and sending signs of acknowledgment!)

The love for our children does not change when they die. It's not like we can whip out pictures of our deceased children in their "current" form and show them off (nor would you want us to; we totally understand that.)

We need to talk about their lives, and yes, sometimes we need to feel safe enough to process their deaths too. We just want the opportunity to be able to share the memories we have of them with others. You see, the memories are all we have left to sustain us until the day we are reunited with them. Please say their name. Don't be afraid to share a memory with us. Help us get through the holidays, the empty chair at our table, the holes in our souls that are the exact size of our children gone Home too early.

Say their name. It's personal…and it's music to our ears and hearts.

June 7, 2015

"No one ever told me that grief felt so like fear," wrote C.S. Lewis in his book *A Grief Observed*. My friend, Jessica expanded on that thought after recently losing her son in a tragic accident. She said, "What I perceive that statement to mean is fear in the sense of the unknown. Losing such a critical piece of your being opens the whole world to great unknowns...and that is scary." She's so right. The unknown can be terrifying. The journey isn't linear, it's a day to day, minute by minute jumbled voyage into the unknown that we navigate the best we can.

Out and about recently at various events, I had several conversations with people who have also lost a loved one. (Sometimes I swear there is a neon sign above our heads that make us gravitate towards each other...or perhaps our loved ones on the other side somehow manage to help arrange our "chance" encounters?)

One person had never known grief before until she was suddenly faced with the death of her young, vibrant husband. She was still trying to fathom it. "I just never understood the magnitude of it before," she said." Does it ever get any better?" she asked. She would love to just hibernate, but must instead go back to work, make a living and continue to try to raise her children as both a mother and now, also as a father.

Another person was six years out from the loss of her child;

she avoided leaving the house much for the first three years. She simply couldn't handle any type of celebration, such as weddings, graduation parties or baby showers, because each one reminded her that her son was no longer here.

In her words, "I have turned into a bitter, angry, lonely woman that no one really wants to be around. I miss who I once was, but I have lost my faith, my heart and my soul in that one horrible moment in time."

On the flip side, a couple of my friends who have lost multiple children seem to have dedicated their lives to spreading joy and happiness to others. They greet each day with a smile, despite their broken hearts and do not measure their children's short lives by their last day of it. Instead, they strive to share all the positive attributes that their children might have someday shown to the world, had they lived. (I aspire to be like this!)

After three years, six months and 18 days, grief is still a huge mystery to me; so far, the only thing I am 100 percent sure of is:

- No two people handle loss the same way or on the same timeline, even in the same family.
- Parents grieve differently than siblings, and even different than each other.
- Grandparents handle things differently than parents.
- Close friends, even though they may not be related to the person who died, can be devastated by your loss too, even to the point of PTSD. Even total strangers can be

touched and forever changed by the loss. Perhaps it is the first time that death has touched their lives.
- Maybe they don't know anyone else who has gone through it.
- Maybe they have already endured so much loss that they are numb.
- We only have our own experiences that we can compare that loss to. I only know what it feels like to lose my child. I don't know what it feels like for you to lose yours.

My mother is a good example of this. She used to say to me, "Losing a grandchild is so much *worse* than losing a child; it is double the grief. We are sad for our loss and have to helplessly watch you, our own child, that we love so much, go through your own loss and pain too." She wasn't trying to be mean or unkind. Each of those experiences was the *worst* loss (at that moment) that she had ever known.

The only things in her own experience that she could compare with the pain of my loss were:

- An early miscarriage in her first pregnancy.
- Losing her own parents (who died peacefully at a respectable old age.)
- Losing her sister, who was hit by a car in the prime of her life (died at age 44)

Eventually, I realized that Jilly's death probably *was* the most painful death she had experienced yet. In the natural order of life, mom expected her parents and possibly her siblings, to go before her, but never in her wildest dreams did she expect to outlive a grandchild.

I understand where she is coming from... or at least I do now. I can tell you that I certainly did *not* understand in the beginning. When Jilly died, several bereaved parents reached out to us. Some were 35 years down the path, one mom was just 20 *days* ahead of us on this journey after burying her oldest two sons together. Each had their own "words of wisdom" that they shared to try to help us cope.

One said, "She was your child, but she was only on loan from God. She is safe in His arms." She was right. I didn't have to like it, but she was right.

Another said, "You think that this is the worst part and it *does* feel that way, but it is going to get a whole lot harder." He was right too. (Forever grateful for that warning... because it did get much harder!)

A third couple said, "Grief scrambles your brain for a while; you won't remember many, many things, but what you *do* remember will be on automatic replay every day for a *very* long time. They were right as well.

My memory, especially my short-term memory, seems to be permanently askew. My memory of the morning of Jilly's death, however, still plays like the movie *Groundhog Day* each morning. Every single one of the bereaved parents who stopped by, took us to lunch or coffee, sent a note or called and graciously allowed us to lean on them. They were a healing presence in our pain because they understood in a way that no one else could. In fact, many of them understood what I am now, three and a half years later, just beginning to comprehend.

I now understand that there can't be *any* comparisons when it comes to death. Everyone will someday experience loss. For that person, each one is the most painful loss for *them*. We all walk this path, but we all must do it differently in order to survive. And that is not only okay ... it is as it *should* be.

I remember the first young person's death after Jilly's. I wanted so badly to help the family! I got a box together of all the things that our family had found helpful and stopped by their house. For some reason, I thought that if I did this, if I could give them the "right tools," they could take a shortcut through their grief and not have to endure the pain that we were also going through. My intentions were good ... my heart was in the right place, but I must have come across like a tornado in their already overwhelmed and fractured life. (If you recognize your family here, I apologize for being so pushy!)

At the time, I am sure I wasn't nearly as helpful as I *thought* I was being. I look back at that now and cringe. How dare I? They were handling it in the way that was best for *them*. They didn't need to handle their situation in the way that was best for me.

I didn't need to jump in and "save" them and couldn't have anyway. Grief is so personal that it would be like trying to give swimming lessons to someone who had just survived a plane crash in the ocean. So, I am slowly learning to back off and maybe send a card or a message offering an idea or two. (Usually something like, "Don't forget to get thumbprints; you may want them later.")

I may check in with them in a couple weeks or a month or two later as an anniversary of "that day" rolls around. It is about that time when other family members and friends have gone back to their lives and reality sets in; the struggle gets much harder.

I think of and pray for them often, but especially on the "special dates."

I am trying harder not to force my own coping strategies on them and instead, give them the space they need to grow. It's not that you ever grow past or beyond grief. It's a companion for the rest of our lives, so you learn how to grow into it, like a coat you can never take off. We learn how to tame the wild moments of missing them that threaten to crowd out everything else in our lives.

It's proving to be a much bigger personal challenge than I thought. As a nurse, helping people isn't just part of my job; it's part of my personality; it's how I seem to be hard-wired. I hate watching people struggle.

I have learned that we *often* grow the most when we face our biggest struggles. We must endure the pain to process (and perhaps grow from) the grief, so that we can go on (or not) to the next phase in our journey. There is *no* shortcut. I can't fix anything for them. (My last name is Crist, not Christ!)

One day at the cemetery, I struck up a conversation with a grandma who had just lost her young adult grandson. I expressed my condolences and asked about the parents. Grandma said, "Oh, honestly, they are doing just *fine!*" (She was absolutely and totally serious; this was not a sarcastic answer!)

My jaw dropped. "*Fine?* They *just* buried their child and they are doing *fine?*" my mind screamed. How can they be *fine?* I looked at her incredulously and calmly whispered, "No, I am pretty sure they are *not* fine. I am pretty sure they are in shock, as you probably are, but haven't yet realized it. I will keep them and you, in my prayers."

I now realize these parents are probably learning to give the standard answer that we all give when people casually ask, "How are you?"

We try our best to smile (sometimes through unseen tears) and say, "Fine." And most people, God bless them, believe it. Maybe if we say it enough, we can magically convince ourselves to believe it too. The ones whose lives have been touched by the loss, however, just give us a sad knowing smile that is normally missed by the rest of the world.

We hold each other's hearts and hands and move slowly away from the last moment we had on Earth with our loved one. We collectively move forward into the next moment without them by our side and look longingly ahead to the time that we will be reunited with our loved ones. We will never be the same person we once were. (We miss that person too!)

I know I have grown along this journey. I am learning... we are all learning, and we are all doing the best we can.

16

AT 1900 DAYS

January 2016

Jilly, today marks 1900 days since you got your wings and instantly flew from our arms to God's embrace. I never imagined I would make it this far. Heck, I never imagined I would survive the first week! But alas, we have. We have been up and down on the rollercoaster of grief. The pain on most days is not as sharp as it was that first two years.

It no longer hurts just to breathe. My heart will always ache from the hole in it that perfectly fits your size. I don't think that ever goes away. Some days, it is a little wave of missing you, other days, a tsunami still comes out of nowhere. I am moving forward and as you know, I take you with me everywhere I go.

You are just a little less visible than when you walked the earth with us. Those who told me I had to "let you go" were wrong. I don't. And I won't.

I look for signs from you ... no, I *expect* to get signs and you deliver on a fairly frequent basis. I love that about you—the thoughtful way you let us know that you haven't forgotten us, that you still love us and that you will not really "leave" us until we are ready. (I probably won't ever be.) I love that your sense of humor stayed with you.

You have come along with me on this amazing adventure, giving me the material and in a sense, co-authoring this work. Even if only family and friends read it and pass it on to their children, it will be a beautiful tribute to honor the wonderful soul that is our Jilly. If anyone finds comfort or ways to help others cope with their grief, it will be an even greater reward. My dream is that someday, the proceeds will finance your scholarship fund, so that we can continue to help those who want to enter the health care field. Some of your best friends have or are finishing their health care degrees and starting to work in their respective fields impacting many people. It is bittersweet, because it could have been you doing those things, but at the same time, because I am aware of how quickly a life can end, I am extra proud of those young adults and their accomplishments. Some of them have started families; I may not get to hold your babies, but it brings me great joy to hold theirs!

One of your besties is getting married this summer. You

would have been in that wedding. That day will be hard, but lovely and sweet. You will be there, beside the other bridesmaids... I am sure they will feel your presence!

Your life mattered. While your last day did not in any way define who you are/were, the weeks afterward affected and changed so many people in so many ways. That event was the stone thrown into the pond, watching the ripples that have come from that day is amazing. It is said that grief is love with no place to go. I choose to find a place to spread that love.

I miss you, Jilly Bean. I am closer to seeing you again by 1900 days. My life counts too, and I am doing the best I can to live it and be a good friend, good mom and good influence on those around me. I love you forever, I love you for always, as long as I'm living and beyond, my Jilly you'll be.

♥ ♥ ♥

February 18, 2016
Jilly's 24th Birthday and 5th One in Heaven

Happy Birthday, sweet JillyBean! You left your cozy liquid wonderland 24 years ago today and came forth into this side of life. I remember feeling ecstatic that I had another daughter and also kind of sad, because we were no longer one with each other. I loved carrying you *beneath* my heart and as the years passed, I loved carrying you in my arms, *next* to my heart as we lived out our adventures.

However, you were destined to change the lives you touched, and I knew that from the beginning. From the serious "old lady" toddler to the vivacious spunky prankster of a teenager you became, you left footprints all over hearts of every age, size and nationality. Those 19 years weren't long enough for us to have you, but apparently it was long enough for you to do what you and God had planned. He must have missed you terribly in Heaven. I can understand that, because I haven't ever gotten used to your absence here. I am not sure I ever will.

I miss you so very much, my precious, funny little rose. Every day, you are in my thoughts. I carry you in my heart now, your memories nestled in every molecule and every beat of my heart.

Some days, that is still just not enough. This fifth birthday that you celebrate in Heaven is probably the hardest one yet for me... I am not sure why. I am struggling with my grief. Witnessing my mom go through the final stages of her life, I think the grief has finally caught up to me. I can no longer out run it. Maybe it's time I don't try and instead, turn around and face it; feel the pain, the longing, the grace, the *immense* love. Those things hurt.

I asked another bereaved mom how she was able to stay standing after losing her twin babies, and then her 21-year old daughter recently. *All* her children. *All* of them. My dear God, I couldn't do it. I would surely curl up and die myself without your sisters here to love on.

She replied that she is still standing *because* of her daughters.

I didn't understand. She explained that she would want her children to go on if she was the one who died. She would want them to have beautiful love filled lives ... and she knows that is what her children also want for her. She is living for them and they are living *through* her, until they all meet again.

Wow. Just wow. Is that what you have been trying to tell me all along, my sweet girl? I know you aren't as far away as we think, you have shown me that repeatedly. I know you are safe, loved, happy and close by. I feel the breath of your soul whisper softly in my ear once in a while.

I will try my best to live *for* you, appreciate the beautiful love-filled life that I have.

I will try to let you live *through* me. Happy 24th birthday Jillian; I guess we are both growing up. I love you with every fiber of my being, with every thought and every beat of my heart.

Until we meet again ... enjoy your "angel food" cake.

Love forever,

Mama-Cita

♥ ♥ ♥

Baby Addison
A Different Kind of "Jilly Wink"

I BELONG TO A PRIVATE Facebook page that has a pretty exclusive membership requirement. You must have lost your child to be accepted. (Talk about a tough initiation!) Unfortunately, the group numbers in the thousands.

Fortunately, this group of parents "get it" the way no one else can or wants to. I totally understand that . . . I thank God, every single day for those who don't get it and pray they never ever have to. I wouldn't wish it on my worst enemy. I can go online to this support group anytime of the day or night and find someone struggling with the same issues I am on any given day. It's wonderful, but sad at the same time.

Before Jilly's birthday this year, I was really struggling with a deep depression. A small dose of antidepressants and some therapy wasn't even able to pull me out of it. For many of us in this "club," that is common; the anticipation of a special day, like a birthday or anniversary is often filled with anxiety and is sometimes *worse* than the actual day itself. Once the day has passed, it is as though a heavy weight has somehow been lifted off our shoulders.

So, as the gray skies of February and bone chilling cold rolled around this year, I was filled with dread as Jilly's birthday approached. Although she has only been gone a bit over four years, this was the 5th birthday Jilly would celebrate in Heaven; a milestone of sorts. I didn't feel like launching lanterns or balloons as we have always done in the past.

In need of a new idea, I went to my online support group and was discussing this with other parents. One mom suggested buying a birthday cake for another child, instead of for your deceased one. I have known all along that lovingly serving others often helps relieve my sadness, which is why in the past, we have collected non-perishable goods for the Food Pantry, the homeless shelter and goodies for the Humane Society, but for some reason, I just didn't have it in me this year.

Erica and Sierra (Jilly's sisters) knew of my struggles this year and God bless them, planned a surprise birthday party for Jilly, inviting a few of my closest friends. It was a surprise to me since I wasn't in on the planning, although I am sure we didn't pull anything over on Jilly. One way or another, my daughters were *not* going to let me sit in my closet sucking my thumb and falling apart that day, like I really wanted to do. (Uncharacteristic for me, by the way, but I really felt I had reached a new low!)

February 18th arrived; Erica got me out of the house and took me to the store. She informed me that we "needed" a birthday cake for Jilly, as a "couple people might stop by" and like it or not, we were celebrating her birthday that day—darn it, and *that was that*!

I went to the bakery section of the store and looked at cakes, fighting the tears that threatened to spill over my already reddened eyes and down my face, giving away my intense grief over this day. It's embarrassing to lose control anywhere, but it's especially hard in the middle of a store in the birthday cake section! If you ever see a parent suddenly run out of the store crying and leave a cart full of groceries, you can be pretty sure they are going through this same thing over some innocent trigger, like their child's favorite food, a song on the overhead radio or walking by the greeting card section.

Erica and I picked out a festive cake. I was sad that Jilly would not be here to eat it with us; in fact, I was downright morose and feeling pretty sorry for myself. I was talking to her in my head, as I often do, asking her how she was celebrating her special day in Heaven, because she loved birthdays. I was telling her how much I really needed a Jilly wink that day.

And then, I "heard" her answer.

It's all about the love, Mom!

Suddenly, I remembered the suggestion from the other grieving mom about buying another child's birthday cake.

On a whim, I asked the bakery lady if anyone was by chance coming in that day to pick up a birthday cake for a child. (What are the odds, anyway?) She looked through the cakes, talking out loud, "Well, let's see. This one is a retirement cake, this one is a going away cake; oh wait, there *is* a birthday cake!"

I held my breath.

"Is it for a boy or girl?" I asked.

"It's for a little girl," she replied. "She is turning 5 years old today." (Jilly's 5th birthday in Heaven, this little girl's 5th birthday... hmmm.)

"What is the name on the cake?" I asked.

It immediately brought back a sweet funny Jilly memory. Let me backtrack here for a minute and explain. Jilly was a baby magnet. She loved babies more than just about anything else on this planet. Throughout her life, Jilly coveted those "realistic" lifelike baby dolls. She saved every dollar she earned for months to buy one that looked like her, so she could pretend she had a real baby. One of her assignments in high school Family Relationships class was "Mock Parenting" and to Jilly's delight, the teacher sent the students home with a realistic "Robo-Baby" that the student must care for as if it was a real child. When I took the class in school, we had to carry around a boiled egg for our "baby." Times certainly have changed!

The "baby" she brought home could cry at random intervals, signaling hunger, wet diaper, needs cuddling, etc. The student must take the baby everywhere they go for the whole weekend, as the only way to stop the baby's crying is a key bracelet that the student must wear that matches the computer in the assigned doll.

Jilly was over the moon for this assignment! She named the "baby" one of her favorite names...Addison. She did very well, taking the baby on dates, to the store and even took pictures of her. She was so proud of it despite being in high school and I believe with some maturity, would have been a good mom if she ever had children of her own.

By Sunday night though, she was tired of "Addison" disturbing her sleep every couple of hours. She tried to pawn her off on anyone who would hold her and eventually ended up burying her under a pile of clothes in her sister's closet and going back to bed. (She was a young teen after all.)

I have no idea what grade she ended up getting on this assignment, but Jilly realized she was not quite ready for motherhood, even though she still loved "Addison."

So, there we are, years later, standing at the bakery counter in the store, and the lady says the name of the child who is turning five today... Addison!

"Buy the cake, mom! Please?" I heard Jilly's sweet, giggly voice say in my head.

We bought the cake, attached a note that said that we wanted to do something special to honor our now 24-year-old daughter, who was celebrating her 5th birthday in Heaven, eating angel food cake with God, and we hoped that this 5-year-old child had a great birthday here on Earth.

That night I went to bed happy, as I thought of a family here on Earth who probably smiled as they picked up a birthday cake for a daughter they adore, paid for by a stranger who also loves a birthday girl in Heaven.

Sometimes, Jilly astounds me with her signs. I shouldn't be shocked anymore but usually, my response is, "How does she *do* that?" Case in point... Jilly's cousin recently had twins. They were born prematurely at 31 weeks, a boy, Hunter and a girl, Emma.

Jilly aspired to be a neonatal nurse who took care of premature babies. She *adored* the idea of twins. (She also had a dog named Emma.)

The day after the twins were born, I got up and went downstairs. It was just Mark and I at home and two dogs. No one had been here for a few days except for us and certainly no babies had been in the house.

In the middle of the room I spied this on the floor... a baby shoe. I had never seen it before. It doesn't belong to me and didn't belong to any of my children. It is obviously old and very small. It would fit on a premature baby.

I have absolutely no explanation for it being in my living room the day after the twins were born. How *does* she do that?

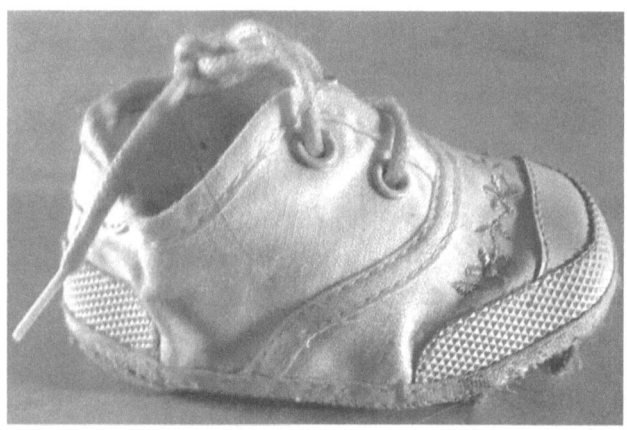

17

SIX YEARS LATER

January 7, 2017

There hadn't been a really good Jilly wink for a while, but she made up for that. I had shoulder surgery recently. As the anesthesiologist was giving me the "happy juice" in my IV, I felt it start to hit, melting my body into a completely relaxed state. The last thing I remember was saying to myself, "C'mon Jilly and Dean (my step-dad), let's have a chat, or at least give me a sign that you are with me."

I sank into the warm velvety blackness of general anesthesia. According to my husband, I woke up smiling... although I don't remember a visit with Jilly or Dean. The surgery went well, and I came home to recuperate. At about the same time I was in surgery, my sister in Pennsylvania was sending me good vibes, thoughts and prayers as she went grocery shopping.

One of the things she bought while thinking of me was a bag of pears. (She and I both love pears!) She had one pear for dinner and then decided to take the rest of the pears out of the bag and put them in a bowl for a quick snack; no one else had touched the pears before this. She finished arranging them and the pear on top caught her eye. At first it looked bruised; a closer look at it made her laugh. Apparently, Jilly was closer than I thought during my surgery. She knows my sister is open to signs as I am and would pass this one on if she made it obvious enough.

Jilly always signed her name crossing the J. To me, it looks like it says I ♥ Jill.

What would you say?

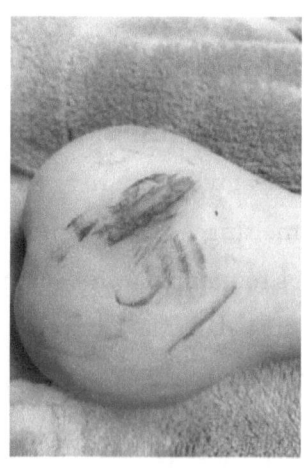

♥ ♥ ♥

February 8, 2017

*J*DREAMT OF JILLY AGAIN last night. She was at Central Michigan University, one of the places she loved. It was always an exciting time for her to visit her friends that attended school there.

In this dream, she suddenly just appeared in my arms. "Oh!!!" I cried. I was so surprised; it was so unexpected. I could feel the outline of her body pressed against mine. I could feel her heart beating next to mine and her bony little ribs as I rubbed her back. I felt her familiar "tummy hugs" that only *she* could do the right way, in spite of her trying to teach everyone else the "proper" way to do them. It was divine. I was radiant with joy and basking in it.

Just as suddenly, she was out of my arms and running away from me. 'What the___?" I thought. I took off chasing her. She would run down a hall and I would pursue her as fast as my legs could carry me, sure I was going to catch her. Just as I reached a corner, she was around it and all the way down at the end of another long hall...and another...and another. I was exhausted when I came around the last corner and found her up on a stage, singing in a band, slightly off key and with theatrical gusto, as usual.

I held my arms out to her, willing her to come back into my embrace. She shook her finger at me, silently saying no. I reached out further. Again, she said no with a nod of her head and a wag of her finger while she continued to sing. I didn't understand. I waited until the song was over and once again reached for her. She backed away, staying just out of my reach and explained why as gently as she could.

"Mama, I *can't* let you catch me. If you did, you would try to take me back home. You wouldn't be able to help yourself because you love me so much. I know that... but you can't take me back home, mom... because I am already "Home." And please believe me when I tell you that I am having the time of my life. I am so happy. There is only joy here. You will catch me eventually and when you do, you won't ever have to let me go again unless we both agree on it... but that time is not just yet. I love you, mom."

I slowly put my arms back down. I knew without any question she was absolutely right. As I woke up in the next breath, I didn't feel sad. I felt nothing but gratitude.

Gratitude for the journey we are on, for being able to share part of that journey here on earth and for the reminder that she is only a short distance in front of me on that journey. Someday, when I catch her again, we will have the sweetest embrace and then continue our journey... together. Eternally together.

Birthday Week, 2017

OH, MY SWEET JILLY Bean; we are heading into your birthday (on Earth) week and you have been busy letting us know that we better not forget it! (Like we ever could!) I wonder what you would be doing at 25? We usually celebrated your birthday with three of your best friends, since the four of you were all born within 20 days of each other; three of us mamas all worked together as nurses on the pediatric floor.

Last week, your sister Erica found a quarter under the bed covers. Who puts a quarter in their pajamas? Not Erica!

Today, just to prove a point, you got three of us! (One of your bestie's birthday was yesterday, but you were rarely on time for anything anyway.)

First, your name was scribbled on a "post-it" note on Erica's work desk when she arrived there after a near miss accident on the way to work. Someone came extremely close to rear ending her. (She even had the thought to relax, because she felt she was going to get hit.) Erica didn't write your name on that sticky pad and doesn't know why it would be there. Thank God, she is safe.

I think you were letting her know that you are here with her more often than she realizes. Next, my sister got into her car and found a quarter on the seat along with a blue glass stone that says Gratitude on it. We both attended a conference last year that handed out those blue stones. She has packed and unpacked her car many times since our trip last year and that was never on the seat before.

I suppose it could have fallen out of her purse. Along with a quarter. And lined up next to each other cozily on the seat with nothing else in her clean car. Yeah, right. I found it amusing that Gratitude showed up like that...this week we have been giving out Jilly presents in honor of your upcoming birthday, because we are so grateful that we had you for 19 years.

My sister works for a child safety hotline. Unfortunately, she gets many calls each shift but this particular call involved a young woman with Jillian's "exact" birthday. Of course, the odds were one in 365.

And your sense of humor? Oh yes, still there. One of the places we dropped off Jilly presents was at the funeral home, to the lovely ladies who have lifted the spirits of our family at some of the lowest moments in our lives, time and time again. Just a "thank you, we love you, Jilly loves you", kind of thing. I was showing them some of the designs on the presents we have made so far. One is a "Red Solo Cup" fabric. I was telling the ladies how that was the last song you taught me in this life, the day before you went Home. We were coming back from Ft. Wayne, just you and I and that song came on. I asked you, "Are they really singing about a red plastic solo cup?" You laughed and said, "Yes, and it's a great song!" Then you proceeded to teach me the words...loudly, with lots of gusto and slightly off key.

The ladies asked if a had more of a specific design, as they all wanted the same one. I told them I did and ran home for a minute to grab more. When I got back to the funeral home a few minutes later, I opened the door and walked into music playing on the overhead system. The song? Yes, "Red Solo Cup!"

I asked, "Did you guys put that song on?"

"*No!* It just came on the radio when you walked in! That is too freaky! We were just talking about it and it came on!" (It was a popular song six years ago.)

Welcome to my life...I don't make this stuff up! Oh, my sweet girl...thank you for telling us that you are still close by, you are safe, but we can only see you on special occasions! I love you, Jilly Bean!

♥ ♥ ♥

February 18, 2017
(Jilly's 25th Birthday)
Finding a Place for all the Love to Go

I READ A PHRASE SOMEWHERE that said, "Grief is love with no place to go." I couldn't have stated it any better. That's exactly what it feels like for me. In my five plus years of this journey since our Jilly Bean's passed into her new life, I think that is one of the things that has caused me the most pain...especially on her birthday. As parents, our child's birthday is usually one of the happiest days of our lives. We are forever changed on that day, our hearts expanding to hold all the love that this new life brought us. They are each little 'miracles'... a gift lent to us from God for a while. We watch them grow into their own unique person with a personality unlike anyone else.

As our children celebrate their birthday milestones here on earth, we might throw parties, buy or make presents and invite friends to share in the anniversary of the day the child was born. If we are lucky, extra special birthdays might come to pass. Soon, they are 5 and starting school. Then they hit the double digits at 10. It isn't long before they become teenagers and suddenly, celebrating with family takes a backseat to celebrating with friends. At 16, they can drive. At 18 they can graduate. At 21, they become a legal adult. Each of those birthdays brings out so much love.

Special birthdays at my house as a child were 6, 11 and 16. I know my mom probably stayed up many nights trying to figure out how to space those years so that no two children in our family had a big celebration that year, since we didn't have the means to have big parties. It wasn't a bad idea. I tried to make my daughter's sixth, 11th and 16th birthdays just as special as mine were.

My love for her had not faded at all. In fact, it seemed to be stronger than ever, but I couldn't physically GIVE her that love anymore. I couldn't buy her presents. I felt all that love for my sweet Jilly and I couldn't figure out how to channel it. My love for her had no place to go. It is a struggle that many bereaved people go through.

Since her death, I have figured out that the best coping mechanism I have in dealing with what should be a happy day, is to put all that love somewhere. For her 21st birthday, we took up collections of needed items for the animal shelter. For her 22nd, we gathered food pantry donations in her name. Another year, we made backpacks for the homeless. Still another, we took treats to those who put their lives on the line every day for others.

Last year (on what was probably the most difficult birthday yet) we bought a birthday cake for a total stranger; a little girl celebrating her fifth birthday on earth, just as Jilly was celebrating her fifth birthday in Heaven. Instead of giving presents to Jilly, we give other people presents from Jillian. That way, it feels less like grief and more like the celebration we might have had shared with her if she were still here.

Since I had surgery this year, I was limited in what I could do for several weeks. One of my physical therapy exercises inspired our birthday gifts from her. I was finally able to do something productive with my pain, both physical and emotional! I ended up making dozens of hot/cold therapy packs to bring comfort to athletes with sore muscles, new mamas with cramps, tired teachers and coaches, colicky babies and grandparents with achy stiff joints. I can't begin to tell you how much joy it has brought me as I surprise people with these. I have chosen the recipients randomly. Some that I know, but also many that

I have never met before and may never see again like:

- The bus drivers that sat in the parking lot waiting hours to take a group of athletes back to their own school.
- The baristas at a coffee shop that have been on their feet all day.
- The nursing staff at a long-term care facility.
- An elderly, frail gentleman in line behind me at the bank (who really looked like he needed a hug more than anything else), who watched me hand them out to the tellers and timidly asked, "May I have one too?" (Of course, you can!)
- The volunteers at a fundraising event I am so blessed to be a part of.
- And many others who are usually not thanked nearly enough for doing what they do every day.

It's been so much fun to make them and give them out! I have put much thought into the fabrics, thinking of very special people as I select it. It feels almost as though I am shopping for gifts for Jilly again, except it's even better somehow.

The reason I tell you this is not because I need a pat on the back or thanks, although those things are nice. You can't have givers if you don't have people willing to receive. The point of sharing this is to offer an idea for those who are desperately searching for a place for their love to go. Be creative and consider trying something that not only keeps your memories alive, but benefits others. I believe you will be pleasantly surprised at how good it feels and the peace it gives you. Furthermore, it contributes to the legacy of your loved one.

I know that Jilly planted this idea. She certainly has been quite busy letting me know that she is thrilled with it. For the first time in over five years, I can hardly wait to celebrate her birthday. She will be 25...another big milestone. A quarter of a century. I miss her more with each passing day and I also celebrate that I am another year closer to seeing her again. I will celebrate that she walked with me on this journey for 19 years here on earth. I will celebrate that she is probably throwing a huge birthday party in heaven and that Jesus is her guest of honor. (She tells me he loves a good party too!)

I celebrate that she is safe; she is loved beyond measure; she is missed and most of all, I will celebrate that she is remembered.

If grief is love with nowhere to go, I am truly blessed that I have found such a beautiful place for my love for her to go; it goes to my fellow man, woman and child.

Happiest of birthdays, my sweet baby. I know that from where you are, each good, kind thing that we do reaches you as the best present possible. I hope you are showered with those presents from this side as you dance in the presence of our very best friend, the Prince of Peace.

June 23, 2017
The Best Winks

"I'M SORRY, BUT I'M afraid the odds of you getting pregnant naturally are slim to none. Your best chance would be to freeze your eggs and try in-vitro fertilization before you get much older."

These are the words that Jillian's big sister, Erica, heard on February 17th, the day before Jillian's 25th birthday, after several weeks of testing. It is already a difficult day each year without that jaw dropping news on top of it. Since Erica was nearly 28, the fertility specialist suggested harvesting and freezing her eggs as soon as possible... to the tune of $10,000. It would wipe out her college fund, but if that was what she wanted to do, her dad and I were all for it. If it didn't work out, she could always adopt. Erica was beyond sad. As her mom, I was sad too. Another daughter that could not give us grandchildren; at least not without a lot of effort—and a miracle. If her 'furry children' were any indication of her parenting abilities, she would have made such a good mom!

After weighing all the options, we decided to go ahead and pull the money from her college fund. When she moved back home, we would find another fertility clinic and get her eggs harvested. It was a leap of faith but she felt she needed to do it. Erica moved into my recently deceased stepdad's house with her "children" (her pack of dogs) and threw herself into getting the house updated. After weeks of painting, replacing floors, fixing hardware and deep cleaning, she was too tired to think too much about the devastating news she had just received. She started a business and began building a new life for herself here with her family close by for a support system.

In the meantime, Jilly must have been busy helping God pick out babies for her friends. Jillian's longtime boyfriend, Randolph, had finally moved on after hitting bottom with his grief and met a girlfriend. Ironically, she was a gymnast on the same team that Jilly had been on. They became pregnant around Jilly's birthday in February and are due in November, the month that she died! The timing was incredible, but there were more surprises in store for us. The morning of Randolph's gender reveal party, I heard

Jilly whisper in my ear, "It's a girl, mom." I laughed at my own wishful thinking, but on the way to the party, I told Jilly that if it really was her giving me that information that I would need another sign. A few minutes later, I drove by a Dodge Stratus (Jilly's car), saw a man with a beautiful huge purple butterfly painted on his shirt (Jilly's sign, and when is the last time you saw a *man* wearing a butterfly on his shirt?) When I walked into the party, there were purple and green flowers (Jilly's signature colors) gracing the tables. As they popped the balloons and pink glitter fell softly to the ground, I smiled. It was indeed a girl!

One of the girls on Jilly's cheerleading squad is pregnant and is also due in November. The foster mom of the dog we adopted (another good friend of Erica's) became pregnant by in-vitro with a daughter and is due in November too. Another of Jillian's close friends is due with another son the first week of November as well. She already had one child who has been fascinated by all things Jilly from the time of her infancy. As a baby, Aubree would giggle and laugh at something unseen in the corner that was entertaining her. She sleeps every night with a stuffed "Jilly Bear." All these babies coming fast and furious are all due in November. Jilly would have been in baby heaven, stealing them out of their mama's arms for kisses and hugs, rocking them to sleep and dancing to slow music with them.

Within a couple of months of Jilly's death, we had been told by a psychic that someday, a baby would arrive "with Jilly's fingerprints and handiwork all over it." We would know without any doubt that it was heaven sent. Which baby would it be? I was and am still close to her boyfriend, Randolph, and to several of Jilly's high school friends. Would one of those babies be that special little Jilly wink? Or maybe it will be a future baby, as her very best friends are planning to get married this year. (Another emotional challenge—Jilly would have been in those weddings!) Her friends are all growing up and moving on. Jilly is forever 19.

Each pregnancy announcement brings us both joy and sorrow. Erica and Sierra are okay some days, edgy and hormonal on others, as each pregnancy was revealed to them. Sierra even caught baby fever, wondering when her turn at motherhood would come. (She wisely has waited to finish college first.) But for Erica especially, it hurts. Even though all these other babies will hopefully be a part of my life (and I am very grateful for that), I'm also acutely aware that Jilly won't ever have children. She won't be there to spoil these babies, or her own nieces or nephews someday. She won't be there to coach her sisters in the delivery room. There are no more chances for a fifth-generation brown eyed child. (My grandma, my mom, me, and Jilly are the only brown eyed girls in the family.) Erica has green eyes and Sierra has blue eyes, as does the young man Sierra will likely marry. Without some random quirk of nature, the odds are remote. It sounds like such a minor detail, wanting a brown-eyed grandchild to carry on that trait, but with my mom in the last season of her life, I will be the only brown eyed person left in my family. I can always hope for a miracle.

The sun continues to rise each day, as it always has and with it, we became more accustomed to Erica living back in town and more grateful as she continued to work on my step-dad Dean's house. We all kept busy running from the grief that is so fresh in our hearts.

It had only been a few months since I found Dean's body permanently asleep in his bed one afternoon. Each time I pull into the driveway, I still expect him to answer the door. I miss him more each day. November this year will be especially difficult with both Jilly and Dean's "Angelversaries" within same week. (What rotten timing!) Both funerals were the week of Thanksgiving, which is our favorite family holiday. I can imagine Dean saying, "Well that month was already full of grief; I didn't want to mess up another one by dying in the middle of summer or something!" It's all I can do to get through those two weeks.

One night, Erica and I unpacked her moving boxes and came across her fertility testing supplies, now mostly outdated and we wondered what to do with them. On a whim, she took out one of the pregnancy tests and just for fun (or perhaps out of pure spite) decided to pee on it. Her cycles have been irregular for years, either bleeding or spotting throughout the month.

She finished the test, threw it in the sink and ran out of the room screaming.

"Well that was quite the reaction," I thought. "Poor girl must be really hormonal. All these tests are bringing back her frustration and disappointment. Grief quakes are like that.

They come out of nowhere, knocking you to your knees when you least expect it."

A minute later, she came back in the bathroom, scooped up the pregnancy test and screamed again.

"Mom ... *look*!" she cried.

My eyes stared intently at the test and my mind could not quite grasp what I was seeing. I looked at Erica and she looked at me. We both looked at the test again. Our jaws dropped.

There were two pink lines. The test was positive!

"No way!" we both said at once. It couldn't be! The specialist said she couldn't ... "Her ovaries weren't right ... we should freeze her eggs ... the tests showed the odds were remote to none ..."

Erica noticed that the tests were about four months past their expiration date. We "Googled" it and from what we gathered, expired pregnancy tests can sometimes give a false positive result. Well that would certainly explain it. Or would it?

It was 3:00 in the morning, so we did what any normal mother and daughter would do in this situation. We jumped in the car and drove to the store to buy another test ... or four. We got home, Erica repeated the test, then another and another. After five tests, the answers were all the same. They were all *very* positive. There were two pink lines on every single test.

I knew that there had been someone she had become quite close to before she came back home. She hadn't ruled out a long-term relationship with him but wanted to give herself time to live on her own and do some soul searching. He is 11 years older than Erica and his marriage to his ex-wife had never produced children either. His parents, approaching 70, have no grandchildren; it was the end of their family lineage and they had accepted that.

Well, let me tell you, Auntie Jilly had different plans for Erica. I have no doubt that she begged God to put a baby (or two or three or four) in her sister. She can be very persistent, at least she was on Earth. If she set her mind to something she wanted, she would just wear you down until you gave in. (It drove me nuts on more than one occasion.) I sometimes wonder if God has a special timeout chair for her in heaven when she gets to be too ornery.

God also has more wisdom than any specialist on earth, no matter how much schooling they have had. He has carried us through our grief, time and time again. What looks like a tragedy or an impossible situation usually ends up working out for the good of all concerned—if we are patient enough. We have learned to put our trust in him and just sit back and wait to see how it all plays out. His ways are not my ways, they are so much better!

It turns out that not only is Erica with child, she is also due the very week Jilly died.

The baby's father's last name, according to Wikipedia, means "Son of Laurence." My father-in-law's name was Larry, who died nine weeks before Jilly did. I had only received a wink or two from him since he crossed over and didn't think I had received any from Dean, but I was wrong. Here's another tidbit; the baby's father shares a birthday with my beloved Nanna (grandma) who was the second generation only brown eyed girl. And guess what else? He has *brown eyes!*

Now really, what are the odds of all those things lining up like that to create such a perfect opportunity? Is this possibly the best Jilly wink yet? Did she have help from my stepdad, Mark's dad and my grandma? I have no doubt she did. How could God resist all that persuasion?

Shortly after we told my husband that we were going to be first time grandparents (which thrilled him to pieces) he went camping. Sitting out by the fire one night, he was silently contemplating this new turn in our life path and wondering what the odds of all this being "just a coincidence" were, when something shiny caught his eye. He bent down to check it out and started to laugh. There, sticking out of the dirt next to the metal fire ring, was a quarter. (*Well, of course it was!*)

For now, I call this unborn child, "Baby Chuckles" because I know several of my loved ones are laughing in heaven at the orchestration of this little miracle. I can't wait to see what Jilly has in mind for this baby, her first living niece or nephew. I believe that this is the baby that has her fingerprints all over it that was predicted five years ago. God will take the hardest week of the year this November and fill it with joy instead of sorrow. In future years, I will have something else to look forward to that week, God willing... and what a story to tell the baby!

July 21, 2017
Update

*J*uly 13th was a special day to Jillian, as it was her ex-boyfriend, Randolph's birthday; he was the one she loved the most and longest. He was finally able to move forward after her passing and is expecting a baby daughter this November. July 13th also happened to be the day that Erica was scheduled for her ultrasound to find out the gender of the baby she is carrying. The baby didn't cooperate very well; its hands covered its face as if it was playing peek-a-boo. It had a leg up by its cheek, much like a trick all three of our girls did on the beam as gymnasts. An agile little one, it is.

The popular vote was that Erica was carrying a girl. In fact, one cousin went so far as to say, "If it isn't a girl, there has been some mistake!" My husband, Mark, was just as sure it was a boy, since there are no Crist boys. The baby's father only has one brother and his parents have no other grandchildren, so a girl would be extra special, but a boy would carry on their family name. The new parents to be didn't care either way, so long as it is healthy. Alas, when it came time to peek at the gender reveal parts of the anatomy, it rolled over and showed its butt to the camera. Nope, not telling! It did not offer up any clues on the ultrasound to the untrained eye, so they left the appointment with a sealed envelope from the sonographer, having no idea what the gender was.

On the evening of Jillian's Memorial Scholarship mud volleyball tournament two days later, we would gather friends together and reveal the baby's gender. Since Erica's first "children" were her dogs, we tied bandanas around their necks with "Big Brother" and "Big Sister" labels on them. Erica and Chuck would open a bandana and a pink or blue bow would give the answer to the big question. Jillian's godmother, Kathy, a very good friend of the family (whose children Erica used to babysit), is also our local funeral home director. We gave her the honor of opening the envelope and selecting the correct color bow. Since she usually must deal with the other end of the life process, we wanted her to be a special part of this joyous occasion. Except for Kathy, none of us would know until the big reveal moment.

We sat Erica and Chuck on the swing in the backyard with family and friends holding their breaths in anticipation. They called over the first dog and opened the bandana. It was a black and white zebra bow. (We just had to draw out the suspense a little!) They called over the second dog and slowly opened the bandana. Out popped a beautiful *pink* bow.

It's a girl! *Of course,* it's a girl! She has made herself such a presence already... so many people had absolutely no doubt it was a "she." Apparently, she is also already a gymnast, just as her mom and aunts were! We are over the moon with excitement. I have an entire "Barbie" attic, leftover from the girls' childhood days that is ready and waiting for this precious little girl!

A couple of days later, the talk of baby names naturally

came up. Erica and I had perused the entire baby name book on a road trip the week before and she had picked a few that appealed to her. Chuck wasn't crazy about any of them though, so they started again from scratch.

The three of us sat talking after the gender of the baby had been revealed. I asked if he had thought of any names. He laughed and said, "I kind of like Brooke, because if you take out one of the o's, it is what we will be once we are parents! *Broke!*" (He has researched the cost of raising a child but will spare no expense for this baby!) I knew that Erica wanted to use Alexis for a middle name in honor of Jilly. *Brooke Alexis*. Hmmm, I guess it has a nice ring to it. It's not a common name. I don't know anyone named Brooke. I don't think that Erica does either. The subject quickly changed, and we didn't bring it up again.

Later that night, I was chatting with a Facebook friend who lives in Florida. Her name is Ashley and she has followed Jilly's memory page for years. We have quite a bit in common; for instance, she also has a sister named Jillian, whose nickname is Jilly or Jilly Bean too. Both of Ashley's grandparents died 4 years apart *on Jillian's birthday.* Her other grandparents' anniversary is on the day of Jilly's Papa Larry's passing.

Ashley notices that the number 19 seems to pop up around her a lot. She works as a vet tech and every year, she sponsors a spay or neuter in our Jillian's memory. In fact, as we were talking that night, she mentioned that a dog named Emma was coming in the next day for a spay. Emma is our "grand-dog,"

Jilly's fur baby Staffordshire Terrier.

I decided to let her in on the story of Erica's miracle baby and subsequent gender reveal. We did not discuss anything else. About six hours after I had the discussion about baby names with Erica and Chuck, Ashley wrote this to me:

"Congrats on Erica being a mommy, Sierra and Jilly becoming aunts and ya'll becoming grandparents! Definitely so many Jilly winks! I'm beyond over the moon! She knows how to send those signs! And it's a girl! Since Jilly's middle name is Alexis, and my sister Jillian's middle name is Brooke, I think that Alexis Brooke or Brooke Alexis is the cutest name! Just saying!"

Oh my ... I had just had that conversation a few hours earlier and the only three people who knew about it were Erica, Chuck and me. I thought we were alone. I was wrong. Apparently, Jilly can (and does) eavesdrop on conversations. We all thought that was a great, "in your face" wink.

Three days later, Mark and I went to Babies R Us to browse the items that the happy new parents to be had put on their registry. We chose a stroller and pack-n-play crib and had them taken up to the register where a blonde, blue eyed young girl in a purple (remember, it's Jilly's favorite color) blouse waited on us. As I was digging in my purse, Mark nudged me and whispered in my ear, "Check out her name tag!"

Her name was *Brooke*. I didn't even ask what her middle name was. I was fighting the urge to whip out my camera and take a picture of her nametag, which probably would have made me look like a creepy stalker.

The next day, I treated myself to my weekly latte at the coffee shop. I know all the baristas there, so when I pulled up to the drive through window, I was surprised to hear a new young lady say, "This is Brooke, what can I get started for you today?"

Jilly must be talking God's ear off. I sometimes wonder if he ever says, "Jilly, could you please be quiet for just five minutes?"

Nope. Not a chance. By the way, they did not name the baby Brooke!

February 18, 2018
Jillian's 26th birthday
Two More Winks

*I*T DOESN'T SEEM POSSIBLE that you are celebrating your 7th birthday in Heaven. Where has the time gone? That is a good thing to ask, because it means we are seven years closer to you already; more importantly, we have survived the separation.

I use the term "separation" loosely, because, we are not separated by anything except time. You are still you and we are still the same. You don't miss out details in our lives and you let us know that by sending quarters and other signs.

This week in fact, you have sent two great winks for us. Oh, how you loved your animals, Marley the turtle and Emma, your puppy. They are both over 10-years-old now. Your big sister, Erica, is the guardian of your turtle. He had grown from a little baby quarter-sized turtle to one who is bigger than an outstretched hand. He needs lots of space, therefore, he requires a big aquarium. He is one spoiled turtle! He has a platform for basking in his heat lamp and he splashes around happily in the tank getting his exercise when he is bored. Imagine Erica's surprise when it was discovered in the middle of the night that, most of the water in Marley's tank was no longer there. *Uh-oh.* It had soaked through the floor, the walls, the baseboard and the ceiling into the basement, right into the small room where Erica kept all her off-season storage items.

In a panic, Erica ran downstairs to pull items out of that

room before the water damage got worse; she opened the door to the storage room...low and behold, a quarter lay on the floor at the entrance to the room. I don't think for a minute that you had anything to do with the leak in the aquarium (no cracks in the tank, by the way, so it's a mystery where the leak came from) but I do think that you were there with your sister, letting her know that you are not missing out on anything in her life...even if your, "Hello, I'm here!" was a bit messy.

Today, we bought your birthday cake. It's a bit of a struggle because we want to celebrate the time you spent with us and honor the day your soul chose our family and yet...it hurts that you aren't physically here to celebrate with us. You always had the most outrageous birthday parties. You preferred homemade birthday cakes but would settle with store bought if it had "whippy frosting." Sierra and I went to the store to pick out a cake and as a way to honor you, we also did our Jilly's birthday Random Act of Kindness. For a few years now, we go to our local bakery on or near your birthday and ask to pay for a random child's birthday cake; a cake that someone ordered and is waiting to be picked up. Today, the bakery staff (after a bit of confusion), finally caught on to what we were requesting and went to search for a child's birthday cake. While she was searching, Sierra and I jotted a note on a card that read, "Happy Birthday to your Angel from ours! Celebrating the love with a random act of kindness today. Pay it forward if you can! Many blessings!

She came back and said there was one cake ready for a little girl.

I asked the name and knew without any question that you were close by in spirit because of all the names in the world, it matched your beloved fur baby's ... Emma. What are the odds of that? It made me smile. We then walked over to buy your cake, searching for a small one that had "whippy" frosting. Right in front of my nose, I spied one ... in your favorite flavor *and* with green and purple frosting, your signature colors.

Thank you for staying close by, even when we can't see you ... we know you are there with us. We love you, we miss you, we'll see you again, our sweet Jilly. Happy Heavenly Birthday!

18

WHAT NOT TO SAY

Let us now address something that has happened to most of the bereaved families that I know. Now, I don't rant... or at least I try very hard not to, so forgive me if this sounds like a rant. It's not intended to be; I prefer to educate.

People say the darnedest things because sometimes, they just don't know any better. They open their mouths and have not bothered to run the words through their brain first. There are many things that you just shouldn't say to a bereaved person, (such as any sentence beginning with "At least...") Some of the worst, cruelest and most insensitive things you can say to anyone who is grieving are:

"When are you going to "get over" it and move on?"

"Aren't things back to normal yet?"

"I want the *old* you back."

Perhaps, with their limited language skills, what they are *really* trying to say is that they hope the pain fades and the memories get brighter with each passing day. People may mean well, but I can't fathom how anyone could think those kinds of statements will enhance a relationship, much less make the bereaved feel better. It feels like you are being slapped in the face when someone says this, and it makes you feel like striking back at them for saying it.

Trust me, no one wants things "back the way they were" more than a grieving family... *absolutely no one.*

We dream about it, but we will never be the same person we were before we lost our loved one. We don't wish this on anyone; in fact, we pray that other people, even our worst enemy, will never have to know or experience what we go through.

For those who have never lost a child, it's almost impossible for you to imagine what it's like. Do you really want to understand it? If so, I want to take you with me on a journey. I want you to get comfortable, as this will take a few minutes. I want you to imagine something while I paint a picture with my words.

Trigger alert for other bereaved parents, the descriptions are very raw and realistic and many on this path have stated that their experience was similar to my experience. Please skip the rest of this chapter if you need to. It's not my intention to disrupt your healing process with these memories.

For the rest of you, try to relax your body as completely as you can.

Imagine your child (or spouse, parent or sibling, if you don't have a child.) Close your eyes and see your child's face. Look into their bright eyes, study their smile. Imagine feeling their soft, warm skin and their body cozily wrapped in your arms for a hug. Can you hear the sound of their unique voice when you think of them? Remember what it feels like when they plant a kiss on your cheek. You are smiling, aren't you?

Try to remember the time they _____ (fill in the blank) that made you burst with happiness. Remember the day they were born and how much your life has changed. Remember a special conversation you shared.

Isn't it wonderful to have a child? Do you remember your life before they were born? What did you do with all your time, energy, resources and money? They are worth every minute you have spent with them, aren't they?

Take a deep breath and let's go one step further. Try to imagine that you have just received news that will change everything about your world.

Someone has just said these words to you.

Your child is dead.

Can you say those words out loud? Try it. Go ahead. Try it.

"_____ is dead."

Imagine them not moving, not laughing, not breathing, but cold, pale and lifeless. Can you even imagine that? It takes your breath away, doesn't it?

Someone needs to go identify the body at the hospital, the morgue or on the scene. It should be a parent or someone who knows your child. Perhaps you found the body yourself. There is no way to prepare you for this. It isn't in the natural order of things. Parents are *not supposed* to bury their children.

If your child died in a car accident (like Jillian), your first instinct might be to race to the scene, as I did. I was in the car alone looking for her when I got the news that is every parent's worst fear. God must have taken the wheel, because I don't remember driving the last 10 miles that separated us; I am sure I was a danger to other drivers, but I just knew I had to get there.

Once I arrived and pulled my car over to the side of the road, I firmly requested to see my daughter. The police officer on scene discouraged it, as most of them do.

"Why?" I asked.

"You don't want to see her that way," she replied.

Rather bluntly, I asked if she was in one piece, and the officer assured me that yes, she was. I inquired about the nature of Jillian's injuries and was told her neck and legs were broken. I firmly repeated my request to see her anyway. I begged the funeral director, (not our family friend, but a total stranger that the police had called to the scene), to please let me see her. He looked at me rather doubtfully and said very gently, "How about if I go look first and get her out of the car? I will put her on the gurney, and then perhaps you can see her."

I knew parents who had lost their children and were not allowed to see them after death. One mom had no idea what her daughter wore in the casket; she was kept from seeing her by people who thought she would never recover from the shock. Others had children who were not "viewable." I understand that police, fire and EMT's don't want another situation to deal with if a parent suddenly becomes unstable from the shock, but one way or the other, I was *going to see* my 19-year-old "baby." But let's go back to our imaginary journey.

Now, imagine what it might feel like to go into a state of shock upon hearing this news. Many people describe a deep physical ache in their chest and arms as they yearn to hold their child again. Unfortunately, that unique ache will last a very long time.

It feels as though someone has pulled your heart from your chest while it was still beating, stomped on it and then reinserted it back into an invisible wound in your chest, expecting it to function normally. It physically hurts when your heart is broken.

You might begin to shake violently. "*Noooo!*" your mind screams. This is a bad joke. It isn't real! They have the wrong person! It isn't *your* child, it can't be!

But sadly, it is. Your child's identity has been confirmed by sight, dental records, tattoos or jewelry. You beg God to take you instead.

Suddenly, you feel as though you have been dumped in a pool upside down. You can't find your way to the top. Your body goes into auto-pilot. It hurts to breathe; in fact, you must actually *think* about breathing.

Next, you must break this news to the rest of your family. You somehow figure out how to say those awful words (that you have already come to hate) repeatedly to relatives, loved ones and friends. They will remember that moment forever. You must listen as each one reacts to this news with screams, cries, anger or shock. You lose track of who knows and whom you still must tell. You keep telling the story repeatedly, but it just seems like a horrible dream... it can't be real! Each time you retell it, you tremble. After the tenth time or so, you become numb. Your body simply can't keep up with what your brain is trying to tell you.

Your child is dead. You go into a different stage of shock. You can't get warm, no matter how many blankets you wrap yourself in. Your hands feel like ice. You heart starts skipping beats. The tears, if and when they come, are so relentless that you fear you may never get them stopped again. You become dehydrated from crying so much... or perhaps you manage to hold it together for a while before the tears come. You lose all concept of time because it *stopped* the minute your child died.

I couldn't remember the most basic things... eating, drinking, bathing or dressing without someone prompting me to do so. Your body functions in a numb fog. Suddenly, people are in your house with food. Lots of food; it is the universal comfort offering. Everyone wants you to eat. Food tastes like cardboard and sometimes just comes back up if you can manage to get it down. Your body doesn't seem to absorb anything; everything goes right through it. (I still have trouble actually tasting food.) I remember people putting a cup of tea in my hand... I would look at them blankly, and stare at the cup, wondering what the heck I was supposed to do with it. They would have to continually remind me that I needed to put it to my lips and drink it.

Finally, when you can't stay on your feet one more minute, you collapse on the nearest bed, sofa, or even the floor. Sleep is the only respite you get (what little of it comes) and if you are lucky, it is not filled with the images of identifying your child at the hospital, morgue or on the scene, because that is a memory you will never forget.

Now, during this horrible pain, you must plan a funeral that you never dreamt of. First, you must pick a funeral home. (It's a heck of a time to have to shop for one.) Then, you must decide between burial and cremation... this is your *child* that must be put into a container and sealed up forever! You must pick a casket or urn... there is no, "I will think about that next week." It must be done as soon as possible.

You also must pick a date for the funeral. Do you have a large family? How quickly can they make the arrangements to leave their jobs and pets to travel? How long will it take loved ones and guests to arrive? Where will they stay? How long can they afford to stay? How will you feed them? How long can you afford to be off work?

You must pick flowers for the funeral home and clothes for your child to wear, find pictures to display or put on video, choose songs and ask someone to do a eulogy. How do you condense someone's life into a few minutes? If you are doing a burial, you must pick pallbearers to carry your child from the place of service to the hearse.

You must go to the cemetery and pick a *grave* for your child's body to be placed in. The very thought of your child's body being six-feet under the soil is more than you can bear. The thought of reducing their body to ashes for a cremation reduces *you* to yet another round of tears. You must plan all this through the most horrible pain and the most intense numbness you can imagine. It is like trying to eat when you are starving, just after the dentist has injected your entire mouth with multiple doses of numbing medicine and you can't feel your tongue or even speak coherently, let alone eat. Only this is unfathomably much, much worse. You can't feel your soul. Your body and soul are numb and yet in a catastrophic pain unlike anything you have ever experienced. Every nerve ending and emotion you have is hypersensitive. You have never felt deader and more alive at the same time. And yet, you must make important decisions. There simply is no other choice.

You select the clothing for your child . . . right down to socks, shoes, undergarments and favorite objects, like hats, wallets and stuffed animals. You must pick something that hides any injuries, embalming and autopsy incisions. You take the clothes to the funeral home and pick a remembrance pamphlet that will eventually bear your child's name and your favorite verse. You help write the obituary, trying to summarize your child's life in 300 words or less. Some funeral directors allow you to help give your child a final bath, do a manicure and makeup and help style their hair. Perhaps you can put on their socks and shoes.

Are you still upright? Take another deep breath, and let's keep going. Families are usually given at least an hour or two alone with their child before the public visitation or wake officially begins. Imagine seeing your child's body made up and dressed in the final outfit you picked for them to wear. They are lying in the casket on a silky pillow, their head slightly raised and hands folded. They may or may not even look like your child, depending on the skill of the funeral home and the circumstances of the death.

Jillian managed to pull off being the prettiest girl in the room at her funeral and for that I am beyond grateful. Her godmother spent hours fixing her up and hiding the injuries, especially her broken neck, with incredible skill. She explained that everyone's neck looks bigger when you view them lying down. (It's true.)

She lovingly prepared Jillian's body with tenderness and tears. She let us cut a lock of her long beautiful hair for those days that we would desperately need to have some physical part of her to touch. She also took thumbprints on ink and paper so that we could have "Thumbie" necklaces later. (I personally feel this should be mandatory at every funeral home. In your shock, you may not think of that until it's too late and many funeral directors are not aware of this service.)

You go back home and finish preparations while people are coming in and out of your home. You have no business driving in this state of mind.

The day of the visitation has now arrived. You get there a few minutes early and already people are making their way into the funeral home. The music you have picked plays softly in the background and a slideshow is flashing images of your child's life on a small screen. You are moving around in a thick fog. Perhaps you have frail parents or grandparents. You worry if they can handle this. Right now, you can't take care of them too.

Imagine greeting other parents and adults who came to offer their sympathy. You can see it in their eyes as they look over at your child's casket, "If that were *my* child, oh my God, I just couldn't bear it! I would crawl into a hole and die! How on earth are these parents and siblings still standing?"

They look at your child's pictures, mementos and flower arrangements, file past your child's casket and allow themselves just for a fraction of a second to imagine themselves in your shoes. They cry tears of sadness for your loss and perhaps, secretly thank God that it isn't them. (It's normal to think that!) They offer what words of comfort they can, but nothing can fix your brokenness. Some have no words…just a hug and tears. You understand, because you don't have any words either.

Many people, in their attempt to take away your pain, will say words that they think will comfort you. These offerings sometimes bring more comfort to *them* than *you*. Here are some examples.

"They are in a better place now."

(While I am sure that heaven is nice, the *best* place I feel they could be is with me!)

"At least you have more children."

(Which one of your children could you stand to give up? Will you give him or her to me right now (and often without warning) and allow me to take them to another part of the world where you won't see them for the rest of your life?)

"God wanted her/him more."

(God has enough people in heaven; couldn't He just leave my child here?")

"She/he wouldn't want you to be sad."

(Did you get an email from them or something that said that? How do you know?)

"Only the good die young."

(So, my grandma, who was 92 when she died, was *bad*?)

"It's a blessing that God took them now. They could have grown up to be a horrible person." (Seriously? I would take that chance!)

"God only gives you what you can handle." (Guess what, I can't handle this! He must think I can bench press a Buick or something!)

"Time will heal all wounds."

(Liar, liar, pants on fire! This wound is gaping! My soul is crushed! The wound will be fully healed when I am reunited with my child. This is not like an injury to my heart, it's an amputation! How do you heal that?)

"I don't know what you did to deserve this."

(I don't either! Did Mary deserve to watch her son Jesus die? What could we have done that was so bad that God needed to take our children from us? Was it because I disobeyed the speed limit by five m.p.h. last week? Or maybe it was something I did when I was young and stupid that made me deserve this?)

"You will see her/him again someday."

(Can someone please tell me exactly how long that will be because I desperately want and need that to be today!)

"Lean on God, He will carry you through." (God is holding me tight, but I have been questioning Him since this happened, and my relationship with Him is very tenuous right now. We have a massive amount of things to talk about later.)

"I know just how you feel. I lost my _____." (No, losing your grandparent, parent, dog, cat or pet fish is not the same. You expect to bury them. You never expect to bury your child! Only if you have lost a child as well, can you even begin to understand. Perhaps siblings and spouses come close, but I do not know. I have not lost either yet.)

The children (no matter what age) who come to see your child are stunned. For many, this is their first experience with grief. Death is suddenly very real, and they see that it *does* happen to young people. They hug you, sob and stand in little groups by the casket, not believing what their eyes are telling them. Some are filled with remorse and regret. Perhaps, the last thing they said to your child was not very kind. There are no take-backs; it is too late for apologies. You overhear snippets of their conversation. "I know just how they feel," one says to another. "I lost my dog last year." You thank God, they *don't* know just how you feel and try to comfort them as best as you can. They will never forget this event. It will likely help shape who they become.

Some reach out gently to touch your child's body and are shocked at the unfamiliar cold stiffness of the waxy, pale skin that used to be so warm and vibrant. They draw their hand back and bring it to their face in tears. It faintly smells of formaldehyde and cologne or perfume. They walk away and sob some more. Some get hysterical and friends gather round quickly with tissues to support them. Many are now in shock, like you are. Children aren't supposed to die. They repeatedly ask why? You don't have a good answer. You have been asking yourself that very question for days.

You hug more people than you have ever hugged in your life and have said, "Thank you for coming" for what seems like a million times. You are exhausted by the end of the day, but once again, sleep is elusive. Tomorrow will be the hardest day of your life. You dread the sunrise.

Are you still with me here? Take another deep breath . . . please. It gets harder.

Imagine the day of the funeral is now dawning; the world has continued to spin, while you can hardly move. Your feet still feel as though they are encased in concrete. You hurt all over, inside and outside, as though you have been beaten within an inch of your life. You haven't slept more than a few minutes at a time for days and that sleep is not at all restful. You keep hoping you will wake up from this nightmare.

You don't.

The sun had *the nerve* to rise this morning as it always does, but the sun stopped rising for you a few days ago. How dare it?!? You pick out an outfit to wear to the funeral that will haunt you from now on when you see it in your closet, because it will remind you of this day. It is probably something dark to match the black void in your life. You don't really care how you look at this point, because when you look in the mirror, you don't recognize the person looking back at you. Your clothes don't fit like they should. Maybe you have forgotten to eat much of anything for several days. You dread this day. It still just doesn't feel real.

You walk into the church or funeral home knowing that this day will be forever etched in your mind, just as the day that your child was born is etched in your mind and the last conversation you had with them will remain forever etched in your mind. Every time you walk into this building in the future, your mind will see your child's casket there.

You listen to the special songs that you somehow picked, which by the way, I hope weren't your favorites because you will cry for many years when you hear them again! You try to concentrate on the eulogy that someone spent hours writing and hear some beautiful tributes that others want so desperately to share with your child. You realize how much this child touched the world and then all too quickly, the funeral is over. It's time to say goodbye, knowing that the next time you see your child will be the day you die yourself... and only God knows how long that will be. It might be days, but it could be decades before you see their sweet face again. You pray that God makes that time as short and bearable as possible, because a part of you is dead already. It happened just a few days ago when your child died. However, because you are still walking and breathing, no one has called the coroner for you yet.

The people who came to the service file past the casket one last time and say goodbye. You give more hugs and thank them for coming.

It is suddenly time to close the lid on the casket. The jewelry is removed and given back to you. The pillow where your child's head lays in the casket is slowly cranked down to a flat position, tucking your child into the depths of this box. They have already gone somewhere that you can't follow, as badly as you want to; you must wait your turn. This is just their shell; the body that held the soul you have loved so deeply. The casket looks so deep and your child, no matter how old they are, suddenly looks so small and vulnerable.

As we closed the lid on Jilly's casket, I went into a panic... *Why didn't I bring her favorite blanket to cover her? She might get cold! Maybe I could just run home and get it? We could just drive the whole funeral procession by the house... would anyone mind?* There is no rationality in your brain at that point. The casket is carried carefully by the chosen pallbearers and is loaded into the hearse. No one this side of heaven will ever gaze on your child's beautiful face again.

If your child is buried, the hearse drives to the cemetery and the casket with your child's body is placed over a gaping hole strategically covered with artificial carpet. "*NO!*" your mind screams, "Oh God, please don't put my child in that deep dark hole! Please let me take her home with me, where she belongs." The preacher says a few words... and it is finished. You are led away from the casket and placed in the car. When you return later, the casket is gone; in its place, there is fresh dirt and the flowers you picked out from the funeral.

The funeral is over... you are beyond exhausted, physically, mentally and emotionally. You are touched with gratitude like you have never known before for all the people who came to share this day, this sorrow with you. You will remember bits and pieces forever, but unless someone videotaped the funeral or took pictures, you will eventually start forgetting some of the details. That will frighten you.

Remembering sucks. Forgetting is even more terrifying. It is a parent's instinct to protect their child... and when their child dies, it is a parent's instinct to protect the memory of their child.

We had pictures and videos taken. I had a friend unobtrusively and respectfully photograph every flower arrangement and group of people who came. (I don't remember half of them being there.) My brother taped her funeral. My husband can't watch it. I have a friend who has videos of her child's very short life after birth. All were taken in the hospital as her baby was attached to tubes and a ventilator. She has never watched it. She just can't... and that's okay.

I have only watched her funeral once or twice, but sometimes listening to her service comforts me because it was so moving and beautiful and unique. I have the pictures if I need to see them. It brings me some weird, unexplainable security knowing that I don't have to worry about forgetting the details. I didn't care then and still don't care what other people thought of that idea. I am glad we did it. I would encourage others to do it if they feel it will help them.

Soon... it is all over. The next phase of your life must begin. By now, it has been just three to seven days since your child died. It feels like forever already.

The company, friends and family all must go back to their own lives. You are left holding a shadow of your former self. You are forever and ever changed. There is no going back to the "old you" or the "way it was before." It is impossible!

Life must go on. You are expected to run a family, cook meals, drive and go back to work. Many employers are kind enough to give you a week or two off, but you may only get paid for three days. You must keep up the house, pay the bills and move forward, even though a part of you is stuck forever in the last hours or minutes of your child's life and the days that followed. You are a zombie. The lingering, merciful numbness that persists for a while will let your body catch up to the news your mind has given you.

Your child is dead. It still doesn't feel real. And believe it or not, you have just gone through what is probably the *least* difficult part of the journey.

Relationships will change. Your friends will change. They want to make it all better, but of course, they can't. They still love you dearly, but they just can't relate. (Thank God they can't relate!) *You* have changed. People you never knew before will enter your life and become very important to you. They are other bereaved parents; the ones who will let you talk about your child endlessly. They understand. You have a bond.

Spouses grieve differently, as they each had a unique relationship with the deceased child. Siblings lose not only their sister or brother, but for a time, sometimes a very long time, they also lose their parents. Each of the children also had a different relationship with their sibling. Regrets, memories, guilt, what ifs, whys, sadness, despondency, anger... it all happens. The family must be rebuilt. They each turn to whatever brings distraction from the pain. They try to run from it, but it is always there. For me that distraction was going back to work after 13 days. I would have gone crazy had I not been able to have some control somewhere in my world. It probably saved my life. I am sure it saved my sanity.

Realizing how truly fragile life is, parents become fanatical about the safety of their other children, loving them more than they ever thought possible and at the same time, terrified of just how much they *do* love them. They now understand the pain they will have to endure if the unthinkable happens and they lose another child. (I am now friends with five families who have lost two or more children and a few families that lost their only child.) They come to realize... they have *no* control over this. If it is meant to happen, it will happen anyway. No one, even the siblings in the family are afraid to die anymore. Your own death has lost its sting. Some family members may turn to self-destructive activities in an effort to feel pain... any pain, instead of the raw numbness.

Somehow, the days quickly turn into weeks and then months. One year passes and the family has endured (yes, *endured*) all the "firsts" like the family holidays, birthdays and eventually the anniversary of the death. It is starting to feel more real, but you still have a painful lingering numbness, alternating with grief quakes. There will be days that it will take every ounce of energy and willpower that you have just to get out of bed, and those days never come when it's convenient!

Your faith, if you have one, can take a beating or it will pull you through, sometimes both! If you don't have a faith in some higher power, some life after this one, I honestly don't know how you would get through it. I wouldn't have survived. The only thing that keeps me going is my belief that I will see my loved ones again in heaven.

Now for some strange reason, those who have not walked this path seem to think that this horrendous pain magically disappears after about 12 months! (Or sooner; some are expected to be back to normal in a few weeks!)

They couldn't be more wrong. It doesn't disappear, not by a long shot.

Everyone deals with grief differently, but often the second year hurts even worse than the first one did. Each day that takes me away from the last time I saw Jilly alive makes it more real that she isn't coming back to life as we know it. I fight panic when I think of it even now. The first year, I could almost pretend that she was away at college, even though I knew she was dead. I still expected her to walk through the door. Day by day, my mind and heart are starting to accept that it won't happen. The numbness is beginning to fade, and reality is setting in.

I know she doesn't need her body anymore, but it doesn't stop me from wanting to hold her again in the familiar vessel that housed her soul. On the other hand, each day that passes, brings me one day closer to seeing her again. I no longer fear death, but actually look forward to the day she takes my hand and leads me Home. I will stay here for as long as God plans for me to, but I smile when I think of holding my daughter in my arms once again, forever this time.

Let's go back to our journey. In addition to trying to process the death and shock of losing your child, you have insurance claims, outstanding bills or debts that your child may have incurred, canceling cell phone contracts, for instance, and other services your child may have used. One mom I know called the cell phone carrier and informed them of her son's death. Their response? "How do you plan to pay for the remaining contract months and penalty for early termination? He has a two-year contract that must be paid for!" (True story!)

You must figure out how to pay for the funeral and eventually select the headstone if you have one. By the way, most funeral directors expect payment up front because they *must* in order to stay in business. Funerals are expensive; they can easily run between $5,000 and $20,000. Headstones are several thousand more. Did you think ahead and have a life insurance policy on your child? How many people have that kind of money just sitting in the bank? You may have to take out a loan or refinance your house. You might also have to go through the wreckage of the vehicle as we did, pulling out personal items before the vehicle is totaled and the car is reduced to scrap metal. There may even be lawsuits or criminal charges and court dates. Insurance companies usually do not call you and tell you that you may be entitled to some form of financial compensation to help with expenses. You don't think of that yourself, and sometimes by the time someone mentions it, the statute of limitations has passed and it's too late.

There are thank you notes to write, dishes to return and follow up calls to make. Getting Jilly's taxes done for the last time undid me. It was so *final*. Mail continues to come for your child. You treasure each piece, even the junk mail and it kills you all over again at the same time. Family pictures are awkward. Someone is missing. How will you ever learn to smile again?

Are you overwhelmed yet?

What are you supposed to do with their room, their clothes and their most prized possessions? Keep them? Give them away? Put them in storage? Redo the room? Don't touch it? Every family must deal with it differently. It may be a while before you can look at their pictures and some families never can. Others sleep with their child's picture or urn. Hearing your child's voice on a video is painfully bittersweet. You don't ever want to forget, but sometimes can't bear to listen to it either. There are no new memories to record, no new pictures with your child. They remain forever the age they were when they died.

Are you still there? Are you in tears yet just imagining it?

Now, imagine that after you have experienced what is known by the experts across the board as the worst, most difficult loss anyone can have, some well-meaning individual has decided that you have had *enough time to mourn*. You need to "get over it" and move on. It might be your boss, your friend or even a family member. "Get over it, already!" they say. "It's time to let them go and get back to normal," they say. As you stare at them with your mouth agape, you wonder *how*? How do I do that? How do I let go of a part of myself and still survive? How do I just turn off that part of my heart and expect it to still beat? It's like having your leg cut off and pretending that it isn't. You try to give them the benefit of a doubt . . . how could they possibly know what this journey is like unless they have lost a child?

You eventually *do* learn how to navigate this new life, very slowly. It's a one step forward, five steps back, day by day thing as you learn to survive this loss, but it is at your own pace, which is often agonizingly slow. It can't be measured in days, weeks, months or years. It is often measured only in seconds and minutes. You truly don't know how strong you are until you have to be . . . .and now, you have to be.

You are a completely different person by now. It will bring out your best and your worst traits, depending on where you focus your energy. Some days, it is all you can do to just function somewhat "normally". You might feel completely alone in a crowded room. If you acknowledge "signs" from your deceased child, you risk being labeled as crazy.

The first time you laugh, you might feel guilty. Is it okay to laugh when your child is dead? (The answer is yes, but it still shocks you when it happens!)

You will always feel vulnerable. You have experienced the greatest loss there is. Will you ever "get over it?" No. Never.

Did you get over your child being born? Of course not! It changed your identity.

Which of your children could you go the rest of your life

without seeing and "get over it?" If you have one, I will happily trade you so that I can have mine back!

You will start to have days that are filled with fewer tears and memories that bring a smile, but those days take their sweet time in coming. Eventually, you learn to put on the mask and say that you are fine when people ask, so that they don't start avoiding you. You can pick another bereaved parent out of a crowd by the haunted look in their eyes. It is the same look the person in the mirror gives you every morning. With a lot of practice, you eventually learn to cover the sadness. You move forward an inch at a time, ferociously holding onto the memories of who your child was during their life or wondering who they would be today.

The tears eventually slow down and then only come with the triggers...a song, a scent, a favorite food or an important day or event. We have been given a life sentence; the experience is permanent. The timeline of our lives is now measured before and after "that day."

Now that you have read through this journal of sorts, maybe you can begin to understand the grieving parent's journey a little better.

I hope that when you see a bereaved parent, you offer a simple touch, a hug, an, "I am thinking of you," or sometimes, share a memory of their loved one. You aren't "reminding" us of our children...we will think about them every day for the rest of our lives, no matter how much time passes. The tears we might shed are ones of gratitude that you cared enough to mention our child's name. (Sweet music to our ears!) Mostly, remembering us in your prayers keeps us going. Somewhere, I believe God takes all those prayers and covers us with the warm, protective blanket of coping as we crawl, then stumble and finally learn to walk this rocky road.

After you pray for us, please go hug and kiss your children. Tell them you love them. Always, even when they are in the throes of temper tantrum toddlerhood, or hormonal, know-it-all teenagers. Every chance you have, *tell them*. Please tell them! You are blessed to have that chance.

Pretend that it is the last thing you will say to them or the last thing they will ever hear. It very well might be.

My last words to Jillian and hers to me were, "I love you." Thank God, those were our last words to each other!

You never know; you might be the next one to walk in our shoes...and if the unthinkable happens and you must join us in the club no one wants to belong to, we will pull you into the safety net of our hearts and take your hand as we all walk each other Home, where our children wait for us with open arms. We will understand you when you don't even understand yourself.

You will never *ever* hear another bereaved parent tell you that you need to *get over it* and move on.

We know better.

LOUISE CRIST

♥ ♥ ♥

19

IN MEMORIAM

What we have once enjoyed deeply we can never lose. All that we love deeply becomes a part of us. -Helen Keller

Most people have a date on the calendar that they can look at and say, "I remember what I was doing on that day in the year ___." It is a significant date for one reason or another and a memory is carved into their hearts, minds and souls. September 11th is one example. For years to come, people will be able to say, "I remember that day, I was _____ when I heard the news." I have several of those significant days. My children's birthdays, my wedding anniversary...and this day, April 3rd.

Sue Ellen Machemer
July 22, 1963—April 3, 1980

*I*n 1980, April 3 fell on a Thursday. It is an anniversary of a significant emotional event in my life; a day I will never forget.

It was the day before Good Friday, ushering in Easter weekend and a much-anticipated week off school for Spring Break. It was overcast in the morning and almost, but not quite warm. It rained before the sun set on the horizon that night. I was a senior in high school, 18 years young and very naive. I did not know when I woke up that morning that before the day was over, my life would change forever. God was preparing me for another event which would take place 31 years in my future.

The school day was our usual routine. I talked and laughed with friends about Spring Break and Easter plans. At lunch, I saw my friend Sue across the road from the high school, walking away from her car. Odd, since I hadn't seen her in typing class 3rd hour. I waved from the door; she waved back, her sunny smile in place as usual. Sue was in Pom-Poms, Christian Athletes, Flag Corps Co-Captain (I think it's called Color Guard now) and she shined in Young American Dances, where she was way more talented and graceful than I could ever hope to be. She was slim and tall for age 16, had wavy, sometimes unruly dark hair, expressive brown eyes and sun-kissed freckles that dotted her nose and cheeks. She also had a shy smile that could light up a room when she chose to bless you with it. Beginning to come out of her shell and find her place as a leader in her sophomore class, she was blossoming into the trailblazing young woman her family knew their only daughter would someday become. I smiled as I watched her walk down the road and then went to band class.

The school day ended with smiles and shouts of, "See you later!" as we all looked forward to a much-needed spring break. I hadn't been home from school very long when Sue's mom, Ellen, called. She asked me if I had seen Sue, who hadn't come home from school yet as expected. I figured that since I saw her at lunch and she wasn't in school, she had skipped school and I wasn't about to get her in trouble. I told her mom, "Nope, I haven't seen her!" Her mom thanked me and asked me to call her if I heard from her. I remember feeling sorry for Sue when her mom got a hold of her eventually . . . she would probably be grounded until she was 21!

As it turns out, while her mom was busy calling Sue's friends trying to track her down that Thursday afternoon, two young teenage boys were out exploring an abandoned railroad bed next to a shallow creek. They were walking along the path when they made a horrifying discovery: Sue's body face-down in a ditch. She had run out of gas near the school and another classmate had helped her put gas in from the can she had borrowed from the service station down the road from the school. (That's why I had seen her walking away from her car earlier.) The classmate was 17 and kind of cute; he came from a nice successful family. He had talked Sue into giving him a ride home and convinced her to drive down an abandoned railroad path, telling her it was a shortcut to his house. There, her life was taken by a boy that most of us would have let in our car without a second thought.

Easter Sunday was Sue's visitation at the funeral home. Her parents greeted hundreds of kids by wishing them a Happy Easter. I made my way to the casket, where my friend's pale, still body lay dressed in a mint green skirt and vest with a white blouse; probably her Easter outfit.

"Happy Easter?" I thought. "How can this Easter be happy?" We were frightened. We were angry. We felt so vulnerable, so robbed of our innocence that things like *this* could happen to good people. Six hundred people attended Sue's funeral the next day. She was the Flag Corps co-captain, so we made a cordon into the church. Her parents and three brothers walked under the arch created by our flags as we stood proudly in our uniforms, saluting our fallen comrade, their daughter, their sister, our irreplaceable friend. The rain had just started to drizzle, and it appeared Heaven was weeping with us. Her oldest brother Melvin, a gifted musician, played Sue's favorite cantata on the piano while her other brothers, David and Rob, sat quietly in the front row with their parents, Mel and Ellen. They all wore the look of, "I can't believe this is real" painted on their shocked faces.

The pastor read the poem, *To all Parents* by Edgar Guest.

"I'll lend you for a little while, a child of Mine," He said.
"For you to love the while she lives and mourn for when she's dead.
It may be six or seven years, or twenty-two or three,
But will you, till I call her back, take care of her for Me?
She'll bring her charms to gladden you, but shall her stay be brief,
You'll have her lovely memories, as solace for your grief."

"I cannot promise she will stay, since all from earth return,
But there are lessons taught down there I want this child to learn.
I've looked the wide world over in My search for teachers true
And from the throngs that crowd life's lanes I have selected you.
Now will you give her all your love, nor think the labor vain,
Nor hate Me when I come to call her back again?"

I fancied that I heard them say: "Dear Lord, Thy will be done!
For all the joy Thy child shall bring, the risk of grief we'll run.
We'll shelter her with tenderness; we'll love her while we may,
And for happiness we've known forever grateful stay.
But should the angels call for her much sooner than we'd planned,
We'll brave the bitter grief that comes and try to understand."

After the poem, he said something that rocked my world. He told those 600 mourners, most of us young kids, that we should "pray for the one who did this, because Jesus came to this world for that person as much as He did for Sue, for you and for me." I let that sink in. Wow.

Watching her family at that service, I marveled at their faith. It was unshakable. They seemed comforted by their beliefs. I could not even *fathom* how her parents were so full of grace, of love, of mercy and forgiveness when their only daughter had just been murdered at the tender age of 16. She had barely started to date. I don't think she had even been to her first prom yet.

I wanted the peace they possessed. I wanted that faith. I made up my mind in that moment, that if, God forbid, I was ever in a similar situation, I would try my hardest to be the same positive influence for others that Sue's family shared with the hundreds of kids in the church that morning. I searched their faces for hate and found none. Only sadness for Sue, a faith in their God and love for the outpouring of people and support they were receiving from the community. Even after the killer was caught, they did not hate. They visited him in prison, where he was given a life sentence without parole at 17-years-old; they grieved with his parents, whom they have become good friends with over the years.

Each family had lost a child; Sue to Heaven, where they knew she was safe; her killer to prison, where his parents fear for his safety daily. He received their full forgiveness. As he matured into adult-hood they encouraged him to turn his life around, and by all reports, he is a model prisoner. He deeply regrets his youthful actions. Both families survived; they grew in ways they couldn't have imagined and helped other grieving parents move forward.

God was preparing me even then, in the innocence of my youth, for the day when I would also sit in the front pew of a church, at the head of Jillian's casket. I would listen to the same words that had changed my life in 1980. One of her favorite teachers recited the same poem that had brought me comfort when Sue died. Would I take care of her until He called her back again?" Would I? *Oh, yes!* In a heartbeat, I would!

I had made that promise to God to care for her the night Jilly was born. She was *His* girl before He lent her to me. The week Jilly went back to Him, I was given a peace beyond my own human understanding and now understood the forgiveness and mercy Sue's parents had shown 31 years earlier. The forgiveness I felt toward the driver left me free to love . . . and love, I did.

Just like Sue, Jilly's life had never been more powerful than it was in that one hour, as she reached hundreds of people in the church that morning through her physical death. I had resolved to be a point of God's light for Sue the day of her funeral . . . to make the world a better place because she was a part of it and by extension, a part of all of us. Many of Sue's friends made that same silent pledge. Would Jilly's friends do the same for her? So far, the answer is yes. I am seeing this in countless ways of generosity and love for others among her friends.

I thank God for the example that Sue's family gave us in

the face of an unfathomable loss on that rainy April day so long ago. I had hoped that no one who sat in the church that day or at the visitation for Jilly, would ever have to bury a child. Sadly, at least four of us at Sue's funeral have buried children already. However, if they must walk that difficult road, I hope they will remember the example that Sue's family set for me...and hopefully that *our* family set for those behind us on this path.

It is one way that Sue lives on, just as Jilly does, in our hearts, minds and souls. I still dream of Sue 31 years later; I miss her, but I can smile instead of cry at the memories. I am positive we will meet again.

I also take comfort knowing that, although they hadn't met each other on Earth, Sue knows my daughter Jilly in Heaven and they are joyously dancing their way among the stars together in a beautiful display of love while they wait for the rest of us to arrive back Home.

Hugs and kisses my beautiful, dancing souls of Light.

Rick Laney
July 2, 1960—June 13, 2014

*M*Y HIGH SCHOOL SWEETHEART died last weekend. Rick and I had a close friendship for several years as teenagers but had gone our separate ways after college. Each of us found our spouses, got married and started our own families. Although I am sure we crossed each other's minds many times, we had only talked briefly once in the last 30 years. When we did, it was as if we had just spoken last week, instead of decades ago. We picked right back up where we left off with the same ease and laughter that we once shared. Our cheeks almost hurt from smiling so hard at the memories we shared.

Sometimes, relationships are like that...you go a long, long time without any contact, but that doesn't seem to matter when you finally meet again. You just *know* that the relationship will stand the test of time. Although I shed tears at the loss of seeing his familiar physical body, I have no doubt that I *will* see him in another form again someday and we will get to talk for an eternity if we want to. It is the same way with Jillian, my dad and all the others I love who have gone Home before me. Our love will be there just as easily when we meet again as it was the last time we were together here on earth.

One of Jilly's friends posted something very profound. "Every year we unknowingly pass the anniversary of our future death." What if we knew ahead when that day on the calendar approached? Or, what if we knew the year but not the exact day or vice versa? Would it change the way we live? How would you spend tomorrow if you knew it was your last day? Most of us would not sit around saying, "Oh goodie! *Bring it on*! I am just going to sit here in my chair, or just lie in my bed and wait for death to come and get me!"

Think about it. We might get busy telling people who are important to us how much we love them and tying up loose ends so that our loved ones didn't have to after we're gone. Those 24 hours would not be long enough. We would probably spend it doing something that made us happy. But we don't live our lives that way ... because we think that tomorrow will always come.

For most, it does. For a few, it doesn't.

I *know* I will see them again, and it will be forever and ever ... but in my human-ness I also want "forever" to be right now. I tend to focus on what I don't "have" instead of what I *do* have. In reality, I already have all that I need, but I just don't have it all at the same time or in the same way. There is a good reason for that! God is pretty smart; His plan is much better than mine. We don't eat breakfast, lunch and dinner all at the same time, do we? Of course not, we need time to process things. We can only hold so much!

I thought about it ... what if Jilly (or my other loved ones) came back today? I would be so happy and excited to see her that I would want to hold her and never let her go, not even for an instant. I wouldn't be able to bear being apart from her again, because having her out of my sight is often overwhelming. I doubt seriously that I would even be able to interact with those around me. I wouldn't get anything done, because you can't do anything else while you are hugging someone! I most certainly wouldn't go to work, go shopping or do anything that would allow either one of us any kind of freedom to come and go. My house would be in shambles, my cupboards empty and I would start to smell funky after a few days.

I wouldn't be able to take my eyes off her. I would not be able to focus on much of anything except her... including *living* the life and serving whatever special purpose that God has planned for me. I would miss a lot of opportunities to grow. I wouldn't be living, only existing from day to day; just waiting for that awful time that she would be separated from me again. I would be living in constant fear... instead of living my life with the absolute faith that we will have *all the time we need and want* in eternity "later" on. "Later" could be as early as tomorrow or it could be 50 years from now in human terms... but in the scheme of eternity, it is only an instant.

We will have all the time we need to catch up... just like catching up with my friend after many years. I will be able to pick right back up where Jilly and I left off when we see each other again. The next time, there will be no need to worry about letting her out of my sight. She will be right there, as close as my thoughts and in my embrace whenever I need her to be... forever and ever.

In the meantime, I think that I might have some living I need to do...and lots of opportunities for growth and development. Maybe some of you will join me and grow with me on this journey. Our loved ones on the other side will wait patiently for us. Each year, we unknowingly pass the anniversary of our future death. Someday, we will not pass it. We will land smack dab on it. I want to try to do that gracefully. Food for thought.

H. Dean Dixon
December 23, 1944—November 12, 2016

Known by most as Dean, but also called Bumpa Dean, Deanie or even Harold, if you really wanted to get his attention. There are also a few names I can't repeat in polite company but were always spoken with affection.

Where do I begin to tell you about this man's life? How do I sum up in just a few minutes all that he was to so many people and all the adventures he packed into his 71 years?

Dean got off to a rough start. He was born to a young mother (she was 14 when she gave birth to him) who tried her best to provide for him and just couldn't do it with the limited resources she had. Her own mother was still having babies and couldn't be of much help either. Dean caught the eye and won the heart of two older women who ran the dry cleaners in his town and spent quite a bit of time with them. His mother loved him enough to let these ladies adopt him and give him a better life than she was able to give him. He was always grateful to her for that. His adoptive moms raised him to adulthood with good values and morals. He called himself an alley rat... and one of the other "rats" he hung out with, went on to become a lieutenant governor of Arkansas!

Dean graduated from Newport High School in Arkansas in 1962 and was voted the cutest boy in his class. By all accounts, he was a popular guy. He joined the Air Force and served four years, mostly in England. He also discovered false courage in the bottom of a bottle during those years. He eventually looked in the mirror and faced the demons that would have killed him had he stayed on that path of self-destruction. Most of his extended family had moved to Michigan by then, so after his discharge from the Air Force, he moved back to Michigan to ponder his future. About a year after he turned his life over to a Higher Power and put his faith in God, he met my mom.

Now whoever said God doesn't have a sense of humor and purpose, didn't know Dean very well. I didn't meet Dean until he was 29 years old. Mom met him after she and my dad divorced, and he fell head over heels in love with her from the beginning. She started bringing him around to be an older male role model for my brothers. (At least that's what she said at the time.) He was a nice guy and he definitely softened mom up a bit, convincing her to give us a few new freedoms we had not previously had. He had become a steady presence in our lives for about 18 months... and in the middle of an argument about him bossing me around about some small thing (which, in my 13-year old mind was probably something super important), I discovered something that would change my world.

"You can't tell me what to do!" I yelled. "It's not like you're *my dad* or something!"

He barely skipped a beat before yelling back, "Actually, I *am*! Your mom and I eloped a while back! That makes me your stepdad and you have to mind me!"

I was hurt; not because she had married him, but because no one asked me to be the flower girl. It turned out to be one of the best decisions Mom would ever make. Whatever possessed him to take on a 42-year old divorcee with five children ranging from nine to 20 years old, I will never understand... but what a lucky day that was for us, the day he said *yes* to our family.

He grew up right along with us children as we all transitioned from moody adolescents to college students, then brides and grooms, parents and some of us even becoming grandparents. I remember telling him in the beginning that he would *never* be my real dad. I had a dad; I didn't need another one. Boy, was I wrong! He became so much more than a father to me. When my beloved biological dad passed away, Dean announced that the "father of his children" had died. He claimed us, warts and all and made us *his* children. He could have thrown in the towel and I am sure that at times, we tempted him to do that, but he never walked away from us.

Each of us had our own unique relationship with him. I can't tell you what that was like for my siblings; I can only tell you what my own experience with Dean was.

When an airline strike prevented my biological father from being there, this wonderful, loving man beamed with pride as he walked me down the aisle on my wedding day. He fawned over me like a mother hen when I became pregnant with his grandchildren. You could have pinned a medal to his chest the day he stood outside the delivery room listening as I gave birth to Erica and he officially became "Bumpa Dean." Since he had never witnessed the miracle of birth in person, I invited him to watch Jillian and Sierra's births three and six years later. He videotaped that for us, which was another memorable "Dean moment."

Dean loved the University of Arkansas sports, all of them. The Arkansas basketball game was on TV during Jillian's birth. He was so torn. Dean really wanted to watch the birth, so he dutifully put his eye to the camcorder lens and tried to focus on the task at hand. There I am on the delivery table pushing and Arkansas scores. It was a tight game. In the video, Dean is taping me, then the TV, then me, then the TV. It makes me dizzy watching it. Afterward, he was walking around the room with the camcorder, giving a running commentary, "Here's the new mama," he says, as he walks around the foot of my bed while they are stitching me up, "And here's the baby's head. Oops, that's not the baby's head! The baby is over here across the room!"

For Sierra's birth, we made him stay planted in a closet by my head, with the camcorder firmly on a tripod. That birth video was *not* rated R. As a grandpa, his love and devotion for our family grew by leaps and bounds. My girls had him wrapped around their cute little pinkies. In all his Bumpa Dean years, he only spanked a child once. Erica had bit him for some reason as a toddler. He tapped her little bottom, (padded by two cloth diapers mind you, so it couldn't have really hurt her) and she looked at him in shock. Tears welled up in her little eyes as she stuck her quivering bottom lip out and said, "Thanks a lot Bumpa Dean. I love you and you smacked my butt!"

A dollhouse was delivered to our living room the next day. I told him that he really couldn't afford to spank her again. He never did. He was such a softie when it came to his grandchildren. He was so proud of them and wanted to do all he could to help them succeed.

Having been born and raised there, Dean was an avid Arkansas Razorback fan. He could make the best "Pig Sooie" noises when his team won! He had season tickets to the basketball games and never missed a Razorback football game, always wearing his favorite T-shirt or jersey for good luck. I think they may have lost the day he died because he wasn't there to yell at the TV. He loved golf, both playing the game and even working the P.G.A. events when he got a chance.

He was the happiest when he was outside enjoying the sunshine... especially if that involved going to an auction. He loved finding great deals. Mom's cousin shared this story about Dean's adventure of getting the best deal at an auction once.

The cousins, named Marion and Joanie, had gone to an auction with mom and Dean looking for bargains. Mom found a doll that she just had to have, but lacked the confidence to bid on it, so she asked Dean to do the bidding for her. Dean positioned himself away from Mom as the doll came up for bidding. He thought he had the deal all sewn up for a bargain price of $20. Suddenly, someone started bidding against him from across the room. The price quickly started climbing higher and higher. It was getting too steep for Dean, but he knew how much my mom wanted that doll. Mom's cousin could see both sides of the room, but Dean couldn't. He craned his neck to see who wanted this doll so badly, and there...across the room, he spied the competitor who was driving up the price of this darn doll.

It was my mom! *"Vera! I've got this!"*

They got the doll, but it cost him $45. Those cousins said, "Believe me, we will remember our dear friend and buddy Dean with the fun-loving way that one can only experience by knowing him." He loved bossing...that was his thing. He wisely found a way to do what he loved and find a way to get paid for it.

After graduating with honors from Western Michigan University, he went to work for the State of Michigan in correctional facilities. There he could boss people around all day long and get away with it. The prisoners didn't have any choice but to obey. He told it like it was, no-holds-barred and they respected and loved him for it. He was the same way with other officers. He got away with saying things to people that you can't begin to imagine, because he did it with humor and sincerity.

After he retired in 2000, Dean got a hankering to move back to Arkansas with visions of attending all the Razorback games and schmoozing with Sam Walton's (of Walmart fame) family. Moving was his other "thing." My mom and dad had moved 29 times in their marriage of 20 years. Mom vowed she was done with moving... she wasn't going to move *ever* again. However, Dean *was just getting started.* He moved Vera another seven or eight times after they got married. They were up in their "Michigan summer home" when Mom had a massive stroke in June of last year. With the intense care she would now require, Dean had to move her again... over to the local nursing home, Maple Lawn. It was so hard for him to be apart from the love of his life.

Now Dean had a mindset, even without having any medical training, that Maple Lawn was simply unable to run without him there to tell them how to do their job, although he turned green with anything involving even the simplest of medical procedures. He had high standards for mom's care and more than one nurse's aide was terrified of disappointing him. He was consistent, charming when he wanted to be, harsh only when that didn't work. But he really appreciated how much they cared for her there.

When he developed pneumonia in September and had to

wait three weeks to see her in person, it broke his heart. He was utterly devoted to mom until the very last day of his life. He spent the last three months trying to make it easier for us children should something happen to him first. They were wed for 41 years. Wow. Since he was 12 years younger and playing 18 holes of golf just a few months earlier, I never imagined that *she* would outlive *him!*

On a Saturday afternoon in 2016, I went to his house to watch a Razorback game with him. He wasn't answering his phone, so I let myself in. I followed the oxygen tubing down the hall into his bedroom and was shocked and devastated to find that he had peacefully gone Home in his sleep.

I can't even begin to express how much our family will miss him. He was everything I could have wished for, not just in a stepdad, but in the *real* dad he became over the years. For those of you who are not familiar with the *Velveteen Rabbit* children's story, it explains how one becomes real.

> "What is Real?" asked the Rabbit one day, while they were lying side by side near the nursery fender, before Nana came to tidy the room. "Does it mean having things that buzz inside you and a stick-out handle?"
>
> "Real isn't how you are made," said the Skin Horse. "It's a thing that happens to you. When a child loves you for a long, long time, REALLY loves you, then you become Real."

"Does it hurt?" asked the Rabbit.

"Sometimes," said the Skin Horse, for he was always truthful. "When you are Real you don't mind being hurt."

"Does it happen all at once, like being wound up," he asked, "or bit by bit?"

"It doesn't happen all at once," said the Skin Horse. "You become. It takes a long time. That's why it doesn't happen often to people who break easily, or have sharp edges, or who have to be carefully kept. Generally, by the time you are Real, most of your hair has been loved off and your eyes drop out and you get loose in the joints and very shabby. But these things don't matter at all, because once you are Real you can't be ugly, except to people who don't understand."

Our Dean became a *real* dad. And he was more beautiful to me with each passing year. The love we shared will have to last until the day that it is our turn to go Home to God and back to those who are still so very *real* in our hearts.

Clifford H. (Cliffie) Bowers
July 4, 1989 – December 23, 2017

*T*oday, December 29th, was a sad day as I attended the funeral of Jilly's best friend Sonya's brother. Cliffie was a 28-year-old, funny, helpful larger than life soul whose presence on this earth influenced hundreds, if not thousands of lives. His passing brought up many emotions for me, especially since he died the same way Jilly did, also right before a major family holiday.

The first wave of emotion was shock and sorrow, both for his beloved sister, Sonya and his awesome parents, Linda and Big Cliff. To make things worse (if there can be such a thing when it comes to losing a child), his maternal grandmother died the day after Cliffie, leaving his mom to plan two funerals during the Christmas holiday. They had also said goodbye to Big Cliff's mom earlier that summer. How much can one family take? Did I have the right to complain about some mundane thing like not being able to find matching socks this morning? Geesh, the things we gripe about; they are *not important* in the greater scheme of things.

The second emotion was helplessness. Reliving Jilly's death and the aftermath of it, Mark and I recounted all the things that his parents might be feeling right now and what would likely come later. Everyone handles grief in their own way; Mark curled up in a fetal position on the floor several times in those early days and he wondered if Cliffie's dad might react the same way. Mom might fall apart, or she might go into organizational mode, trying to make some sense of what was happening. A tragedy like this can make you run to your "fallback" mode of operation. Cliffie's sister lived in another city a couple hours away. Delivering the news to the sibling of the one that passed is excruciating. It's even worse over the phone, believe me. They were able to tell Sonya in person, thank God. I remember calling her mom, Linda, the morning Jilly died and begging her to get to Sonya at college to deliver the news herself. You have to act pretty fast now-a-days, or you will read about it on Facebook before you have finished telling everyone in the family. (Don't get me started on that social ineptitude! Always let the family post first! If you really need to reach them, send a private message.)

Any season of the year is heartbreaking when you lose a child, but I personally think that family centered holidays, such as Thanksgiving and Christmas would seem to be particularly bad timing. Plans have been made, presents may have already been bought, dinner plans are already in progress. The holiday is about togetherness and never has the absence of one person been so loud and so deafeningly quiet.

Charles Dickens wrote, "And can it be that in a world so full and busy, the loss of one creature makes a void so wide and deep that nothing but the width and depth of eternity can fill up?"

Most of Cliffie's family is from our area and I knew that

their family gatherings are large and loud and full of love. To keep the family tradition or not? Is it something you want and need to do? They were all in shock at this point, appearing on the outside to be functioning, while on the inside they might feel like they died too.

The third emotion was compassion. Those first few days, we instinctively knew what would be asked of them, because death doesn't happen conveniently, on days that you really don't have anything going on and you can afford to spare the rest of your life for this task. Cliffie died on a Saturday morning, the day before Christmas Eve. There would be arrangements to make immediately, such as choosing a funeral home, then selecting a funeral date. They would have to find a church that would accommodate 500 people and write the obituary. I dare you, try to sum up the life of someone you love in 300 words or less. Those of us in "The Club No One Wants to Join" stood by for support, wishing we could wake them up from this nightmare and realizing all we can do is offer hugs, prayers and food like everyone else.

We remarked again and again how important support is. It's as if people are bringing back a piece of your shattered heart. The tears flow and the hugs and prayers mend quietly and slowly. We cry with each new family that joins. We are the witnesses to our children's lives when they can no longer speak for themselves.

By Tuesday, they would probably go to the funeral home and select the items needed for the funeral. They would have chosen something to bury him in, which would mean spending time at his house, going through a room full of his scent and reminders of his life. They would pick the pallbearers, if they hadn't already. Many people would want to speak at the funeral, but they would have to select only a few, there were so many Cliffie stories! Picking the pictures for the slideshow would be another daunting task. Each photo brings back a memory.

The visitation would be at his mom's church from 4:00-8:00 p.m. We arrived at 5:00 and didn't get through the line to see Linda and Big Cliff for a couple of hours. We recognized so many of the "kids" there from Jillian's funeral, a few with their own children now in tow. Jilly is forever 19, so it always amazes me that her friends did not stay that age, as silly as that sounds. We reached the family and the first thing that we recognized was that their eyes have all changed. The sparkle is simply gone, it left with Cliffie. It will come back but will never be as bright as it once was.

Sonya was a pallbearer for Jilly's funeral (All girls! Woohoo!) and it was her mom, Linda and her friend Marcy, that orchestrated Jillian's balloon launch at her funeral, to which I am forever indebted. I knew they had been at Jilly's funeral, so they knew the difference between a somber cold funeral and a healing celebration of life. Jilly had the latter. It was perfect for her ... we cried, we laughed, we clapped and rose our voices together in unison for her. Several people told us, "When I go, I want a funeral just like that!"

Cliffie's funeral *was just like that.* (It ended with the song that made people giggle, "Jeremiah Was a Bullfrog," if that gives you any clue.) I should backtrack here a minute and tell you that almost immediately after receiving word about Cliffie, I sat down and had a few words with Jilly. "Honey, please find Cliffie right away and be his tour guide in Heaven. Let me know that you have him by sending me an unmistakable sign."

The funeral was packed, with another 100 people still standing, as I knew it would be. It was such a wonderful outpouring of love for this family. They had three eulogies and several songs by friends and cousins who were brave enough through their grief, to get up in front of a large crowd to speak and sing. Talk about love.

Midway through the service, with Jilly heavily on my mind, I watched as two of his friends went to the front with a guitar and a cornet (trumpet). They sat down and began to play "Freebird" by Lynyrd Skynyrd, Jilly's signature song. We played that song at the end of her funeral service. I've never heard it played on guitar and a trumpet though; it was achingly beautiful.

Today that memory came back to me. It may be purely coincidental, or it may be that Cliffie's family remembered us playing "Freebird" for Jilly, but I personally took it as Jilly's way of telling me that she had found Cliffie and all was well on the other side. Some close friends who had also lost a child heard that song on the way to the visitation last night, followed by Elton John's, "Funeral for a Friend." Both of our "angel girls" knew

Cliffie and adored him. How could you not? I have never heard anyone say a bad thing about him. He was a high school athlete, placing 2nd in state in Track and Field, Homecoming court, an all-around good guy who would make it a point to come all the way across the room to acknowledge you with a friendly greeting. He was also a prankster from what I gather, and he loved pizza, so I wondered how mischievous Jilly and Cliffie could be as a team on the other side! She would be with Sonya's big brother on that side, and Sonya would continue to be here for Erica and Sierra as they all learned the sibling grief path together.

We will move forward into a New Year, 2018...leaping into an unknown. For some, new lives and new relationships will be created. Others are entering their final year on this side and they don't even know it. It's yet another test of faith.

For many of us in "the club," it's one more year that we leave our child in the past. As the years go by, it becomes more unbelievable that so much time has passed since the last time we saw our child on this side. We never get over it...it is just *different*. Our group never hesitates to say their child's name. We can't make new memories with them, but it's up to us to become the keepers of the memories we do have, however fleeting they were.

Our children will not be forgotten. Jilly isn't, Cliffie certainly won't be.

♥ ♥ ♥

*M*y friend Linda shared these thoughts with me and perhaps it resonates with readers who struggle with the holidays.

From the soul's perspective, what better time for a soul to go home than around Christmas? It gives special meaning to, "I'll be home for Christmas," the ultimate Homecoming —to be with loved ones they have longed for years to see again and be with.

When I think of how badly my own mother longed to be with my younger brother for seven years after he passed, it makes so much sense, because holidays were never the same for her or any of us for that matter. Although she transitioned in our earthly spring, I can certainly imagine her great joy celebrating her first Christmas on the other side with him, dad, her parents, grandparents and seven brothers and two sisters. She was the last of her generation to go Home. Although releasing them from our presence is the hardest thing we ever must do, it helps to remind ourselves that they are so happy to be "IN-JOY-ing" their current reality. Remembering that helps us realize they aren't sad not to be here, because they ARE, right here, right now and present with us, just in a different form.

And, according to another friend of mine who glimpsed the other side, "If you think the lights at Christmas are spectacular to look at here on Earth, just *wait* until you see what they look like from Heaven!"

LOUISE CRIST

Our treasured children, Loved in Joy and awaiting us at Home:

Colin Albright
Zack Alldredge
Tamara Avra
Kayla Babick
Whitney Bahlman
Brice Bassett
Joshua Beatty
Angie Bevilacqua
Jeff Biddinger
Becky Blair
Cliffie Bowers
Jared Brandstatter
Holly Jo Burgett
Brooke Butler
D. J. Caldwell
Lalo Carrion
Brandi Cechini
Bethany Cocco
Andy Cole
Cary Coleman
Joseph Daniels
Scott Danielson
Toby Dantes
Holly Denger
Kyle Desmond
Gregg Doster
Ryver Duckham
Kenny Dunn
Gerald "Jerry" Federan
Broc Fejes
Bridgette Fleagle
Bruce Flippo
Jimmy Gaglio
Joshua Gallup
Bethany Gibson
Ryan Gilmore
Carrie Gleason
John Greathouse
Tom Greise
Dylan Hackworth
Tyler Hartzell
Sara Haskin
Sarah Haylett
Brier Quinn Henry
Melissa Higbee
Jennifer Hoard

Always Remember to Kiss Me Goodnight

Dana Holicki	Valerie Rathbun
Jeri Holt	Tara Jo Reynolds
Tuff Hower	Lindsey Rockwell
Jason Huss	Stephanie Schabow
Kellie Jewell	Forest Sharp
Leaigha Keiser	Jamie Smoker
Trevor Kent	Victoria Sousa
Derek Klingaman	Casey Starks
LaDene Korfmacher	Maddox Luck Starr
Kurt Krenzalek	Raivyn Summerfield
Adam Lackey	Cami Szafranski
Sue Ellen Machemer	Ronald Tesch Jr.
Mike Mast	Zachary Thacher
Rob Mate	Aaron Thorp
Ryan McBride	Ronny Todd
Corey McCurley	Xachary Trayling
Danielle McCurley	Megan VanWagner
Natasha McGinnis	Shawn Waring
Stacy McVey	Katie Weis
Matthew Mills	Dana Weller
Rick Morey	Lisa Willson
Tony Ochsner	Heather Wilson
Kevin Oliver	Tyler Wirtz
Brian Porter	Eric Wood
Harlyn Radley	Michael Wood

And a special hug for these families with more than one child in Heaven:

Jersey Bridgeman & her uncle Nathaniel Fairchild
Siblings Christian and Jordan Blansit
Siblings Micha'ella and Andrea Capella
Siblings Tyler and Evan Clendening
Siblings Macy and Sydney Donay
Siblings Kyra and Noah Jones
Siblings Rick Laney, Lynn Laney Davis, Laura Laney-Litke and her son Keaton Litke
Siblings Johnathon, Catherine & Noah Simmerman
Siblings Byron and Manny Smith
Siblings Mackenzie, Madison and Kayla Wagoner

20

MARRIAGE AFTER LOSS OF A CHILD

It is true that when you lose a child, you lose a piece of your heart. It is devastating and affects every aspect of living for the rest of your life, but marriages take a particularly hard blow. With non-bereaved couples divorcing at a rate of about 50%, child loss boosts that number to approximately 65% and some sources say as high as 80%. This is a scary statistic to be sure, but it doesn't mean that your marriage is automatically doomed just because you have lost a child. I am by no means a marriage counselor, nor do I pretend to be. The words written here are a compilation of feedback from other parents traveling the same road I am on.

I have several friends who are couples that have lost a child, knowing upwards of forty families on this same path. I asked what kept their marriages together. If the couples were divorced or separated, what drove them apart? Most couples I know who have lost a child are still married between 2 and 38 years after child loss. A few have lost multiple children.

Here are some of their responses:

- "We have an unspoken rule that we can't have meltdowns at the same time. Someone must remain standing to hold the other person up. It's perfectly okay to have those knock-you-to-your-knees meltdowns, but if both of you do it at the same time, you may never get back up again. It's like drowning in grief. Someone has to be the lifeguard and stay calm."
- "To divorce after the death of a child, especially if there are surviving children, would mean enduring one more loss in addition to the one you already had. It wouldn't be fair to anyone."
- "Both of us in this marriage have lost a child. Neither of us is going through this alone. We make it a point to remember that the other person hurts just as much as you do, even if they don't show it in the same way."
- "It's really important to give each other space, physically and emotionally. Each parent has different coping mechanisms, strengths and weaknesses. Try to be supportive of the way your spouse grieves. If you need to

talk about your child and your grief and they can't, join a support group online or in person. Your spouse can't lend you what they don't have to give."

- "Without some sort of faith in a higher power or a life beyond this one, it's very challenging to keep a marriage going. In this case, there is no looking forward to seeing your child again and no hope that your child is being cared for on another level. You don't necessarily have to attend a church, although that can be a great source of support. If you don't believe in a grander plan than this world offers, it's too easy to give up." Many parents have a hard time attending the church where their child's funeral service was. My mind always sees Jilly's casket sitting by the altar when I walk in; this is not uncommon. A few (thankfully rare) churches see grief as a lack of faith on the part of the parents.
- "The emotion that you feed grows bigger and more out of control every day that you feed it. If your natural defense mechanism to extreme stress is bitterness or anger, that is probably how you will react. If your natural defense mechanism is to respond with love and forgiveness and see that everything is in divine order, you will probably feed that mentality instead. The choice is always yours. You might feel both ways in the same hour, but eventually, you return to whatever your core values are. Child loss will bring out your best and your worst traits."

If your marriage was strong prior to your child's death, it may make you closer. If your marriage was already rocky, it will either be the "final straw" or it will be a huge opportunity for growth. The first year is harder than you can even begin to imagine, but many parents say the second year is even more difficult; the numbness of the first year is gone but people often expect you to be "normal" again. You are never the same after child loss. It changes you permanently. Many parents are in such a fog the first two years that they simply don't have the ability to care for their spouse's needs, in addition to their own.

Of course, much of this depends on the circumstances of the loss; was it stillbirth, SIDS, murder, sudden accident or unexplained death, suicide, long term illness or a special needs child?

For example, in the case of a special-needs child, both parents are somewhat cohesive already because they invested so much energy in taking care of the child throughout the course of their life. When a special needs child dies, there is an enormous void left in the time and routines of taking care of that child. The parent's lives usually revolved around medical routines, doctor visits, check-ups, frequent hospitalizations, etc. and suddenly that is gone now. Although, they may have anticipated a shorter lifespan for the child, it doesn't make it any easier to lose them. Special needs parents usually gravitate towards other parents of special needs children. There may be a support system already in place, but as each child dies, the whole group goes through fear and loss all over again, knowing that their child could be next.

In the case of babies "born asleep," the parents never got a chance to get to know the baby. They say hello and goodbye in the same moment. The mother sometimes feels guilt, as if there was anything that she could possibly have done during her pregnancy that might have prevented the miscarriage or stillbirth. The father may feel guilty that he was not somehow able to protect the baby. A "normal" pregnancy brings couples closer together, anticipating the birth of a "perfect" baby. To lose that child before the parents ever got to know him/her is to lose a part of yourself and your future. Each couple must deal with not only the loss of this infant, but also the grief of losing their dreams of the future as new parents. They must return home from the hospital with empty arms and an even emptier heart to a nursery that is still awaiting a baby. I can only make these statements based on what other parents have told me, since I have not personally lost a child through miscarriage or stillbirth. I have had friends whose children were diagnosed with a terminal condition while they were still pregnant, and delivered their babies knowing that they wouldn't survive. The anticipation was horrible for them. The same goes for preemies. The parents didn't know from one moment to the next if their child(ren) would survive.

SIDS is a bit more complicated, as it is usually one of the parents who finds the baby in the crib when they don't awaken from sleep, adding another layer of "why and what if." These parents were just getting to know their precious child. Everything is going along normally in their lives. Their family was adjusting to another member in the safety and sanctuary of their own home when suddenly, it's over...almost before it began. They must deal with police investigations and autopsies. Sometimes they are young enough to have more children, but that doesn't "make up" for the child that they lost. That child was unique and irreplaceable. It's not like going out and buying a new set of shoes for the one's that the dog chewed up. Sudden unexplained death of a child or young adult is similar and frighteningly common. Knowing what took your child is painful enough...not ever finding out the cause of their sudden passing is almost unbearable. They just go to sleep one night and for no explainable reason, don't wake up.

In the case of a sudden accident, the blame game usually happens first. The child may be the driver in an accident, with no witnesses and no answers as to why the accident occurred. The child is there one minute and then in an instant, or shortly thereafter, they are gone. There is rarely time to say goodbye while the child is conscious and coherent. These parents especially wonder, "What was my child's last thought, last words, last actions? Did they suffer? Were they crying out to me for help and I couldn't be there? Did they even know what hit them?" Perhaps they were the passenger in a car or hit by a drunk, drugged or distracted driver. It's very difficult *not* to blame that other person because that is the first natural reaction. "That person *stole* my child's life," they might say, especially if it is not the first offense for the person who caused the accident. It would be challenging for anyone to have compassion for someone on their second, third or twentieth drunk driving offense, especially if they had killed someone in the past.

In our case, the driver has enough guilt for the accident without us adding to it. She is serving a self-imposed life sentence in her mind for accidentally killing her best friend. There is nothing I could do to her that would be worse than the loss she lives with every day. She can't answer specific questions about the accident as a result of her brain injury. She only remembers tiny fragments of it, and I am grateful for that. If she someday remembers and wants to tell me about it, she will. I loved her then, and still do.

Even if the child somehow survives the initial accident, they may be kept on life support, vacillating between life and death long enough for the family to be able to say goodbye to the body or to donate organs, thus allowing part of their child to live on in others and give someone else a chance at life. These families are true heroes in my book.

In the case of murder…whoa, I think that is one of the toughest. My experience with this was unique because I only know four families that have had to deal with this situation. The first family's only daughter was murdered by a classmate and most people would experience rage or anger at the person who took their child's life; this would be a natural reaction. In this case, however, I witnessed the way they handled it with such extraordinary love and grace that I figured all families were supposed to deal with their grief that way. Indeed, that experience made a huge impact on the way I handled Jilly's death. The family not only forgave the murderer and prayed for him, they also became friends with his parents, realizing that they too, had lost a child. One lost to murder, the other lost to a life sentence in prison. I was fortunate to have them as mentors very early in my life.

The unique thing about murder is that it becomes very public and there are usually trials, court proceedings, sentencing and parole boards. It never stops, even when the trial is over. Those who were not part of the immediate family, but knew the victim, become frightened if parole is sought and especially if it's granted. The young boy who panicked and murdered my friend at age 17 during an attempted rape, is still in prison decades later. Both sets of parents would like to see him paroled, but the community he grew up in will probably never forgive him, even though he has expressed much remorse about that one stupid decision that changed so many lives. I am not sure how well he could function on the outside since all he has known in his adult life is the prison routine. Interestingly enough, both sets of parents in this situation are still married.

Another dear friend lost her son to murder as well, but it was premeditated. Her son had been robbed a couple weeks before and when he did not put up any resistance, the gang members came back and tried to rob him again. When he resisted this time, he and his roommate were both shot and killed over stupid material items that you could buy anywhere. Her son survived for a few minutes, long enough to tell the police what happened and who shot them, making it easier to catch and lock up the murderers. It has taken a huge physical and emotional toll on this single mom and her surviving son. The murderers showed little or no remorse for their actions and were probably juvenile career criminals before they took two lives that day. The mother in this case, had already buried her parents and two siblings (most of her family), so her support system was not nearly as large as the first set of parents. She chose not to attend the court hearings and relied on the parents of the roommate who was killed to keep her informed. It has been nearly two years and there has still not been a sentencing, but when it does come, it will likely be 20 to 40 years with time served and possibly early parole. How fair is it that? The person who snuffed out her son's life can eventually walk free, while her son can't enjoy one more minute with his family? The grief eventually became too much for her to bear, and it contributed to a cascading decline of the mother's serious health issues. Sadly, she followed her son to Heaven two years later.

What about suicide? Another case in which someone finds the body. The entire family is in turmoil. "Why didn't I see this coming? Was it something I said or did? What kind of parent doesn't know this is going on inside their child's head? I could have stopped them if I had known!" are common thoughts. None of this is usually true, but it doesn't stop the thoughts from coming. Add to that guilt, the anger of finding out that someone else might have been involved in what was that last straw for that person... perhaps a classmate, a co-worker or boss, a spouse or girl/boyfriend. Someone or something must be blamed.

Occasionally, it's an impulsive rash decision that wasn't even on that person's radar the day before. Occasionally it is literally a "flip of the coin." Sometimes people self-destruct over years instead of suddenly. Alcohol, drugs, eating disorders, thrill seeking behaviors and mental illness can all take a toll on a person insidiously... each day one day closer to death but because it happens so slowly, it's still a shock when it happens. I've lost several friends this way and it isn't any easier than my situation in which Jillian died instantly.

In each of these situations, most of the parents remained married. Some are even closer than before child loss, others have stayed because they didn't have the energy to do otherwise. One of the parents took to their bed and became reclusive; the other parent simply doesn't have the strength to "live again" in a normal way.

In my own personal experience, I immediately searched for things that I knew could help me cope. I fell back to my normal response to stress; writing, staying active (okay, *running* from the grief if I am honest, by staying overly busy) and surrounding myself with supportive people and other parents who had been through child loss. I dragged my husband to some of these meetings; I believe that talking with other fathers probably helped him realize he was not alone. I devoured books on grieving, taking what was useful from each and tossing the rest that didn't resonate with me. I had to go back to work or I would not have an income; that also turned out to be a blessing.

For eight hours a day, I could focus on something else besides Jillian, even though she was at the front of every thought all day. I was able to pour my love for her into caring for my patients. I am a natural nurturer, whereas my husband is not. He prefers his solitary grieving, doing things that make him feel more alive, such as creating a beautiful garden, whitewater kayaking and sitting in a tree stand during hunting season. (That was especially difficult the first couple of years for him because that's exactly where he was when Jillian died.) I suddenly became aware of each new family in our community that lost a child and learned the importance of supporting them, even if we were total strangers. (I'm sure I overwhelmed a few!) We would send a card or show up at a visitation of a total stranger, just to offer a hug. I started a local group for bereaved families that get together once a year for a candlelit dinner in memory of our children. We say their name, talk about them, share our growth and our tears. It is a terrible "club" to have to join, but the people in it are some of the most amazing, strongest and most loving and supportive people I have ever met.

I can't say that my own marriage has gotten stronger or

better; just different, much like our grief. I wasn't sure it was going to survive our loss, but so far, it has. Before Jillian died, Mark and I survived his cancer diagnosis and treatment. (He is currently in remission.) We thought that was the biggest test we would ever face. We were wrong. Cancer did bring us closer somehow, probably because we knew our days together might be numbered. We had both lost our fathers to cancer. After burying our child, neither of us fear death any longer. The first one to go will be the lucky one to see her first. We know what it's like to be the one left behind and we both fear having to be that person and reliving yet another loss.

In by gone days, periods of mourning for families were observed for up to a year. Decades passed and in previous generations, child loss was not discussed at all... not among spouses, families, children or communities. The deceased child was simply not talked about. Mothers gave birth to stillborn babies and were not allowed to see them or hold them. The fathers decided what to do with the child's body and once the mother woke up from the anesthesia, she was simply sent home to deal with it. There was no such thing as "closure" in those days. My grandmother lost several children to miscarriages and a 4-year-old twin to meningitis in the early 1920's. In response to her grief and depression, she was committed to a mental asylum. The treatment back then was insulin shock therapy. She was injected with insulin until she went comatose. I'm not sure who thought putting someone into a diabetic coma was a good cure, but she finally died from the complications of diabetes that this bizarre treatment eventually caused. She never left the sanitarium.

In my lifetime, I have witnessed funerals lengthening from the standard of three days from the time of the child's death up to a more realistic time frame of five to seven days or more. (I couldn't even tie my shoes for three days, much less plan a funeral and attend it! By the way, who decided that when you give birth to a baby, six to twelve weeks off work is customary, but when you bury one, three days to a week is enough?)

Those whose marriage did not survive usually blamed a strained or doomed marriage to start with and the extra added stress was the final straw. This is especially true in blended families. The natural parent thinks that the step-parent doesn't "get it" and can't grasp the enormity of the grief. The spouse who is not the child's natural parent sometimes (but not always) can't grasp why the person they married is not recovering from the loss faster. They can't deal with their spouse spending days or weeks in bed mourning. They want desperately to fix them, but sadly, they can't. It is one more thing that is beyond their control and sometimes they just don't have the energy or strength to keep fighting. One partner usually moves forward in grief faster than the other, but they may stay in that same spot for years; eventually, the other parent passes them by. It's not a race to the finish line; it's about survival.

I guess the biggest indicator of a marriage surviving loss is communication and support. Communicate with someone, ideally your partner. If you can't do that, find a good counselor and do it with them. Talk to other bereaved parents who seem to be dealing with their grief in a healthy way. Learn to read non-verbal cues, body language and signs of stress. Play fair, do not blame your spouse for the child loss. (Chances are good that they have already done that anyway; grief is rarely rational.)

If you are lucky enough to get signs from your child, be open with your spouse about that and help them to notice them too. If you need to take separate vacations for a while, do that. What one person finds healing might not appeal to the other. I honor Jillian by raising funds for scholarships in her memory. Usually, this involves months of event planning. While it is stressful, I think of all the good that will come out of it. Mark, on the other hand, is the opposite. Every single thing he touches to help me get ready for the event (even though he enjoys the activities that day) just remind him that Jilly is no longer here. We agree to disagree, and I try not to put too many tasks on his shoulders during the event, as he is doing the best that he can to hold it together, while I am walking around smiling most of the day. He finds giving out the scholarships difficult; I see it as one more way to say her name in public, encourage people to not forget her and help young students at the same time, making Jilly proud.

Every couple that experiences child loss should eventually seek out a good grief counselor; however, they may not be ready to do so for months or even years. Incidentally, run, don't walk away from anyone who tells you that you need to get over it!

My biggest meltdown occurred when I was least expecting it, about two and 1/2 years after Jilly died, and it was a doozy! It was so ugly, so intense and so frightening, that I didn't think it would stop and I thought I would lose all control forever. I seriously pondered whether I needed to commit myself to an inpatient treatment center because for a brief moment, I was contemplating just ending the pain.

When I had curled into a ball on the floor and wailed until no more tears would come, I reverted to my core values and realized that I had not lost control forever...just for those hours. Guess what...that is normal! I would never be the same, but I would be reasonably "okay"...and I felt much better afterward. Mark has gone to a counselor a few times; I go monthly to maintain my sanity and am grateful that I have found a counselor skilled at a therapy called EMDR. It helps with managing the Post Traumatic Stress that came to live in my body the day Jilly died. I also insisted that both of my surviving daughters get counseling as well.

A marriage will grow if you feed it with love and tenderness. It will disintegrate if you starve it. Loving your spouse can help you find strength to give to surviving children. Even a one-minute hug every day is a start. Love each other. When life throws bricks at you, pick them up and build a monument with them. Let your child's life be about their *life*, be careful not to define it by their death. I don't know about you, but when I die, that's the most I can ask of those I leave here on earth.

It is also true as has been said, you don't know how strong you are until there isn't any other choice.

This is what Jilly's little sister, Sierra, wrote about her experience with sibling grief:

"No one can put into words the heartache I felt from losing a sibling. The wave of emotions, the pain, the tears (so many tears I thought that my tear ducts were empty) and the crushing chest pain are the most extreme train of emotions I've ever felt. Unfortunately, people that have never lost someone close to them don't understand the magnitude and finality of death. We've all been to a funeral and always feel sympathetic for the families of the recently passed loved one. You can't even begin to be empathetic for these families until you have experienced it first-hand. You can always say 'reassuring' words, but it wasn't until after I lost my sister, that I realized that these words aren't actually reassuring at all. It doesn't make me happier to be told that she's in a better place; in that moment all I can feel is that the perfect place would be here with me."

"There isn't a single day that goes by that I don't wish she was here with me. I miss making memories with her everywhere we went. I will no longer be able to make new memories with her."

"Even throughout the mix of emotions and frustration, I am thankful. I am thankful for another day alive to help serve others. I am thankful for my family and their support. I am thankful that I have a guardian angel watching over me constantly and that she continuously shows me signs to let me know she hasn't left my side. I am thankful for all the lessons she has taught me."

"But what I'm most thankful for is that she taught me how to teach. She's taught me valuable life lessons that I probably wouldn't have learned until I was much older. She's taught me the true meaning of life: to love. Love is the strongest energy in the universe. Fear and anger will not get anyone anywhere in this life. I've reached out to others who have felt the same as I do. Teenagers, adults and even elders have come together to help one another heal. I have learned to share the love Jill gave the world every day effortlessly. To help others when in need—I can't think of a better way to honor her life than to continue that love and compassion every day."

♥ ♥ ♥

Depression

Many have commented on how strong they think I am. The truth is, I am a big coward; there are definitely days I want to just throw the towel in on this whole "grief thing." I was and often still am, terrified by the enormity of my emotional pain. My fear was that if I let the grief catch up to me and let the tears deep inside me flow without restriction, I might never be able to close the floodgates. So, I ran from it, but it caught up with me anyway.

The other night, I "ugly sobbed" like a toddler for at least two hours. It was a complete meltdown, including those little sighs toddlers do when they have cried for an extended period of time. The waves of grief washed over me again and again, but believe it or not, it was healing.

The way you have dealt with past grief in your life affects the way you handle grief in the future each time you encounter it. I went through almost a whole box of Kleenex. I don't think I have cried that hard since my dad died when I was pregnant with Jillian. I know that at the other end of this pain is eventually some peace and even joy. I have survived grief before; I will survive this one too.

All of this is a *normal* part of grief....and it *does* hurt. This is often a time when those who love you can "hold your hand." They can't fix the pain, but they can be there to watch over you while you go through it. Words are not even necessary; just their presence helps. They can be your anchor in the storm, simply allowing you to feel what you need to feel, making sure you are safe...sometimes safe from yourself.

There were times during this episode when I had some really dark, depressing thoughts that were overwhelming. There is a fine line between feeling the expected depression you go through in bad situations and the severe depression due to a chemical imbalance in your body.

Autumn and the beginning of winter are peak times for depression, *especially* if, like me, you are sensitive to lower levels of sunlight. I have had Seasonal Affective Disorder, commonly known as the "winter blues" since I was a small child. I knew it was not normal for a 6-year-old to feel sad when the Christmas tree went up, but I did not understand that it was the lack of sunlight and changing of seasons wreaking havoc with my serotonin levels. (Serotonin is the *happy* hormone. When I don't get enough sunlight, even a few minutes a day, I become depressed because my body is not making enough serotonin.)

A dear friend (who went Home a year or so before Jillian did) saved my life several years ago. He was also a psychologist and he talked me into trying an antidepressant early one winter when the blues hit extra hard. He told me that they help restore the proper levels of serotonin by helping your brain build little "bridges" so the happy hormone can jump from one side to the other, giving you back some balance.

He explained that depression is an illness just like diabetes is. If you were a diabetic, you would take insulin. Without it, you might die. You wouldn't be ashamed to take insulin, would you? If you are severely depressed, there are therapies available so that they can learn to cope with the internal pain that they feel so often. Without it, the world can look too bleak and hopeless and that too can be fatal. Depression tends to be genetic. Both of my parents struggled with it. Jillian also struggled with it. I recognized the symptoms in her around the time she hit puberty (again, a time of huge hormonal shifts) and got her help.

It is nothing to be ashamed of. It happens to people of every color, nationality, age, income level and gender. Depression is a chemical imbalance that robs you of nearly everything in your life that usually brings you pleasure. Your joy goes into hiding. You sometimes lose your will and desire to live.

I thought, "Well, I might as well try it, because I can't keep going this way. I am so miserable I can hardly stand myself."

Oh my gosh! What a difference it made! I went from being mopey and despondent to my normal fairly optimistic self in 2 to 4 weeks. (Some people take a little longer.) I felt normal again! I wish they had therapeutic medication like that when I was a kid! They are not for everyone, but if you are at the end of your rope, they can often help. Your family doctor can help, or you can go to a counselor who can point you in the right direction for getting help.

If you are feeling depressed, please hold on to that rope. The pain you are feeling is not permanent. It is intense, overwhelming at times, scary and it is painful, but it does not have to be permanent. If you leave this world now, you may miss meeting people in your future who will change your life—and whose lives will be changed just by you being a part of it! If any of you out there know exactly what I am talking about and start to develop a plan or have suicidal ideas that persist for more than a few minutes, or you are by yourself when this happens, or you just feel you can't go on... *PLEASE* call someone! Call a friend, a co-worker, a family member, clergy, teacher or if you find yourself making a suicide plan and are tempted to act on it, call the **National Suicide Prevention Hotline at 1-800-SUICIDE**

(273-8255.) There is someone there 24 hours a day to listen and help. I recently was told that if you can just make yourself get up and walk for 10 minutes, you will probably live to see another day because walking also increases your serotonin levels.

You are valued and loved as a part of this world, even if sometimes it does not feel that way. If I hadn't gotten help, I might not be here still writing this book. From what I understand, my posts have been helpful to some people; maybe they are part of my purpose in life.

Today may look awful, but tomorrow just might be the best day of your life. You don't want to miss out on it. Please hold on a little while longer. Ask for help. Get on some antidepressants, if that is appropriate for you. Get some counseling. Get out in the sun; let it shine on your face for a few minutes.

Please don't give up. You are needed. You are loved. You would be so missed!

Suicide's pain is multiplied by the agony of those it left behind.

LOUISE CRIST

LONELY WALK OF YOUR NOVEMBER

I tried to catch up to you when
It came time for the souls surrender
But now I am looking for my way home
Left behind in your November

With great beauty, you walked in this place
With a smile and touch—soft and tender
They say they will miss you for all time to come
Lonely here in your November

I look through the pictures from our youth
Summertime fun—June to September
I've cried and laughed until I cannot see
The memories of our November

With no regret but with hidden sorrow
I'll let go of your hand forever
Go on now Jillian—walk with God
While I walk alone into December.
~ By Michael Huggett

(Father of Hannah, who became Jillian's best friend. Her mother Susan and I went through our pregnancies together, worked together and delivered our girls in the same hospital nine days apart.)

January 7, 2015
Loss...

I HAVE BEEN THINKING ABOUT that word a lot lately. Here are some of the meanings of the word LOST in the dictionary: "To be deprived of or cease to retain. Unable to find. To become deeply absorbed. Destroyed or killed. Fail to reach one's destination. Be unable to control one's emotions. Fail to win. To no longer have a clear order about one's purpose or motivation. To misplace, forget, lose track of, leave behind, fail to keep sight of and be unable to comprehend an explanation."

You can lose a game, lose sleep, lose your way, lose your marbles, lose your cool, lose your heart, and lose your mind... but can you really *lose* someone you love?

"I'm sorry for your loss." I have heard it countless times. I have said it myself more times than I care to remember. Sometimes, it's all a person *can* say. They are five words that are spoken when nothing else quite sums up your feelings of compassion and sympathy.

When a child loses their parents, they are labeled an orphan. When one loses their spouse, they are called widows or widowers. These losses (whether they are anticipated or not) are usually unbearable.

Losing my daddy was the most painful loss I had ever known... but I also knew that the odds were good that my parents would go HOME before me. I also fully expect that either Mark or I will someday have to plan a funeral for each other... and one of us will have to be first. I may even bury one or more of my siblings if I live long enough. That will be excruciating too. But I expect it as the natural order of things.

But what do you call a parent who has lost their child? A young sibling who has lost their brother or sister, their best friend to the sting of death? There is no word to describe it because this pain is also unfathomable to those who haven't experienced it. To those who have, no words are necessary. We believe that it is *not* how things are supposed to be. You aren't supposed to plan your child's funeral. The only word I can think of that even comes close is *lost*.

We are unable to comprehend this situation. But what exactly, did I lose?

Jillian's earthly body ceased to function, that much is certain. Her shell is tucked safely away in a beautiful ivory box beneath the grass and snow. I miss holding that body with each and every breath that I am allowed to take, with each heartbeat that I still have, and she no longer does. But did I *lose* her?

I didn't lose our past... that much is etched forever in our minds, our hearts, videos and countless pictures. Nothing and no one can take those away. I have those precious memories that we shared as a family. The times I felt so full of love toward my daughters that I thought my heart would melt. The laughter at the antics they would pull. The moments of bickering over really stupid stuff that teenage girls fight over, like hairbrushes and curling irons and who left dirty clothes on the bathroom floor again.

There are priceless memories of Mark teaching Jilly to hunt and fish and not be afraid of new adventures. She would watch a situation, measure it up and then jump in like it was a mosh pit, full of joy. He never could get her to keep to a budget though!

And then there are my unforgettable Mama/Jilly moments... the look of being the only big brown-eyed one of all the siblings reflecting back at me, as they had done for three generations before her. She looked most like me but acted mostly like Mark. I thought I wrote the book on being stubborn as a child. She quickly corrected that record.

Her compassion toward animals, strays, friends and underdogs was evident every day. She lived and breathed for her friends and family. When she loved, it was 100% and she was fiercely and deeply devoted to those she cared for. I am happy and proud to say that number was seemingly endless.

No, I didn't lose our past. Did I lose our future? Well, yes... and no. Our future is still there. She waits for us to come *Home* someday, anticipating (as we do) the indescribable joy at the reunion we will share at some point. She will be waiting, arms outstretched, love lighting up her beautiful face as she pulls us into an eternal tummy hug. It makes me smile just thinking of it.

We *will* be together again in the future, I am positive of that. We didn't lose our future, but it's not the way I planned it. That is on hold for now.

Our present, with her physical death, is not what we ever imagined for ourselves. There are days I wake up and think (as many other bereaved families do), "This is not my life! This isn't real!"

It is as though a great cosmic finger has hit the pause button in the middle of our favorite song. The verses are left unsung. The haunting melody is forever stuck in our head on repeat.

She lived like each day was her last one on Earth. And one day, it was.

Have I lost her in the present? Kind of. She is right here next to me whenever I think of her, even though my human eyes are unable to see her in the same manner I was used to for 19 years. I know she is there.

But I do I miss the familiar sound of her chuckle, the scent of her clothes and the silky touch of her favorite strand of hair that she twirled. I miss the loud sound of her kiss on my cheek and the way her voice carried through the house when she would randomly announce, "*Mother, you are my mother! I do love you, Mother!*" in her weird nasal singsong cadence. I even miss the crazy stunts she would pull with her buddies and the amount of food they could consume in a late-night snack raid (with ketchup, of course.)

As I watch her friends grow older, marry, graduate and start their families, I am as happy and proud of them as she would be (and is). Yet a part of me thinks, "That could have been/should have been/might have been Jilly!" She would be trying to steal her friends' babies for a weekend of "Auntie Jilly" time. I don't think that Aubree, Landon or Eldon's feet would have hit the ground for a moment if she were physically here. She would have carried them everywhere and swatted away any hands that tried to pry them from her arms. She might have taught Bella to ride a bike.

Although, I do think these babies know her anyway. Perhaps she got to hold and hug their souls before they arrived in their precious little bodies. Perhaps they can feel or somehow "see" her... and that is why they suddenly smile at the wall, or coo at "nothing." Maybe it is really Jilly making goofy faces at them that only they, in their innocence, can see.

Did I lose our status as parents of three daughters? Nope, nope—and nope. We *have* three daughters. We always *will*! One of them just went *Home* ahead of us. She may be *there*, but she is still *here* in so many ways.

Did I lose my daughter? No. I know exactly where she is. She is with God...and He is everywhere. Therefore, in my line of thinking, she is everywhere too. Jilly is right *here*, in the hearts and memories of those who love her and those she still loves in return.

Every day...every minute...eternally. She isn't misplaced, like a big chunk of our plans for her were. Our lives will never be what they once were. That is the loss I grieve for the most.

21

NEWS FLASH!

My Shack

Many years ago, I was fortunate enough to stumble across a book titled, *The Shack*, by William P. Young. I read it many times, bought copies and gave them to my friends. It impacted me *that* much. The idea of God being a personal, loving friend was not new to me. However, I wondered how someone who had lost a child would keep that friendship going with God. I had personally witnessed this in my teen years, when two of my friends died young. One was a car accident, the other was murdered. In both cases, their parents were the epitome of forgiveness and grace under pressure. I determined in my heart way back then at the age of 15 and again at age 18, that if anything like that were to ever happen to me, I wanted to show people God's love the way they did on the days they buried their daughters. They both taught me that our children are only lent to us for a season. Sometimes, many seasons, sometimes for what seems like only a minute. Our children are not *ours*, any more than we are *theirs*, although we seem to have this preconceived notion that they belong to us and therefore we have some control over how long they will be here. Nothing could be further from the truth.

They are "Papa's" children on loan to us. Because I had read *The Shack* and taken to heart many of its ideas about Jesus and God (Papa) and the Holy Spirit, I believe that my heart and mind were much more open when Jillian died, than if I hadn't already pondered that possibility. God had been preparing me for many years to walk this rocky path. Jillian herself had been preparing me from the tender age of about five, when she began to share with me some of the "knowings" of her heart...that she would die young, would never have babies and never get to do many of the things most children do. I distinctly remember asking her what she wanted to be when she grew up. She looked through me with her big, brown, wise old eyes and said, "A grown up would be nice."

In the movie, *The Shack*, the main character struggles with his relationship with God all his life and when he loses his daughter, he spirals into *The Great Sadness*. It is such a deep dark pit of hopelessness that only God can fix it because there is absolutely nothing on this earth that can help. *The Great Sadness* is like wearing a heavy uncomfortable full-length coat in the blazing heat of summer's hottest day. No matter how unbearable it is, you can't take off the coat. The "what ifs" and "coulda, woulda, shouldas" weigh your soul down into a pit of agony. Only a deep and personal conversation and eventual relationship with God or whatever you choose to call this higher power, can change your perception of that pain; changing the coat which you have been given a life sentence to wear into a tolerable garment.

First, God climbs into the pit with you. Then, as he holds and cradles you in his arms and lets you scream and wail like a toddler in a tantrum, you begin to see that his presence brings a light into that dark cavern of your heart. Slowly, you notice that there is and always has been, a ladder that will lead you out of there. You just couldn't see it before. The ladder is intimidatingly tall, stretching from the depths of your despair into a place where you can't see the top.

The ladder is called "trust." You must *trust* that God knows what he is doing, loves your child more than you ever possibly could and loves you with that same magnitude. Your child did not die as punishment to you or anyone else. Your child obeyed when God called him or her Home, never questioning it. That is a very hard pill to swallow!

The Shack recently came out as a movie. I not so patiently waited for it to hit the theaters. I invited several friends who had also lost children to see it with me for the first time. I smiled as I watched the visuals of the Trinity interacting with each other. I chuckled at their sense of humor. ("Wait, God! Did you just call me an idiot?" followed by, "If the shoe fits honey, if the shoe fits!") Every question I had asked about *why* was answered in a way most people do not expect.

When the main character places his daughter in Jesus' arms, it brought back memories of doing the same thing; both at Jillian's birth and at her death 19 years later. I wept as my heart remembered those special moments in communion with God. I walked out of the theater wanting to shout to the world, "My daughter is with PAPA! And she's beautiful and perfect in every way and happy beyond anything I could ever hope to imagine!" How could she not be? She knows that the same God who is loving her every day also holds me in his caress.

I wanted to hug the little old lady sitting next to me, bent over by years of arthritis and obviously, in poor health. I wanted to admit to her that I was jealous that she would probably be in Papa's arms before I would. It gave me some hard questions to ponder and discuss with others. I went back to see the movie a second time...and a third. It gave me *that* much comfort. It was as if someone went into my heart and mind and somehow put it on the big screen for me to watch how beautiful and messy and perfectly orchestrated it really is.

Does this mean it doesn't still hurt to wake up each day and know that Jillian won't walk through the door? Does it mean I don't still grieve for all that I didn't get to experience with her on this side, like watching her become a nurse, get married, give me grandchildren or live to be a ripe old age?

No... not at all. I still grieve those things quite often. I still think about and miss her every single day. But now, I am also able to think of her somewhere with Jesus, perhaps on a peaceful warm beach, kicking back in a comfortable chair, sharing a pizza and shooting the breeze about topics we haven't even dared to dream about yet. The weather is balmy, she is tan and warm and basking in perfect love. She's smiling her goofy, "I am so happy" grin. I get glimpses of that smile now and then. I can't reach her yet, but someday, when I get to the top of the ladder God has placed before me, I will. What a glorious day that will be.

Meanwhile, I take these words from the last chapter of The Shack to heart, when God says: "If anything matters, everything matters. Because you are important, everything you do is important. Every time you forgive, the universe changes; every time you reach out and touch a heart or a life, the world changes; with every kindness and service, seen or unseen, my purposes are accomplished, and nothing will ever be the same again."

Thank you, God, for taking my sweet daughter Home with you. May her legacy on earth be kindness and love and may this world be a better place because for a season, she was a part of it. I look forward to the day I catch up.

The Legacy

No one reading this book is guaranteed tomorrow. Not even one of us... but we all assume we will still see the sun rise in the morning. When my step-dad died his day to day responsibilities were passed on to me as the executor of his trust and will. I am honored that he thought me capable enough to do so. Someday, some of you may be faced with these same responsibilities.

While Dean left a legacy of love and very fond memories, he did the best he could to make things "simple" for me, but I have learned that there is absolutely nothing about being a trustee or executor that is simple. We had been talking about emergency back up plans since my mom's sudden stroke 17 months before.

The day he died, we were supposed to be making the arrangements so that if anything happened to him, I would know exactly what to do... except that didn't happen. We had discussed it the night before, but he said he was too tired and didn't have the energy to think about it right then. He asked me to come back the next day with paper and pen ready for a planning session. He fell asleep that night and never woke up. I found him permanently and peacefully asleep in bed the next morning.

If you were thrust into that situation without warning, would you know what to do? Where would you quickly find all the information that you suddenly needed?

Although this is especially important with aging parents, it is also important for all of us, especially if you are the one that handles the finances in your home. It can help those left behind tremendously if you do a few simple things that will only take a couple of hours of your time. It can save them weeks of frustration, as grief makes your brain foggy enough!

Here are some very important suggestions:
- Get a notebook small enough to fit in a safety deposit box or safe, so that you can store it there when you have completed it.
- Write down all the names of the banks you use, what the account numbers are, and who is authorized on the account. It's a good idea to always have a second person on a check writing account if you are older or in questionable health, even if the only privilege that person has, is writing checks for you. It is a good idea to have a notarized power of attorney in the event it is needed. For example, just to turn off dad's TV service, I had to produce a death certificate, a durable power of attorney (DPOA) and documentation from the bank stating that I was indeed legally able to sign checks and make the decision to cancel the service. Even then, they gave me a hard time—I wasn't disconnecting life support, mind you...I was simply canceling cable service! I haven't even tried to tackle the cell phone account yet.
- Leave instructions for the location of all usernames and

passwords for each of your accounts, your computer, tablet, I-pad and your phone. Don't forget passwords to services like PayPal, Netflix, Amazon and E-bay!

- Write down all the bills you are responsible for along with whom they are payable to and the approximate date they are received and the date they are due each month. Also include how you pay them... online banking? A personal check? (Do you have duplicates in your checkbook?) Automatic deduction from your savings, checking or credit card? Don't forget things you only pay for once or twice a year, like Sirius radio, AARP or AAA accounts, life or auto or home insurance and property taxes. How many credit cards do you have? Those accounts may need to be closed. Copy or scan your credit cards, front and back, along with your driver's license and put this in the safe.

- Note where the money comes from to pay these bills. Who is your DPOA (Durable Power of Attorney)? Do they know all this? Do you have automatic deposits from retirement or pension accounts? What day of the month do those come in?

- Write down where you keep the titles to vehicles and deeds to real estate, especially if there is a mortgage and where to find service records for your vehicles. Also, where are your Social Security number, and birth/ marriage/divorce/graduation certificates and military records? (You

need these for the Social Security and eventually funeral home appointments.)
- Do you have IRA's, mutual funds or life insurance policies? With who? Where do you keep those policies? Who is your broker or contact person? Do you have to take minimum required distributions? Monthly? Yearly? Who is/are the beneficiaries?
- Is there any funeral/celebration of life/burial/cremation preferences? Is anything prepaid? With whom? Where is this information located?
- If you receive Social Security, who is your payee? (That was another adventure ... you must be a legal guardian, as they don't recognize durable powers of attorney.) If one spouse leaves the other behind, there is a one-time $255 (at this time) "death benefit" that needs to be assigned to that person. The surviving spouse's Social Security payment may increase at this time, but it takes a couple of months to finish and file all the paperwork. We found out that when my dad turned 65, my mom was actually due more money than she was collecting on SS. Now they owe us back pay for seven years!
- Where do you keep your tax records? Someone will have to file your taxes for the last year of your life. Is there a will? Where do you keep it?
- Where are all your keys to various vehicles, barns, garages, lawn mowers, snow blowers, lockers, safes and

safety deposit boxes? Does anyone have an extra labeled set?

I am not a lawyer, nor do I have any legal expertise. These are the questions it has taken me weeks to find the answers to, with a lot of help from various agencies. (Thank you, God, for helpful people!)

My head spins with the seemingly endless tasks that need to be completed, all compounded by grief. Please... make it less stressful for those you leave behind.

My New Year's resolution is not only to get my affairs in order, but to teach my girls how to be my trustees while I am still here to show them how it's done! I really miss my stepdad, even if it does bring me great joy and comfort to know he is with Jilly!

Legacy Writing

Another idea you may want to consider leaving for your descendants is Legacy Writing. It is a form of a memoir that gives them clues to what was going on in your life, focusing on your thoughts and feelings. For example, your thoughts and feelings as to how you handled significant events in your life, why you made the choices you made and what your hopes and dreams for them are. Another option is to write and leave a letter (in safety deposit box or with a trusted person) to each significant person in your life to be given after you go

Home. This is a great opportunity to tell them what you may not have said or been able to say previously; keep it positive only please; you wouldn't want to be remembered negatively.

22

OUT OF THE DARKNESS AND INTO THE LIGHT

As we wind up this story, let us first go back to the years 2016 and 2011, so that you can better understand what is, perhaps, the most important chapter in this book.

The Math Assignment
June 26, 2016

Oh, how I love my dreams of Jilly when I am lucky enough to have them. They are so detailed sometimes that it feels like she is right there next to me! In this one, she was in about the sixth grade ... her sassy stage, the one where she would test every limit that I gave her. I could feel her soft skin, her silky hair, see the way her adult teeth didn't quite fit her small oval face yet and her gangly skinny arms and legs made her look just like that—all arms and legs. (The pictures show what I mean!)

I had given her a math homework assignment and she was trying to weasel her way out of doing the whole thing, as she wanted desperately to go to a party to be with her friends. She kept stalling and bringing me half done pages, saying, "Can I go *now*? I will finish when I get back! I'll even help clean the house later if you'll let me go now."

"No, Jilly, just finish the assignment," I replied.

She would go into her room, erase a few things, add a few more equations and come back out.

"Now can I go?"

"Jilly, you know as well as I do that this assignment is not done. If you have time to fiddle-fart around by trying to creatively get out of doing it, you have time to just buckle down and do the darn paper! Now go finish the assignment!"

Dramatically, she went back to her room, slamming the door, wailing about how her friends were already at this party and she was sure she was missing something.

I smiled.

If I drew a line in the sand, Jilly was always the one to stick her toe over it and innocently ask, "What line?" She gave herself about 10 minutes and came out with the passable homework assignment. It wasn't great, but she had finished it. I didn't think she would probably get more than a D on it, but at this point, she had worn me down to a frazzle and arguing with her would be a waste of both our times. Besides, I hated math as much as she did, and she was already way better at it than I was.

Once I relented and let her go, she went back to her room and a few minutes later, emerged in a spectacular dress, all sparkly white, gold and silver and literally made of the stars in the sky. She was absolutely stunning at age 17. I wish I were able to draw what she looked like.

For some reason in this dream, I was photographing this party she was at. I took pictures of her as she laughed and danced; she was her spunky beautiful self, hugging all her friends. It turned out that the party was a wedding reception for a paraplegic gymnast and her paralyzed boyfriend. They had met at rehab, fallen in love and had made the most out of the cards that life had dealt them.

I couldn't help but smile at everyone's happiness for them, at the way they had found love in what first looked like a tragedy. After the party, we helped clean up and Jilly and I went outside to sit on a bench under the stars facing the beach.

"Jilly, I have something to tell you. I don't want to scare you, but I know something about your future that's very important."

I took her hand in mine, gazing into her sparkling mocha brown eyes as I took a deep breath. God, I didn't want to tell her, but somehow, I knew I must be the one to do it, because sometimes it's a parent's duty to be the ones to help our children through life's toughest lessons.

"Jilly, honey" I whispered, barely able to get the words out, "You won't live past the age of 19."

She looked at me, not at all surprised and said, "*Really, really?*" (Like Shrek.)

"Really, really," I replied sadly.

She thought about it for a minute. There was no panic, no crying and no fear in her at all as she mulled this revelation over in her mind.

"Okay then," she said, as she looked in my eyes so deeply it felt like she was looking clear through to the other side of my soul.

"If that is God's big plan for me, then I have to make the most out of the time I have left. I have some things left to do that won't look like anything with a big purpose to you. In fact, it may look like I am "wasting my time" with the "wrong" people, instead of the ones you think I should be hanging out with, since I have so little time left."

She never took her eyes off mine as she said, "Mom, I need to finish this assignment in order to go to the next party. It won't make any sense to you until after I go, but someday, it will . . . I promise. I am not afraid to die mom, and you shouldn't be either. We all die. I will just do it sooner than you, because believe it or not, you will have to work on the harder assignment after I go.

It will take many years...and no, just like you wouldn't let me go to the party till I was done, God wants you to continue what we have started until you are done. It is important work and even after you go, others will still be needed to keep this going. It's like a big circle that doesn't end; the work is *that* important."

I held her in my arms for a long time, just breathing in her scent, feeling her heart beat next to mine and wondering how I got so blessed to have her visit my life, even if it was to be only a "short" time on this side.

She got up and held her hand out to me, helping me up from the bench. I too, had been transformed into the beautiful young woman I was in my prime and was wearing a similar dress made of stars.

"Let's get to it then, Mom," she said. "We have lots to do." As an afterthought, she turned around and said with a big smile, "And about that math assignment...I totally won't need that in Heaven...so can we just skip that for the rest of my life?" (There she goes, sticking her toe over the line again!)

I love these dreams of her! I am confident her sense of humor followed her when she left. God has His hands full with this one, He does!

(This is the closest picture I have to what Jilly looked like in my dream.)

LOUISE CRIST

Always Remember to Kiss Me Goodnight

♥ ♥ ♥

Thursday night, November 17, 2011

Thursday Nov. 17, 2011

Mom! Thank you for all you have given me. Thank you for a ~~bed~~ bed, and food and a place to sleep every night! it means more than you think. I'm so blessed to have a loving family like I have. thank you for teaching me about god. I'm thankful for all you have given me and my family means the world to me! I'm so blessed to have you! I love you more than the world! x1000 ☺ ♡ Jilly bean

LOUISE CRIST

♥ ♥ ♥

Thursday night, November 17, 2011

Thursday, Nov. 17, 2011

Dad, thank you for raising me right, and teaching me about god. Thank you for praying with me when I was young. I didnt realize it before but I'm so thankful for having you and mom. You gave me a warm bed and food. I love you and mom and my sisters with all of my heart and you mean the world to me. Thank you for loving me no matter what! It means alot. I love you a.

Your baby Jilly ♡

P.S. give me a kiss when you get home

♥ ♥ ♥

On October 26, 2011, Jillian sat in a circle of women, surrounded by a group of misfits gathered from all corners of society. Several weeks before this, she had made some unwise choices and the consequence was that her attendance in this group was mandatory. To an outsider, she looked out of place... like she had no business being a part of this group, but true to her personality, she pulled these women into her heart, befriending them, hugging them, opening her heart and soul to them.

Jilly was in a group therapy session and they were discussing God. She must have said something profound, because the leader of the group asked her to write it down, so she did. Jilly didn't share this with me for two more weeks. Only then did she open up to me about the experience with these women that truly made her look at her own life and count her blessings.

Little did we know that exactly one month after Jilly wrote these thoughts, her baby sister, Sierra, would stand up in front of her casket and read them out loud to 500 people gathered at the Celebration of her Life. It takes a lot of guts for most people to speak to a large crowd; it's extraordinary when a 16-year-old girl grieving her sister, her confidante, her best friend in the world, can do it. We handed out copies to those who came to say, "See ya later, Jilly" to her body one last time. Many of those copies are framed above dressers, lovingly placed in hope chests and journals and memorized in hearts that still long for her.

♥ ♥ ♥

While most of this book makes Jillian sound like a saint, trust me when I tell you that she wasn't! She was a normal active teenager who believed that part of her mission on earth was to push the boundaries set up by us, her parents, as often as she could.

Mostly she did it in a fun way, for instance:

"Jilly, please pick up your room. Like today. As in the next hour." (Jilly ever so slowly gathers up all her dirty and clean laundry, wads them up together and hides them under the bed.)

"Okay, done mom!" Grrrrrrr. Totally *not* done.

When she would push me too far, she would get the most dreadful punishment I could think of for her: grounding, no contact with her friends. For Jilly, that was the worst thing I could do. Her friends were as important as breathing to her and they were her Achilles heel. Inevitably, after a day or so of being cut off from the outside world, she would volunteer to clean the entire house if I would un-ground her early. She would look at me with those big, brown, sad puppy dog eyes and beg. I always tried to stand my ground, but having certain mom weaknesses, I sometimes caved in.

This was my downfall, because I knew how Jilly was. When you told her if she did behavior "A," then she would receive consequence "XX," you had *better* stick to it. For Jilly, it was a challenge to try to see if she could wear me down. I would draw a line in the sand, and she would stick her little toe over it, smile sweetly and say, "Line? What line? Oh, *that* line? That ridiculous line right there? The one I just stepped over? Gotcha mom!"

We did the best job we could of raising this beautiful gift that was lent to us with the limited knowledge we had at the time. And we still screwed up, as all parents do. In all honesty though, so did Jilly.

Sometimes, what looks like a dark chapter or a failure is really God's way of putting a person exactly where they need to be at a certain time to affect other people, sometimes many people. It gives people an opportunity to figure out exactly what they *are not*.

Let me explain. In her senior year, Jillian, along with two of her best friends, were tri-captains of the high school gymnastics team in what was a school record-setting season. She was pulling high grades in school . . . no small feat for her since she nearly failed some classes in 10th grade; she missed most of a grading period due to a nasty bout with mononucleosis. She had been a varsity cheerleader. She stood up to bullies and yet instigated pranks in and out of school. She had a diverse group of friends: Jocks, Nerds, Partiers, Smarties, Strugglers, Rich, Poor, Loners, Class King and Queen, students born here and those who came from other countries. She was never short of people to hang out with. She was both a born leader and a follower rolled up into one. She never passed up an opportunity to try something new and exciting.

The week of her 18th birthday, she and her boyfriend were in a dramatic disagreement about something. They went to a secluded area to discuss it and while they were there, apparently used pot. They were busted by the police, who found a mostly smoked marijuana joint in Jilly's car. They let her go but told her that if they were going to press charges, they would notify her so that she could turn herself in first. She wasn't quite sure what was going to happen but making that unwise choice to break the law cost her dearly. She was kicked off the gymnastic team, a consequence that was clearly defined in the student athletic handbook that she had read and agreed to. The coach was distraught; the entire team's score could have been thrown out and the team disqualified in a meet that she had participated in a few days after she was caught. I knew how much Coach Kim loved Jilly and that this was a very difficult situation for her to be in. It was a painful consequence to administer. She wasn't allowed to even acknowledge Jillian or the five years she had been on the team at honors night. Though it hurt very much, I supported the coach fully, praying that this lesson, as "expensive" and meaningful as it was, would discourage Jilly from future brushes with the law.

It turns out that the police did indeed press charges and Jilly was arrested and had to post bail to get out of jail. We let her sweat a few hours first, hoping that she was learning whatever lesson she needed to learn about rules. Part of her sentencing was one year's probation, along with some hefty fines and drug counseling for the marijuana. I thought that things were going well at the hearing when the judge told her, "Jillian, you obviously have a lot going for you. Your parents love you, your family loves you and your GPA tells me that you are an intelligent young lady that made a dumb choice. If you complete this probation, this charge against you will be expunged from your record and you will still be able to get into nursing school. (She had signed up for a CNA class and bought everything she needed. She showed up the first day for training and was mortified when she was told that due to the "violation" on her background check, she would not be allowed to take the class.) Part of *my* consequence for her was that she had to write a college essay on her experience in jail, lest she ever forget how unpleasant it was.

Praise God. Prayers answered! A stiff, but memorable punishment without ruining the rest of her life. She could still have the career of her dreams.

And then, the judge did one last thing. He drew a line in the sand.

"But! I promise you this, young lady...if you get even *one* probation violation...even *one*...I *promise* you that I will put you in jail for 30 days!"

"Oh, dear God." I put my head in my hands and thought, "She will cross that line. I know it. She will test him to see if he is a man of his word. It's a challenge she will have to try, just to see if she can get away with it."

Things went well for quite a while. She did okay and I thought that perhaps she would make a liar out of my intuition. She was getting good grades in her college classes, continuing to take her nursing pre-requisites after graduation from high school. We counted down the months until she was free and clear. 12, 11, 10, 9, 8, 7, 6 (holding my breath), 5, 4, 3, (almost there, I started to breathe a sigh of relief) 2 ... 1.

Nope. It wasn't happening. The same cop who found her the first time, found her again ... sharing half a can of beer with a friend in a parking lot, waiting to pick up a drunk friend so that friend wouldn't get behind the wheel. (Oh, the irony of that!) She was arrested on the spot and hauled off to jail.

One month to go. Are you kidding me? The same week that we were putting Mark's dad into hospice and planned what we knew would be his last birthday party? Seriously? I was angry! I begged the probation officer to let me take her to see Mark's dad before he died; he was down to days left on this earth. We had already planned the party for the next weekend. It's one of the few times I have lost my composure, "ugly sobbing" in a public place. I didn't want the last few hours her grandfather had with her to be marred by this. Thankfully, the court allowed it.

Before the preliminary hearing, I asked the probation officer to give the judge a message. "I know this will sound strange, but please give Jillian what you promised you would give her. If you don't do exactly as you said, she will lose all respect for the court system, the police and rules. I would rather she learned this early in life when the consequences are not as costly as they will be later in life. PS. Please don't promise her *anything* else!"

The judge honored his threat. I know it sounds harsh. By nature, I do not belong to the "Tough Love" club. It was one of the hardest things I ever had to do. "Sending your child to jail for 30 days? What kind of parent am I? Over something that isn't a major crime? She didn't do anything that many people don't do and get away with every day! It's even legal in some states! For Jilly though, it was about the principle of the matter. We both know that if he lets her get away with it, she'll keep challenging it until the price is too high." I argued with myself.

I gave it to God.

Jilly reported for her sentencing in mid-October. The court had kindly postponed it until after she had a chance to tell her beloved Papa how much she loved him before he died, a few days after his birthday party. They had allowed us to take her across the state for his funeral and let her get settled back in for a couple weeks afterwards. I had to work the day she was to report for sentencing and there was no way I could get time off. Mark took her to court instead.

Now, Jilly was a tiny girl; she had a Barbie doll figure. When she came walking down the stairs like the little boy in the Christmas Story who must model the bunny costume for his parents, her head was hanging pretty low. Mark wondered how she had managed to put on 20 pounds that week. She showed him what she had on... seven days-worth of underwear, socks and T-shirts. She had on two or three bras and several pair of leggings. She looked like the Michelin Man. Evidently, she had been talking to people who told her that she would have to wear the same clothes that she went to jail in for all 30 days, or she could buy them from the commissary, but it was $10 each for a pair of socks, pair of underwear or per T-shirt, etc.

Jilly was having none of that. I don't know how the judge held a straight face. I know Mark's heart sank when they took her out the door and she waddled into custody. My daughter had gone from a "Freebird" to a jailbird. She received 30 days in jail, another year of probation and lost her license and driving privileges until we determined she had earned it back. (Thus, the reason her friend was driving her car on that fatal morning.)

Oh my, she would be the first in my family to go to jail for as far back as I can remember. I was embarrassed and sad. It wasn't how we tried to raise her. I was also afraid for my petite little daughter in that environment. We could put money in an account for her so that she could call home once a week, at $10 per 5-minute call. She was also allowed to continue to go to her orthodontic and counseling appointments. Every night at the appointed time, she would call me collect.

"We have a collect call from_____."

Hi Mom, I love you and miss you! she would jabber off in one quick breath instead of stating her name.

She had devised this system where she could hear us, and we could hear her voice every night, without it costing either of us anything, because we only accepted one collect call a week. She could save her weekly call for a really long meaningful 5-minute chat and we could set up a visit time for the weekend. Would she remember what we had preached to her about the basic rules of incarceration?

- Don't be annoying!
- Do not make anyone angry! Always be as polite as you can.
- Don't cross any lines!
- Never ever tell people where you live or give them our phone number!
- Do as you are told by the officers and do it respectfully.
- Don't borrow anything from anyone and always be aware of your surroundings.
- Write us letters! Keep a journal.
- Remember that you are still a good girl. You just made a stupid choice.
- We'll be waiting anxiously with wide open arms for you to come home.
- You are loved beyond measure.

The first visit rolled around. I crept cautiously into the dirty visiting room at the first opportunity they gave me, wondering how miserable my sweet girl would be in those icky conditions. The other visitors and I were escorted to chairs facing an open room which had a bulletproof, scratched up glass wall separating us from the inmates. There was a phone on both sides of the wall. I could hear her and see her but could not touch her. I fought back the tears and expected to see a very upset young lady.

Finally, the inmates all entered the room in a large group, dressed alike in orange and white striped jumpsuits. I stood up and waved my arms, hoping Jilly would see me. Our eyes met and she broke out into a mischievous grin. She came bounding over to the phone on the wall across from me and picked it up.

"Hi mom! I'm so glad to see you! Do you like my new jumpsuit? Do I look great in orange and white or what? Can you please take my picture? Oh, and these are my new friends, Kristi and Kay! (She went to grab them and gave them each a hug.) Can we have them over for dinner when they get out? Pleeease?"

My jaw dropped. This was certainly not how I had expected her to be. She was actually having *fun!* I couldn't believe it, but I was also relieved that she wasn't hurt or being mistreated.

The next week was pretty much the same. She told me that she had gotten the entire unit in trouble one night because she continued to make barnyard animal noises after lights out. The officer said, "Not another word, ladies. It's lights out time." Jilly responded with a loud "*Moo!*" followed by snickers and giggles from the other women on the unit.

The following week she told me that the officers had put a stop to her demonstrating her gymnastic skills on a cement floor. "Crist!" they ordered. "No *more* back handsprings! You may not walk to the chow hall on your hands, you must use your feet. And do not try to get everyone in the unit to do your P-90X workout! This is not a health club!"

The routine of getting up at 5 A.M. to eat unidentifiable food, then eat again at 11:00 a.m. and 4:00 p.m. and not getting a bedtime snack was starting to wear thin. The other inmates had showed her how to make "mash-up" food for snacks. It was a combination of potato chips, cookies, candy bars and God only knows what else, all mashed up and eaten with a spoon. (She even made it for Sierra when she was released.) Her antidepressants had been discontinued abruptly. They had also taken her off her birth control pills, so she was on her cycle and very hormonal.

Maybe we were getting somewhere. On the rare days that I was allowed to take her out for one of her dental or counseling appointments, I would swing by the driveway and let Mark and Sierra hug her. It took everything that I had in me to return her to the jail.

On the way out, after dropping her off one day, one of the officers stopped me and said, "Why is Jillian *here*? She is such a great kid. She doesn't belong here, she's got so much more to offer society than this! She's funny and smart and a natural leader. She's kind to others and gets all the women laughing at least once a day."

I responded that she did the crime and knew the consequences, so she had to do the time.

With about one week to go, she got her braces off. Normally that would have been a call for an impromptu photo shoot because Jilly loved to have her pictures taken, but it would have to wait. Instead, the final picture I have of her looks more like a mug shot. Face the front, mouth open, mouth closed, smile. Turn to the side and repeat. She was wearing a ratty stained T-shirt and sweats, no makeup and hair all askew. At least she had pretty teeth for the rest of her jail sentence.

The days dragged on for me. I comforted myself with the thought that she was close by and she was safe, but I could only see her on special occasions. Little did I know how much I would have to lean on that belief in the future.

Because she took every opportunity to get out of her cell, she went to all the meetings that anyone could sign up for and true to her nature, convinced most of her new friends to go with her. She befriended a diabetic and made sure to watch out for her blood sugar spikes and drops. She loved an old woman who had bounced too many checks. She wiggled her way into the hearts of professional parolees, women with some serious addictions and most of the staff.

It was during one of her church meetings that she finally opened up to others, confessed her shortcomings to God and allowed the Holy Spirit of peace to enter her heart once more. She had hit her bottom and didn't like it. She was ready to climb out of the dark pit and see herself for the beautiful girl she truly was. She was so eloquent that the volunteer church leader asked her to write down her words because she was so moved.

Here is that letter, in Jilly's own handwriting.

Jillian Crest
10-26-1(

God has always been an important part of my life. I know there is a reason for everything, even me going to jail. I am not scared in here because I know God is in here with me keeping me safe and strong. I try to use every situation as a learning experience, even the bad ones. Today in church Jen asked me how my life has changed since I've excepted Christ into my life. I said well I have always had Christ in my life since I can remember and I p have prayed every night since I was a toddler with my parents but since I've been in jail I have realized the importance of a lot of things that most people take for granate like family, friends, food, freedom, music, and being able to do what you want when you want. I never give much thought to how blessed I am. I have a warm house, with a comfy bed and an unlimited supply of GREAT food. I have parents who care about me and love me no matter I've done, sisters who have always been there when I needed them, friends who would come sit with me as I cry for hours. We don't ever think about these great things and great people because were used to having that but I've realized from being in here that I am truly blessed because a lot of people don't have what I do, and don't have people in their lifes who care for them like the people in my life. ~~I want to thank~~ Jen said I needed to write this down because its very moving, and true. I just want to thank my parents for always believing in me and teaching me about Jesus and right from wrong. I'm so blessed to have been raised by them. I want to thank my older sister for telling on me when I did bad things or I wouldn't have learned from them. I want to thank my baby sister for being my best friend, and I promise ill be a better ro model because I know you look up to me and I hope you learn from my mistakes. And I want to thank my true friends for all your advice and support through all the stupid little things that I get upset about. I LOVE YOU ALL SO MUCH

On the last night of her jail sentence, she wrote, "One nice thing about being in this hall is that you can see outside! It's snowing! I learned a lot in here, but I don't ever want to come back!"

As midnight rolled around on November 12th, she left the jail wearing only one pair of socks, one T-shirt, one pair of underwear and one pair of leggings. She left the rest of her clothes for someone who might need them but couldn't afford them. (As it happened, the long-term women saved a T-shirt with her name on it and when Twinaroo was sentenced, they gave her Jilly's shirt. She was comforted by it.) Jilly happily skipped out the door, jumping up in the air as high as she could, so that the women could see her from their tiny little windows. "Bye for now!" she yelled at the top of her lungs, "I'll miss you guys! I'll come to visit you! Write me when you can!" (She had given out our address, darn it!)

She spent the next few days basking in the comfort of her family and we loved the change that we saw in her. She took nothing for granted. She was determined not to let anything get in the way of her and her nursing degree. She wanted us to know how important we were to her and how grateful she was to have a nice house, a comfortable bed and awesome food whenever she wanted to eat, day or night. She went hunting with Mark and Sierra on the opening day of the season, November 15th, but fell asleep in the deer blind. On November 17th, she left both Mark and I heartfelt notes on our dresser that I have included in this chapter. It appears she intuitively sensed her time was near. On November 18th, she and I drove to Ft. Wayne for an appointment, had lunch at the mall, went shopping and came home. It was precious time and we had a really deep heart to heart talk. I asked her forgiveness for anything I had ever done to hurt her, and she granted it. She asked for mine as well. I can still feel her tiny little fingers interlaced with mine as we drove down the highway. She taught me the words to *Red Solo Cup*, a popular country song at the time.

We were following a pickup truck that had a large box in its bed, precariously tied down. It made me nervous, so I switched lanes. Seconds later, that box came flying off the truck, bouncing down the road into the lane we had just been in. Jilly grabbed my arm and shouted, "Mom! That could have killed us! If you hadn't switched lanes, we could have died!"

She would die anyway, the very next morning. Jilly had been out of jail for one week. I instantly realized that it could have just as easily been me behind the wheel when she died.

Jilly's visitation (or wake, as some people call it) was six hours long. Mark and I stood in one place the entire time and received hugs from hundreds and hundreds of people, each bringing back a piece of our shattered hearts. One of the very last people to come through the line was the judge who had sentenced her to 30 days. Eyes misting and tears threatening to spill onto his cheeks, he whispered to us, "I am so sorry I took the last month of your daughter's life from you. I'm just so very sorry!"

Looking up at him through tears I said, "You know what, Judge? When she was in jail, we had to get used to the idea that she was close by, she was safe, and we could only see her on special occasions. And now... she's close by and safe... and we can only "see" her on very special occasions. Jilly knew what the consequences of her behavior would be, and you allowed her to have them. Because of that, she spent the last month of her life making a difference to women that she normally would not have ever crossed paths with.

In the sweet treasured handmade card that the inmates sent upon learning of Jilly's death, nearly all of them commented about Jilly's personality and how she lit up the darkness with her humor and her pranks. For just a few moments in that dark and dismal wasteland, Jilly made each one of those women feel very special. She had to be in that place, living among them, to reach them in that way." (The *Math Assignment* dream that followed years later makes perfect sense to me now!)

The judge kept one of her bracelets on his podium, out of sight, for a long time. He said it reminded him that even though sometimes it broke his heart to sentence someone, perhaps it was for a greater purpose than he could have ever planned.

I believe that to be true. I wondered about whether to include this part of Jilly's story. I had been wrestling with it for months, praying and asking for guidance. After all, it was this part of her personality that made her who she was, but I didn't want to shame her or make anyone think any less of her. My answer came unexpectedly in the form of a picture that a total stranger posted on line and seeing the significance, someone else passed it on to me. (Jilly is still sticking her toe over the line with her winks and she obviously still has her same sense of humor.)

♥ ♥ ♥

Organic Jilly Bean Solo Cup Grow-Day 56 of Flowering-3/11/16
Cola Monster 8,720 views

There are several significant things in this picture. First, of course, is the marijuana plant... the very thing that started her down this dark chapter of her life. Then, the name JillyBean, our nickname for her. Solo cup... as in *Red Solo Cup*, the last song she taught me hours before her death. The number 56. Both her dad I are 56 this year. The date, 3-11-16. Her baby sister's 21st birthday; the age she turned "legal."

I believe this is Jilly telling me that it's okay to tell the darkest part of her story. All of that is behind her; she has been forgiven and she had also forgiven herself. Someone reading this story might very well relate to making errors in judgment and learn from them. While it's never something that you wish for... to see your beloved child spend a month in jail, it is not a reflection of who Jilly really was. Or who we, as her family, really are.

God gave Jillian her final assignment in that month that she spent in jail, although we didn't know it when she was having that experience. Even though she might be scared, she was to trust Him and not hide her light under a barrel.

She passed the lesson with flying colors and God promoted her to the University of Heaven. Jilly had stepped out of the darkness and into God's light.

"Well done, thy good and faithful servant." You learned the lesson your soul came to experience... Faith, Forgiveness, Choices, and Love.

Good job, my JillyBean. Until we meet again, go Home, your spirit soaring on the wings of all our love. Get that great big hug from God! We will catch up with you when we finish our own assignments, but while we wait,

Always remember to kiss us goodnight!

Monday
November 21, 2011
11pm

Dear Louise & Crist Family ~

    I want to tell you something that happened the last night Jillian was here in jail with me. She spent her last 3 nights down here in the cell with me and having known her for so long, I felt a bit obligated to watch over her. The last night she was here, before she left at midnight, she and I and another girl put Jillian's mat on the floor in front of the television and proceeded to watch 3 consecutive episodes of Criminal Minds together, which Jillian loved. At one point in the night she and I started talking about how important it is to tell the people you love how much you love them even if you were angry at them for the simple reason that life is too short and you just never knew when something like this would happen? Jillian looked me in the eyes, and she said "You know Kristi, I've always felt like I would die young, and you know, its okay because I'm ready for whenever it happens."

    The last thing I said to her as she was leaving that night was "I love you babygirl," and gave her a hug, and she said, "I love you too." Having those conversations and last few minutes before she left are truly helping me get through her loss and I wanted to share it with you.

    You should all know that in the short time

—pg 2—

Jillian was here, she ~~truly~~ touched the hearts of ~~almost~~ everyone, if not everyone she came in contact with. There was a very special brightness about her that everyone noticed.

It is my belief that Jillian has been transformed into an angel, she was meant for better things than this earth.

My thoughts, and every other female here, will be with you throughout this time and especially on Saturday there will be many prayers said for all of you and Jillian. We are deeply sorry for your loss and hope that knowing how incredibly special your daughter was will give you some peace of mind during this time.

My ~~deepest~~ sympathy to you all.

Sincerely,
Kristi
(and every other
female inmate at

THE END

Just kidding…
The end is never really the END!

It has been seven years since Jilly went Home to God. Although I can use the word "died" and Jilly in the same sentence, anything I can do to soften that painful reality and help me cope works for me! If there is one lesson that I have learned in the last few years, it is that grief is not a one size fits all experience, even in what we choose to call the date of our child's transition from earthly body to their heavenly state of being. Everyone must learn to walk this path once they are thrown on it. I know what it feels like to lose my child, but I have no idea what it might feel like for you to lose yours.

Some parents seem to cope "better" (I use that word lightly) than others. There is *no* right way or wrong way to grieve unless it involves inflicting pain on someone else intentionally. Many "newbies" feel that the depth of their love is measured by the depth of their grief and if they are not constantly in the throes of deep grief, they don't love their child. I have not found this to be true, at least for me and for many other parents I know who have more experience as seasoned grievers, but it sure does feel that way in the beginning! Does it mean that you will "get over it" and be as happy as you once were? No. Probably not. You won't ever get over losing a child. You *can*, however, with time and a lot of hard work, begin to heal, so that a scab forms over that gaping wound and every little thing that brushes against it doesn't kill you. It doesn't necessarily get better, it just gets *different*.

How is this possible, you might ask? Please let me share with you some of the things that have helped me in the last seven years. I devoured books on grief right from the beginning. A couple of them were life changing for my husband and me, so I bought copies and handed them out to newly bereaved parents. (Those are listed at the end of this chapter.)

The loss of your child does not follow the neat little stages you may be familiar with from Elizabeth Kubler-Ross and her work on dying patients: denial, anger, bargaining, depression and acceptance. Many people go through those stages all on the same day, only to do it repeatedly. It's a messy, twisting path that loops back on itself repeatedly. One day, you can be sailing along, finally not consumed every single minute with the details of your child's death; then a grief quake hits when you least expect it, pulling the rug right out from under you. Other days, you can remember the color of their eyes, the way they laughed, or their unique scent and it actually brings a smile to your face without any tears falling. In her book *How to Survive the Loss of a Child,* Dr. Catherine Sanders describes the stages of grief a little differently: Shock, Awareness of Loss, Conservation and the Need to withdraw, Healing, Renewal and Fulfillment.

A good support group is vital. Many can be found online if there are no local groups in your area. I joined several before I found one or two that fit my personal belief system. Sadly, some of these groups can leave you more depressed than before you started, but others are full of hope. I have joined groups that are both secular and religious and both have filled a unique need at the time. Beware of any group that tells you that your child ceased to exist or is rotting in Hell, particularly if it was a suicide or an overdose. There is so much more support out there than that narrow, cruel mindset! Instead, surround yourself with love.

Compassionate Friends is unique in that there are individual groups for any kind of child loss, and any stages of a child's life. There are specialty groups for miscarriage, SIDS, special needs, cancer, overdose, accidental death, murder, drunk driver, sudden death, suicide, etc. Each of these groups cater to the parent who is experiencing this type of loss. There is always someone online to talk to and many larger cities hold monthly group face-to-face meetings. Don't just go once and write it off if it doesn't resonate with you right away. Give it a chance. On the second Sunday in December, Compassionate Friends always holds a Worldwide Candle Lighting Ceremony at 7:00 p.m. in your local time zone. All over the world on that day, candles are lit in remembrance of a beloved child in homes, churches, synagogues and mosques. It's a beautiful tribute; as the candles in one time zone gently burn out, another wave of candles are lit in the next time zone so that for 24 hours, people all over the world are honoring their children.

Last year, I was introduced to a phenomenal group called Helping Parents Heal. It was started by parents who had experienced child loss and wanted the world to know that healing *is* a possible path if you wish to pursue it ... and healing is different than healed. We are healing for the rest of our lives, but I am not sure that we will be fully healed until we hold our children in our embrace once again. I should mention that one of the moms, Elizabeth Veney-Boisson, co-founded this group the same month her son, Morgan, died at the base of Mt. Everest. He was her second child in spirit, so she was not new to grief.

Helping Parents Heal is different from any other group I have been part of because they are so open and accepting of others, as long as they meet the one requirement to join; you must have a child who is now in spirit. There are caring listeners that people can talk to if the need is there. Another thing that makes them different is that they believe that although your child may have died, your relationship with them continues to live forever. You make new memories with them in this way. You don't have to leave them in your past. It is still possible for them to communicate with you and you with them. Some do this through prayer or meditation, writing or journaling, hiking or yoga. Others utilize mediums. Even if you don't believe this sort of thing, you are still welcome in this group, regardless of your religious beliefs. They also have groups around the world and online meetings as well.

In 2018, Helping Parents Heal held their first international conference; it sold out quickly. There were over 500 bereaved parents in attendance, including myself and my sister, Nicki. You would think that all those parents in one hotel would be a pretty depressing atmosphere, right? You couldn't be more mistaken! The conference opened with a tribute to our children on a slideshow, accompanied by a brief welcome from Garth Brooks, singing "The Dance." Lots of tears were shed, but they were happy tears. Bereaved parents are ecstatic when their child in spirit is recognized. There were several breakout workshops, dealing with many topics related to the loss of a child. There were at least a dozen authors in attendance who inspired us with their stories. In addition, there were mediums available for private readings for those who wished to participate. Each medium that HPH endorses must pass rigorous testing before they can be vetted. There were prayer groups, yoga classes, artwork, classes for dads, etc. I think everyone there found something that resonated with them. One of the speakers had been the driver in an accident that took the life of his wife and son. He was uniquely qualified to tell me what I could do to assist Jilly's driver with her grief if she chose.

My sister and I chose to have separate readings with a medium named Nina that we had never met or heard of, just because we wanted to explore that avenue. I have had some phenomenal readings in the past, so this area fascinates me. All mediums are psychic, but not all psychics are mediums, by the way. An evidential medium offers very specific "snapshots" of your loved one as well as current events that might be happening in your life as proof that your child isn't missing out on anything! I went in as one is supposed to approach a reading: no expectations of who might come through, or the information I would receive. Of course, I was hoping to hear from Jilly or my daddy or my stepdad Dean! I did end up "hearing" from all three, but that is not the best part of what happened during this session.

At the end of the reading, I could tell that Nina was distracted and appeared to be in some pain. She admitted that a rare migraine was starting to form. My background in holistic health and Cranio-Sacral therapy has taught me ways to relieve a migraine at its onset, so I asked if she would be willing to let me try to help her. She agreed.

As I centered myself and said a prayer for healing, I placed my hands on her head and immediately felt the warmth radiating from the spot where her head hurt the most. I also heard someone calling the name "Jared." I thought perhaps it was someone out in the hallway, after all, we were in a busy hotel. I kept going, and a few minutes later, I heard Jared's name being called again, a little louder this time. I tried harder to concentrate despite the outside noise. At the end of the healing session with her, I heard Jared's name for the third time, but this time, it was as though someone was standing behind me, whispering it in my ear. I looked around the room and only Nina and I were in it. I asked if she knew someone named Jared. Nina replied that no, she didn't know anyone by that name, nor had any of her clients at the conference had a child with that name in spirit. Oh well, must be my active imagination, I figured. We finished up and I headed down to lunch, which was buffet style for about 400 people. The lines were long, and my sister was at an appointment, so I didn't know anyone else at lunch. I was waiting my turn near the end of the line and turned around to chat with a beautiful blonde woman standing behind me. We made small talk about where we were from and how far out on the path of grief that we were, just a couple opening sentences. Suddenly, a bright light started glowing behind her. I thought perhaps it was the way the sun was shining through the skylight, but when I checked, there was no reasonable source of light that would cause this phenomenon. At that moment, I also heard Jared's name once again whispered in my ear. I turned around to look at who said it, but no one was near enough except this total stranger I had just met.

"Okay, this is a little weird!" I said to myself silently. Maybe it's the Arizona heat and I am not used to it. Then, feeling a little foolish, I thought, "Alright. I'll bite. I don't have anything to lose." I turned to this new friend, whose glow was even brighter now, and said, "Just by chance, you don't have a son in spirit named Jared, do you?"

She stopped what she was doing and looked at me, astonished, as her mouth dropped open. "OH, MY GOD! How did you know that?" she exclaimed with tears forming in her eyes. Keep in mind I had never laid eyes on this woman before getting in line for lunch that day. As we sat in the sunshine and talked over lunch, I learned that her son and Jilly had many things in common. I texted Nina, the medium and told her that the Jared mystery was solved ... and I was having lunch with his mom at that moment.

Many believe that our children find new friends when they go to Heaven and somehow orchestrate a way for their parents to meet on this side. I asked Jared and Jilly to give me a sign if this was one of the things they do. I started seeing "J's" everywhere and the dinner table I was randomly assigned to was Jared's favorite number! People at entire tables found that they had been "randomly" grouped together and shared special similarities. The whole weekend was like that. It was ... *sacred* somehow. The love was palpable everywhere I went.

My new friend and I saw each other a few more times that weekend but made a bond that will strengthen both of our paths for a very long time. The whole weekend was full of that kind of amazing energy. We as parents were there, yes, but I believe our children in spirit were there too, somehow orchestrating "chance" meetings with others. We were told that as we talk about our kids on this side, they also talk about their parents or siblings on their side, praying for us, sending love to us and giving us energy and "winks" as often as they are able.

Waking up on the last day, I glanced in the mirror and had to do a double-take. The sparkle in my eyes had burnt out when Jilly went Home in 2011. That morning, I saw that the sparkle had returned; my eyes were once again full of love and life. I saw that same sparkle in many other people's eyes. The experience was a life changer for me. It is okay to love again. It's okay to be okay. And it's okay not to be okay too when that happens. Our kids understand. We will understand someday that "the end" as we think of it, is not really the end at all. It's a new beginning in another time zone.

Like many of the other parents I met, I aspire to become a Shining Light Parent. The inspiration from this name came from a Gold Star Parent; ones that lost their children at war and received a special gold star that is placed in their window, honoring their child's service. It's a new label created by Suzanne Giesemann for bereaved parents who have "shining lights" in Heaven that they can't wait to reunite with, and for parents who want to become a shining light to others left behind here on Earth.

"A Shining Light Parent is one whose child has left the physical body, but whose light continues to shine as an ongoing presence in a family's heart and home. The term is a more positive one than 'bereaved parent' (which is certainly more appropriate in some of the stages of grief)," Suzanne states. When one's child goes back to God, we need all the positivity energy we can muster up! After I left the conference, I started to see winks from Jilly and other loved ones everywhere...they had probably been in front of me all along, but I simply wasn't paying attention at the right moment. Jilly amazes me with the way she continues to let me know that our relationship is still strong and full of love, it just gets expressed differently now.

As I wrapped up this book and began to look earnestly into publishing it, I got one of the coolest Jilly winks so far. Each year, the hospital I work for sponsors a "Duck Race" to raise money for our Hospice department. People are encouraged to buy a small rubber duck for the race. The ducks are numbered and released into a river. The first one across the finish line wins. I have bought three tickets every year since the race began; one in honor of each of my daughters. Hospice is the best thing ever when you are going through a terminal illness. We got to experience that first hand with Mark's dad when he lost the battle to lung cancer.

The prizes for the duck race vary from jewelry, to camping adventures, to a side of beef to a large cash prize always donated by Jilly's godmother, Kathy. They are awarded in the order the ducks cross the finish line. It's always a fun race to watch and all the money goes to a great cause, so I love supporting the idea.

Mark and I were on a road trip the morning of the duck race, so I couldn't go this year. We were talking about this book and its progress, and I wondered out loud where the money to publish it was going to come from. Would Jilly approve? Did she want me to put her life and death into words for others to read? Would it help anyone? Would she be okay with part of the profits from the book, if there were any, going to the scholarships that we give out in her honor each year?

As we discussed this, my cell phone rang. "Is this Louise Crist?" the caller asked. "Yes." I responded. "What can I do for you?" The woman on the other end asked if I was having a good day. "Yes, so far," I replied. "It's about to get a whole lot better," she said, with some excitement in her voice. "Your duck placed in the Hospice Duck Race!"

"Wow! That's awesome," I agreed. "What did I win?" The director of Hospice informed me that I had won first place. This year the first-place prize was a check for $2018. Jillian's birthday was 2/18. Is it a coincidence that they are the same numbers? Maybe. Her godmother, hand-picked by Jilly herself as a young girl, donated the prize. Another coincidence? Isn't the timing amazing too, since I had *just* asked where the money to publish the book was going to come from? I got the answer to my questions about the book, and a great wink at the same time. I thanked God (and Jilly) for this miracle.

Faith is like that. It's being sure of what you hope for and certain of what you do not see (yet). Hebrews 11:1.

Keep believing. What you believe, you will eventually experience!

Just this week, Sierra bought a new car. She brought it over to show Mark her first "adult purchase" and was showing him the many nooks and crannies. Not to anyone's great surprise, they found a quarter in the back seat, stuck in one of the cracks. Jilly always did like to have the last word.

Wishing you faith, love, hope, comfort and peace beyond your own understanding. Thank you so much for joining me on this journey.

♥ ♥ ♥

ACKNOWLEDGMENTS

In loving gratitude to those who have assisted me on this journey:

God, without whom I would not have survived. You are my beloved heavenly Papa! I was, and always will be… *your* girl first.

My husband Mark. I've loved you from the first minute I saw you. Thank you for studying "the lessons" with me.

To my beautiful daughters, Erica and Sierra. You bring me much joy! I will always kiss you goodnight and tell you I love you, even when we aren't physically together. Thank you for your patience as I poured my heart into these pages. You are my best friends as well as my daughters. And as long as I'm living… my babies you'll be. Thank you to Chuck and Tyler for loving my girls so completely and helping to fill the void that Jilly's passing left. To my sweet Natalie…you have changed my life. I can't wait to see who Jilly helps pick out to be your playmates!

To my sweet beloved Jilly: I love you, I miss you, I'll see you again and next time, our tummy hug will last forever. I'll see you when my chores are through!

My siblings, Nicki (my biggest cheerleader), Van (We make a great team!) Jaime and Tom. I am so lucky to have you for so many adventures in this life. I love you so!

My parents, Vera, Dean, Jim, Donna and Larry. How blessed am I to end up with not just two, but five terrific parents? Thank you for all you have done for our family!

My dearest friends (and their wonderful families): Jeanne and Dennis, Tina and Jeff, Susan, Laury, Mary, Kim, Jessica, Carol, Kathy, Vickie, Wayne and Anna Sue, Heidi, Gary, Linda, Alanah, Kara, Melody and Pat, Karen and Hal, Melissa, Hannah, Sonya, Annie, Cheyenne, Al, David, Cass, Cole and Acie. We have shared the gifts that our hearts and souls had to uniquely offer each other throughout the years, and I couldn't be more grateful to have you in my life. You are loved very much.

My mentor and lifelong teacher, Vivian Oberheu. I adore you. You saved my life.

Our early messengers, Laura and Lynn. What a fantastic difference you made in this difficult journey. We wouldn't be where we are today without your help! A million thank you's will never be enough!

My editor, Jami Lynn Sands and Dayna Linton for your help in making this book a reality.

Neale Donald Walsch, for his wisdom and encouragement to put my journey into a book.

To all the Shining Lights at Helping Parents Heal. Thank you, thank you!

To the friends from all different generations who continue to get us through each day, and especially Jilly's circle of closest friends: You were as important as breathing to her. Never forget that. Thank you for keeping us in your lives.

To each of my many, many classmates, patients and friends in spirit, especially Marina Dutcher R.N., who helped me (and several others) become the nurses that we are today. She changed the trajectory of so many lives while she was here, and changed countless more lives when she went Home: Thank you for giving me a tiny glimpse of Heaven. Each of your children have made the world a better place as you said they would. What a reunion we will all someday have!

And finally, to all bereaved parents, this book is dedicated to your strength, your wisdom and your compassion. The "Club" we all belong to is full of the most amazing people on this side of heaven. It is an honor to know you. Thank you for holding my hand as we all walk each other Home. We will see our beloved children again. Believe it!

With Love,
Louise

ABOUT THE AUTHOR

*L*OUISE CRIST HAS ENJOYED working at the same hospital as a Registered Nurse for over 30 years. In her spare time, she enjoys teaching, traveling, writing, creating and photography. She aspires to be a Shining Light parent with the Helping Parents Heal foundation, a support group for bereaved parents that demonstrates that with time and work, some healing is possible after the death of a child.

Louise lives in Michigan with her husband Mark. They are, and always will be, the parents of three wonderful daughters. They are currently enjoying one exceptionally beautiful granddaughter and a very loved and a very spoiled "rescue" pup.

BIBLIOGRAPHY

(Recommended Reading List in no particular order)

- *The Shack*, by P. William Young (also available in a movie)
- *The Velveteen Rabbit*, by Margery Williams Bianco
- *Home with God in a Life that Never Ends*, by Neale Donald Walsch
- *The Little Soul and the Sun*, by Neale Donald Walsch
- The *Bible*
- *How to Survive the Loss of a Child*, by Dr. Catherine Sanders
- *Permission to Mourn*, by Tom Zuba
- *Knowing*, by Jeffrey Olsen
- *Still Right Here* and *Messages of Hope*, both by Suzanne Geisemann
- *Walking in the Garden of Souls*, by James Van Praagh
- *Tear Soup: A Recipe for Healing After Loss* by Pat Schwiebert
- *To All Parents*, a poem by Edgar Guest
- *A Grace Disguised…How the Soul Grows through Loss*, by Gerald Sittser
- *The Fall of Freddie the Leaf, a Story of Life for All Ages,* by Leo Buscaglia
- Helping Parents Heal Support Group, which has online, Facebook and in person groups available.
- The Compassionate Friends Support Group

www.ingramcontent.com/pod-product-compliance
Lightning Source LLC
Chambersburg PA
CBHW020349080526
44584CB00014B/950